Information and Communication Techı

for A2 Level

Julian Mott and Anne Leeming

Hodder & Stoughton
A MEMBER OF THE HODDER HEADLINE GROUP

Orders: please contact Bookpoint Ltd, 130 Milton Park, Abingdon, Oxon OX14 4SB. Telephone: (44) 01235
827720. Fax: (44) 01235 400454. Lines are open from 9.00–6.00, Monday to Saturday, with a 24 hour message
answering service. You can also order through our website www.hodderheadline.co.uk.

British Library Cataloguing in Publication Data
A catalogue record for this title is available from the British Library

ISBN 0 340 858222

First Published 2003

Impression number   10 9 8 7 6 5 4 3

Year   2009 2008 2007 2006 2005 2004

Papers used in this book are natural, renewable and recyclable products.
They are made from wood grown in sustainable forests. The logging and manufacturing
processes conform to the environmental regulations of the country of origin.

Typeset by Pantek Arts Ltd, Maidstone, Kent.

Printed in Great Britain for Hodder & Stoughton Educational, a division of Hodder Headline, 338 Euston Road,
London NW1 3BH by J.W. Arrowsmith, Bristol.

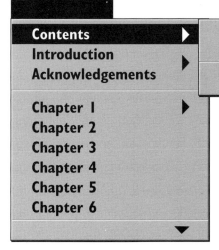

Contents

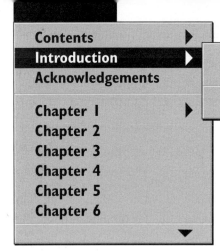

Introduction

This book is designed to cover the final two examinable modules of the AQA A Level Information and Communication Technology specification (6521). These modules are normally referred to as ICT4 and ICT5.

The book follows the specification for AQA board very closely but will also be of use to students preparing for other boards at A level. This book is also suitable for students studying for AVCE ICT.

This book has been substantially rewritten from our second edition and it fully reflects the changes in the AQA specification and technological advances. We have listened to comments from both students and teachers and have included more activities in the chapters as well as providing greater detail and more case studies throughout.

The first ten chapters cover module ICT4. The next eleven chapters cover module ICT5.

Brief answers are provided to questions. Students should be aware that all examination answers should be in sentences. Questions using words like 'explain' and 'describe' require more detail in the answer.

The AQA A level ICT specification also includes a coursework module ICT6. Students studying this module are advised to read Database Projects in Access for Advanced Level by Julian Mott and Ian Rendell published by Hodder and Stoughton.

Information Communication Technology is a subject that is always changing; we have tried to incorporate many new developments into this book. Students are advised to keep up to date with developments; a good way to do this is through accessing some of the many newspaper and magazine websites shown below.

http://news.ft.com/home/uk/
http://www.cw360.com
http://www.guardian.co.uk/
http://www.computing.co.uk
http://www.independent.co.uk/
http://webserv.vnunet.com/news
http://www.telegraph.co.uk/

Some other useful sites include;
http://www.silicon.com/
http://www.howstuffworks.com
http://whatis.techtarget.com/
http://www.bcs.org.uk (British Computer Society)

For information on the specification and examinations visit AQA's site at:
http://www.aqa.org.uk

For further information on the legislation relating to ICT visit the open government site:
http://open.gov.uk

ASK JEEVES provides an excellent search engine:
http://ask.co.uk

Remember that ICT is all around you; the more you relate what you learn to the real world the easier it will be to learn and answer examination questions. Keep your eyes open wherever you are: in a shop, booking a ticket for a cinema or a train journey, gaining information in a museum or buying a lottery ticket. Keep asking yourself how ICT is involved. Parents, neighbours or family friends may have jobs or take part in leisure activities that involve the use of ICT. Talk to them about topics covered in the book that relate to what they do.

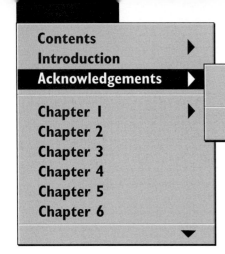

Acknowledgements

Thanks go to Paul Amey of Peter Symonds' College, who produced most of the graphics for this book. He demonstrated cheerful good humour whenever last minute changes were requested.

Thanks also to Richard Carr, ICT teacher at Peter Symonds', who gave up time to review the content of the chapters. He gave vital feedback, ideas for change and valuable material that has been included in the book.

Thanks also to Nicole Stevens and Paul Reed.

The publishers would like to thank the following individuals, institutions and companies for permission to reproduce screenshots or photographs in this book. Every effort has been made to trace ownership of copyright. The publishers would be happy to make arrangements with any copyright holder whom it has not been possible to contact:

www.freeskills.com (page 105), www.mousepointers.co.uk (pages 107 and 108), www.pcadvisor.co.uk (page 154), the Health and Safety Executive (p75)

Organisational structure

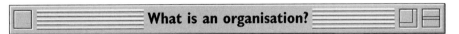

What is an organisation?

An organisation is a group of people with a specific purpose. Here are some examples of organisations and their purpose.

Organisation	Purpose
A multinational oil company	To make a profit
A government pensions department	To pay pensions to pensioners
A bowls club	To arrange bowls matches
A college	To educate students

The purpose of an organisation, whether it is big or small, will determine how it operates.

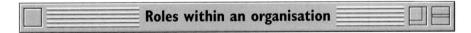

Roles within an organisation

Individuals within an organisation will have defined roles. Activities and tasks are allocated according to these roles, enabling the organisation to take advantage of specialisms and skills.

The allocation of tasks is called **division of labour**.

By specialising, individuals can develop knowledge and expertise in a particular group of tasks. The larger the organisation, the more likely specialisation is to occur.

For example, in a two-person business, the individuals concerned may share all the tasks. In a very large company, there would be separate staff who specialise in accounts, personnel, marketing, sales, etc.

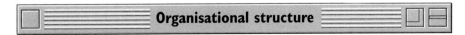

Organisational structure

All organisations must have some structure. A group of individuals are normally responsible to a manager. This can be shown in an organisational chart like the one in Figure 1.1.

Sheila Burnside
Telesales Manager

| Gavin Jones | Hayley Wynn | Gemma Robins | Peter Harrison |
| Telesales assistant | Telesales assistant | Telesales assistant | Telesales assistant |

Figure 1.1 Example of an organisational structure

This is only part of the organisational chart for the whole business. Sheila Burnside is responsible to the Marketing Manager. The Marketing Manager is responsible to the Marketing Director and so on.

At the top of the organisational chart is the Managing Director or the person who has ultimate responsibility for the organisation. This could be the chief executive or the owner.

The organisational structure will:

- determine to whom an individual is answerable
- determine who can make what decisions
- enable managers to coordinate, control and monitor the activities of their staff.

Span of control

The **span of control** is the number of employees who are directly supervised by one person. In Figure 1.1, Sheila Burnside's span of control is the four telesales assistants.

Too wide a span of control leads to a lack of control and is inefficient. Too narrow a span wastes staff.

The nature of the roles of the staff being supervised will help to determine the appropriate span of control in any particular circumstance. A supervisor of supermarket checkout clerks would be able to sustain a larger span of control than a personnel manager. The checkout clerks are all carrying out the same, fairly straightforward tasks whilst a personnel manager's subordinates would have a range of spheres of work, such as recruitment, industrial relations and remuneration.

The span of control should be clear in the organisational structure.

Chain of command

The **chain of command** is the path through the levels of management from the managing director downwards. Instructions go down the line of authority. Problems are referred up the lines to a higher level. Long lines of communication mean messages can be distorted and take time to reach their destination.

The pyramid or hierarchical structure

The pyramid or hierarchical structure (Figure 1.2) is the traditional shape of an organisational structure in a large business. It is common in large public limited companies, the military and the civil service.

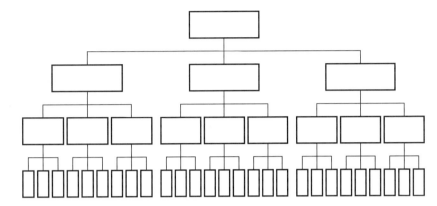

Figure 1.2 The pyramid or hierarchical structure

Roles are clearly defined within a large number of layers, each responsible to the layer above.

At the top of the pyramid is the managing director or chief executive who is responsible for the success or failure of the organisation. Each manager has a relatively small span of control. The chain of command down from the managing director is long.

This hierarchical structure is suitable for large organisations with centralised decision making by the strategic staff.

Problems with the hierarchical structure

- Organisations with a hierarchical structure are likely to be slow to change as important decisions have to be referred all the way up the line.
- Decisions take a long time to be made and take even longer to implement.
- Senior staff can be very remote from the lower levels of the structure.

The horizontal or flat structure

An alternative structure is the horizontal structure (Figure 1.3). In a flat structure there are fewer layers, but the spans of control are much wider. As a result, problems being referred up the line can be resolved more quickly.

As more people are directly answerable to the managing director, the power to make decisions will need to be delegated to middle managers.

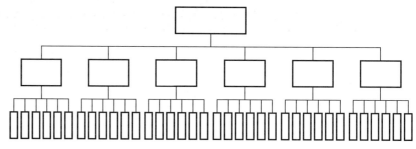

Figure 1.3 The horizontal or flat structure

Parts of the organisation may tend to operate independently of the other parts but are still under the umbrella control of senior management.

Employees have more responsibility which often leads to better motivation. It is more likely that employees can contribute more to decision making.

However, as departments are specialised, different departments may have little to do with each other, which can lead to poor communication across the organisation. Control of top management could be weakened as they have a greater span of control and need to delegate more frequently. Fewer levels usually mean that there are fewer prospects of promotion.

The flat structure is becoming more popular. It allows considerable independence to different units which means that these units can make decisions and change more rapidly. Hierarchical organisations are *static*. Flat organisations tend to be more *dynamic* which mean that they are more flexible and open to change.

The levels of an organisation's structure

There are generally three levels of personnel in a business organisation, although there may be considerably more layers.

The **strategic** level that consists of senior management, responsible for long-term planning and major decision making.

The **tactical (**or implementation) level consists of middle management in charge of one particular department or area of the business. Examples would be a regional sales manager or a training manager. Planning at this level is medium term.

The **operational** level consisting of the workforce who are making the product, taking sales orders, keeping the accounts, and so on. Operational managers include foremen, supervisors and charge hands. Planning is on a short-term, often daily or even minute-by-minute, basis.

How has the development of IT affected organisational structure?

The introduction of Information Technology has tended to lead to flatter organisational structures. One reason is that the introduction of IT and the pace of hardware and software development means that frequent change is inevitable and businesses must be dynamic to cope with the change.

IT systems provide better information on staff performance, thus enabling managers to monitor more people and cope more easily with a wider span of control, a feature of flatter organisational structures.

Some jobs at lower levels may disappear altogether, such as typists in the typing pool as a result of the growth of word-processing. New, direct methods of data entry reduce the number of clerical staff needed. Robots have replaced many jobs on the production line.

All these changes have resulted in the reduction of the number of levels in an organisation.

Over the last decade, the jobs of middle managers have been eroded. Contributory causes include the developments in IT and communications. These have enabled information to be produced in a form suitable for the strategic managers directly from the operational level, without the need for manipulation and interpretation by middle managers. Many decisions that used to be taken by middle managers are now taken by computer-based systems. For example, decisions regarding granting of loans to bank customers and stock ordering in supermarkets can all be made by computer-based systems. Increasingly, operational staff can work without needing direct middle management involvement.

Summary

- Organisations can be structured in a number of ways. They can have:
  - a hierarchical structure or
  - a flat structure.

- Hierarchical structures can be rigid and decision-making can be slow. Flat structures can be flexible and autonomous.

- There are three main levels of hierarchy in an organisation:
  - strategic
  - tactical
  - operational.

- New technologies have affected the organisational structures of many businesses and have altered the way in which decisions are made.
- IT provides information on which decisions can be based at all levels of the organisation's structure.

Organisational structure questions

1. Give an example of one organisation you know which uses a hierarchical structure. *(2)*

2. Explain why is it necessary to have an organisational structure in a business. *(2)*

3. A message has to pass from the chief executive of a company to all the operational staff.
a) Is the message likely to get through more quickly if the company has a hierarchical structure or a flat structure? *(1)*
b) Explain your answer to part (a). *(2)*

4. A company with a hierarchical structure is considering making a whole tier of middle management redundant and adopting a flatter structure. Give two advantages and two disadvantages of this action.

5. The Apex Insurance Company has a hierarchical structure. Instructions from managers to subordinates are normally given verbally, face-to-face. The company is thinking of investing in an internal e-mail system.

Explain how this may speed up communications at Apex.

6. For each of the following types of organisation, suggest decisions which would be made at the (a) strategic, (b) tactical, and (c) operational level:
a) a multinational bank
b) a retail chain of shoe shops
c) a school or college
d) a car manufacturer. *(12)*

7. A small company with a rigid hierarchical structure is planning to introduce a computer system. Describe four concerns a director may have on the effect on the structure of the company. *(4)*

8. Identify and describe the three levels of management usually found in an organisation. What types of information are needed at each level? *(9)*

9. Information is communicated at three levels within an organisation. State these **three** levels. *(3) AQA Jan 2003 ICT04*

Information systems and organisations

Data processing systems and information systems

A data processing system is a computer system that deals with the day-to-day transactions of an organisation. These transactions will be at an **operational** level, for example, recording the loan of books from a library, producing bills for an electricity company or making seat bookings for a cinema.

An information system is a system that processes data to produce information that can be used to help in decision making. Often this data comes from the data processing system. The decisions are likely to be at a **tactical** level or a **strategic** level.

Examples of data processing and information systems

Data processing system	Operational purpose	Information system	Examples of decisions to be made
On-line airline booking system.	Reserving seats for passengers, producing tickets, boarding cards and passenger lists.	The system can provide the airline with the percentage of seats sold.	Whether to continue the service. Whether to put on extra planes for a popular service.
A company payroll system.	Calculating wages and salaries, printing pay slips, conducting money transfers.	The system can provide the company with attendance records and the total wage bill, each broken down by department.	Whether the company can afford to employ more staff or pay them more. Whether to take action over sickness levels.
A school or college timetable system.	Allocating students to classes and printing individual timetables.	The system can provide the management with summaries of class sizes, staff work load and room utilisation.	Whether to split large classes. Whether to cut unpopular classes. Whether more staff and rooms are needed.

In each of three examples above, decisions have to be made. These decisions can be based on information provided by the information system. Use of an information system is likely to lead to more informed decisions, better decision making and more transparent decision making (the reasons for the decision will be clearer).

The use of IT-based information techniques has speeded up the data collection process. Large amounts of data can be processed and analysed, and the information generated can be communicated very quickly. Electronic links improve communications and reduce the need for paper. Decision making can be speeded up.

However, more information may not necessarily lead to better decision making. Too much information may lead to information overload. Information must be at a suitable level of detail. Exception reports, for example, a list of flights with an exceptionally low or exceptionally high number of seats sold, may focus attention on issues to be addressed first. Information may be presented as a summary or in a graphical or tabular form.

Management Information Systems

A Management Information System (MIS) is a system that converts data from internal and external sources into information communicated in an appropriate form to managers at different levels of an organisation. The information enables effective decisions or appropriate planning to be carried out.

An MIS aims to provide a manager with **all** the information needed to make decisions associated with the job as effectively as possible.

The use of MISs has increased as a result of the rapid growth in the use of database systems. An MIS is usually based on data from one or more databases. An MIS allows managers at different levels to access information that is appropriate and in a form suitable for the decisions that they have to make.

Example of a Management Information System

The operations manager of a chocolate factory needs to decide the number and types of bars to be made in a particular week. The following information would help him make this decision:

- the number of each type currently in stock
- outstanding orders still to be delivered
- the sales of each type last week
- the sales of each type this time last year.

This information could be created from the data collected as part of the day-to-day operational data processing system.

The sales manager for the same company will require information on products sold rather than products produced. He will need to be able to compare the performances of different members of the sales force. Information on the products' market share and the nature and performance of a rival manufacturer's products will be needed by the manager so that he can make decisions on which product to promote and on the size and nature of any advertising campaign. Such information is external.

An MIS should produce appropriate information to be used by managers at all levels: strategic, tactical and operational.

Strategic information

Strategic information is used by senior managers such as directors and the chief executive in a business, head teacher and governors in a school, or directors of a charity. Long-term planning is a key function at this level of management and most decisions made will reflect this. An overview of the operation of the whole organisation is required so that an assessment can be made of how well objectives are being met. Actual costs and profits need to be compared with forecasts for all sections of the business. An MIS can produce projections and predictions based on current data, both internal and external, that relates to the business.

The nature of strategic management means that the information that is required at this level can be very varied both in content and in timing. There will be a need for some regular reporting, but depending on the decision to be made, other, 'one-off', information may be needed. External sources will often play a major role at this level.

For example, a company that produces and sells ice cream and other associated products has six factories located in different parts of the United Kingdom. The senior management may wish to close down one factory to reduce costs. This would be a strategic decision and the management would need a wide range of information. An example of internal information would be the increase in labour costs at each factory. External information would include the present site value of each factory.

Most MISs will provide summary, statistical information suitable for senior management. Often, however, such summarising hides crucial detail. The need for such detail would be impossible to predict as it depends on specific circumstances. This lack of appropriate detail could result in incorrect decisions.

A form of MIS called an Executive Information System (EIS) provides aggregated information for senior managers. The manager can display the information in more detail by clicking on hot spots. Such a system would bring together information from a range of internal and external sources.

For example, a senior manager is reviewing company expenditure over the past year, comparing it with the estimated budget. This information is displayed in a graphical form. She then notices that one department is well over budget and decides to investigate further. A click of the mouse button on the appropriate figure results in the details of the budget and expenditure of the department in question being displayed. It appears that the overspend is greatest in the raw materials' expenditure, so our manager clicks on this figure to reveal that prices are as estimated but the department has purchased more raw materials than planned. The manager can investigate sales and stock levels to find out whether these extra purchases were necessary.

Activity 1

The Principal of a college is reviewing the A level results. Describe the information that she would need and the form it should be presented to her.

Unfortunately, the college pass rate is lower than expected. Explain how an EIS could be used to investigate the finding.

Tactical information

Middle managers, typically department heads, have roles that are tactical. Such a manager would be responsible for a certain section of a business and would be responsible to a senior manager. She would be likely to have a number of operational managers reporting to her. In some organisations, such a manager could be responsible for a sales region, a specific factory or group of shops. In another organisation, a middle manager could be in charge of training, customer accounting or IT Services.

Much of the information needed by such managers relates directly to the performance of the organisation and is used for monitoring and controlling purposes. An example would be sales figures for each of the company's sales representatives. Regular reports to assist making tactical decisions are common at this level in a variety of forms: tabular, graphical and pictorial. The information is usually prepared on a routine basis, perhaps weekly or monthly. A factory manager of the ice cream company might consider running an extra shift during the summer months. Such a decision would be based on tactical information.

Exception reports, for example, a list of all sales figures which fall below their target level, provide managers with a powerful tool in establishing areas for further investigation. Successful decision making at this level often depends upon accurate forecasting, for example, cash flow forecasts.

Operational information

Operational managers are closely involved at the productive end of the operation. A supervisor may oversee the workforce on a particular production line. He may need to work out rotas and rest breaks, monitor the rate of production, ensure that hold-ups due to machine failure or delay in the arrival of spare parts are minimised and ensure that the quality of the finished product is maintained within acceptable levels.

The information system could provide him with details of his employees' working hours as well as current stock levels which would help in his decision making.

Nowadays, many operational decisions, such as when to reorder stock, are made automatically by the computer software. The reordering can itself be initiated automatically.

Simple lists and charts will play a major part in operational information. Such a list could be produced by sorting the transaction data that has been processed as part of the normal data processing function.

At the operational level, information is characterised by a high level of detail. For example, in a shoe shop chain, the local shop manager might require a daily, itemised list of all shoes sold, sorted into types, styles and quantities. The regional manager (tactical level) would require a weekly or monthly summary report showing the total sales for each

---

Activity 2

A Head of Department in a school has to order new text books for the incoming AS level ICT class. Another part of his role is to see all students who are not progressing well on the course so that he can offer advice and provide them with appropriate support.

What information could the Management Information System provide him with that will help him carry out the above tasks?

shop in a region. At a strategic level, the marketing manager might wish to forecast sales trends over the next few years.

Case Study 1

MIS – West Yorkshire Police

West Yorkshire Police are the fourth largest metropolitan force in England and Wales with 8000 employees, police and support staff. With the introduction of the Government's Best Value regime, the force needed to use IT for more efficient ways of working and deliver better value for money.

Police overtime payments were the largest devolved part of the budget. Information given to the divisions about the amount of overtime worked was completely out of date by the time it was sent out.

West Yorkshire Police were looking for a system that gave them better financial budgeting and could deliver management information.

The new system records how many hours each police officer has worked and exports the data directly into the payroll system. It includes a MIS which is able to provide information to managers about which division, which group and which week the overtime is worked in. As a result it is much easier to monitor spending.

- Which information is used at an operational level?
- Which information is used at a tactical level?
- Think up some examples of decisions that could be made based on the tactical information provided.

Success or failure of a Management Information System

In spite of many technical advances and the investment of huge amounts of money, time and effort, many Management Information Systems have not fulfilled their promise and have failed to provide the management with the information that they need.

There are many factors that will affect whether an MIS is unsuccessful.

Inadequate analysis

It is important that the IT experts spend adequate time getting to know the information needs of the managers. This can only be achieved once a thorough understanding of the organisation has been gained and a detailed analysis made of the system.

Lack of management involvement in design

It is vital that the management is involved with the design of the system. They are to be the users and it is therefore crucial that any system meets their real needs.

Emphasis on computer system

A poor system will be produced if there is too much emphasis on the computer system and inadequate attention given to the whole system and the data flow throughout the organisation. The system should be designed around the information needs of the managers rather than be based upon what the computer can easily produce.

Concentration on low-level data processing

Many Management Information Systems have failed to provide adequate information as too much emphasis has been placed on the lower level data processing applications. Information is not provided in the right level of detail to enable managers to make the correct decision quickly.

Lack of management knowledge of ICT systems

The management will need to have an up-to-date knowledge of current IT systems and their capabilities. They will need to be able to make informed decisions and not be blinded by the IT experts' knowledge and use of jargon.

Inappropriate/excessive management demands

An inadequate knowledge of the capabilities of current technology may result in management making inappropriate or excessive demands from the system. When the system inevitably fails to meet their high expectations they will be disillusioned and may well not then use the system.

Lack of teamwork

Inadequate teamwork can lead to the chain breaking at its weakest link. Unless colleagues cooperate some work can be left undone, other work may be repeated.

Lack of professional standards

A lack of professional standards can lead to unmet deadlines and a system that does not function as was intended.

IT SPECIALISTS

Have a real, detailed knowledge of the business and the systems involved. A system should be designed around an organisation's needs, not just what works easily on a computer!

Carry out careful analysis of the current system and make sure that management requirements are fully understood

Consider the whole system, not just the parts that require computer use. Consider the complete information flow

Look at ways in which the new system will interact with other systems within the organisation

Consider information needs alongside day to day data processing needs

Work together as a team

Establish regular meetings

Agree and establish professional standards that should be maintained throughout the project

Use agreed project management techniques

Share a common goal

MANAGEMENT

Acquire a basic knowledge of IT systems, especially as they relate to the business. If necessary undergo training. Do not 'leave it all to the computer experts'

Be involved in all stages of design. Assess prototypes and feedback comments

Have an awareness of what can be done using IT at the moment and what cannot be done. Ensure that demands from the new system are technically realistic

Do not ask for too much and resist the temptation to keep changing your mind and demanding extras and alterations to the system

Be realistic

Figure 2.1 Ensuring a successful MIS – the role of IT specialists and management

---

Case Study 2

Passport to nowhere

In June 1999, 'teething problems' with a new computer system at Britain's Passport Agency led to a backlog of over half a million would-be holidaymakers waiting for their passports.

The problem was made worse by changes in the regulations requiring all children to have their own passport and by a 20 per cent increase in applications for passports. Offices were taking nearly 40 working days to process an application, compared to a target of ten days.

Queues formed outside passport offices. In Glasgow the first people started queuing one night at midnight. By 9.30 a.m. over 1000 people were waiting in the rain.

The new system, installed by the German company Siemens at a cost of £230 million, was needed because the old system was not Year 2000 compliant. Siemens said: 'It is misleading to suggest that the delays experienced by the public are primarily caused by failures in IT systems. It is clear that the application demand has exceeded Home Office forecasts.'

The new computer systems were installed first at offices in Liverpool and Newport. This was where the biggest backlogs occurred. Reports suggested that the need to install the whole system before the end of 1999 meant that the new system had not been fully tested.

So what went wrong?

continued ...

Case Study 2 *continued*

Many reasons were given for the Passport Agency's difficulties in issuing passports.

- The new ruling that children had to have their own passports undoubtedly made the problem worse. This obviously meant there would be an increase in the number of passports required and the number of passport applications. Was this taken into account in staffing levels and in the original hardware specification?

- The new computer system went online at the start of the summer – the Passport Agency's busiest time.

- The rush to introduce the complete new system meant that full testing and training had not been carried out.

- The new system was piloted at two offices. It should have undergone thorough testing at one site with real data before going live.

What lessons can be learned from this case study?

Summary

- A data processing system carries out the day to day operational activities of an organisation.

- An information system provides information for the user that can be used in decision making.

- A Management Information System (MIS) provides information in appropriate forms for managers. It converts data from internal and external sources into information. This is communicated in an appropriate form to managers at different levels to enable them to make effective decisions.

- Decisions can take place at different levels within an organisation: strategic, tactical and operational. The level of detail, form and type of information needed is different at each management level.

- Not all MIS systems are implemented successfully. Factors influencing success or failure include:
  - inadequate analysis
  - lack of management involvement in design
  - emphasis on computer system
  - concentration on low-level data processing
  - lack of management knowledge of IT systems and their capabilities
  - inappropriate/excessive management demands
  - lack of team work
  - lack of professional standards.

Information systems and organisations questions

1. A company which distributes car parts has recently expanded and wants to commission a new corporate information system. It needs the system to be successful to ensure the future growth of the business.
State five factors that could cause the failure of such an information system. *(5)*

AQA June 2002 Paper 4

2. A large chain of supermarkets makes use of data processing systems and information systems.
   a) With the use of suitable examples, identify the difference between a *data processing system* and an *information system. (4)*
   b) Describe, with an example of each, the role of an information system in decision making for the following levels of supermarket management:
      i)   tactical;
      ii) strategic. *(4)*
   c) Give an example of how a data processing operation in a supermarket might provide data for a company-wide information system. *(2)*

AQA June 2002 Paper 4

3. Patrick Maddock is the managing director of a medium sized publishing company. He feels that it is time that an MIS were developed. However, he has read horror stories about other businesses that had attempted to install such systems with disastrous results. He calls in a consultant for advice.

Write a report from the consultant, advising Patrick on what he needs to do to ensure that an MIS system developed for his business will be successful. *(8)*

4. The manager of a cinema is facing a dilemma of whether to raise admission prices by a small amount to ensure total income continues just to cover running expenses or to risk a much larger increase. Suggest a suitable type of general purpose package for the manager to use to study the implications of the options. Explain how the manager could use this package to assist the decision making process and the setting of admission prices. *(4)*

AEB Computing Specimen Paper 2

5. Organisations often use Management Information Systems.
   a) What is the purpose of a Management Information System? *(1)*
   b) Why is such a system required by managers of an organisation? *(1)*
   c) Give one example of the use of a Management Information System within an organisation, clearly stating its purpose. *(2)*

NEAB 1997 Paper 4

6. a) What is meant by a Management Information System? *(4)*
   b) State four factors which could contribute to the success or failure of an MIS. *(4)*

AQA ICT Specimen Paper 4

7. a) What is the purpose of a Management Information System? *(1)*
   b) Give one example of the use of a Management Information System within an organisation, clearly stating its purpose. *(2)*

AQA 2001 Paper 4

8. The manager of a local company complains that the company's information system continually fails to provide the correct level of information. State four possible reasons why the system is failing. *(4)*

NEAB 1999 Paper 4

9. Information systems are capable of producing strategic and operational level information. With the aid of examples, explain the difference between these two levels of information, clearly stating the level of personnel involved in using each one. *(6)*

NEAB 1999 Paper 4

10. Describe what is meant by the following terms, and give an example of each:
   a) a data processing system; *(3)*
   b) a management information system. *(3)*

AQA Jan 2003 Paper 4

The development and life cycle of an information system

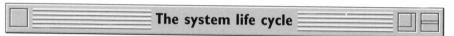

The system life cycle

The process of introducing a new information system is called the 'system life cycle'. The old system may be manual or computer-based. As the term *cycle* implies, producing a new information system is not a one-off exercise involving a few months of activity. A system, once developed, will need maintenance and eventually will be seen as inadequate to meet the users' needs so a new system will then need to be developed, and so on.

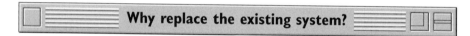

Why replace the existing system?

An information system might need replacing for a number of reasons.

The technology used might have become outdated

New technology may offer a more efficient solution or one that offers additional functions, enabling the organisation to be more competitive.

For example, British Telecom billing systems now provide itemised details of calls, increasing the amount of information available to customers. As new telecommunication companies start operating, British Telecom needs to provide more information to compete.

Of course it is not necessary to replace a system just because a new one can be developed. Often the old system will still be perfectly adequate for many years.

Changes in the organisation

The organisation of a business may alter, changing the requirements from the information system. This might happen for a number of reasons. The organisation might be expanding; restructuring; merging with, or taking over, another company; or diversifying into new areas of activity.

Changes in the demands of the users

What was acceptable to the user when a system was installed might not be a few years later. Users become increasingly sophisticated in their

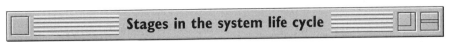

understanding of IT and consequently more demanding in how they expect a system to perform.

The purchase and installation of a new computer system is likely to be expensive. If the introduction of the new system is unsuccessful the cost to the company is likely to be even greater.

As the introduction of the new system is vital to the success of the organisation, formal methods of developing an information system have grown up to try to ensure the new system is a success.

The stages of introducing a new system that have traditionally been used are shown in Figure 3.1. The system is a cycle because no system lasts for ever, and, after a period of time, the cycle will start again with a new study into the feasibility of a new system.

Although the life cycle goes through a number of stages, a particular stage is often repeated a number of times. For example, when a design stage is apparently complete the prospective users or developers may highlight problems that require the stage to be repeated.

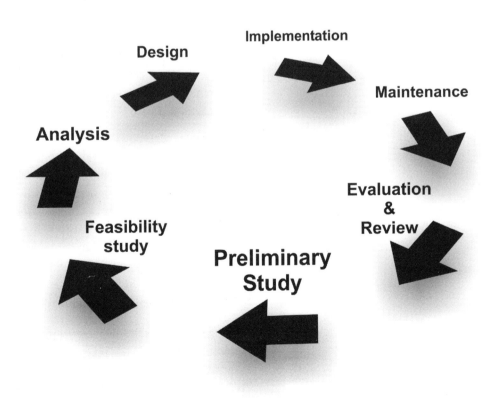

Figure 3.1 The traditional system life cycle

Preliminary study

This is a brief study to look at whether or not a new system is needed. The managers will initiate the study if they feel that the present system is not functioning well or that a new system might lead to improvements in productivity or quality.

Feasibility study

This study looks at the existing system and possible alternatives, including developing a new system or upgrading the old one. The study looks at whether the options are technically feasible and whether they are likely to be cost-effective. The study will include a formal report for the management who will then decide whether to give approval to continue.

Analysis

Once approval has been given to go ahead, the next stage is the systems analysis carried out by a systems analyst. This involves investigating the requirements of the existing system. This usually involves looking at current documents, sending questionnaires to staff, conducting interviews and direct observation. The systems analyst will use formal graphical and tabular methods to represent the current system. Data flow diagrams (DFDs) may be drawn up together with a number of charts showing how data will be organised.

The systems analysts use the information that they have found to produce a requirements specification for the new system.

Design

The design stage for the new system determines how the requirements specification will be implemented. It involves breaking down the problem into smaller sub-problems, designing the fields and tables of the database, input formats, output formats, validation checks and the test plan. Clear time scales are needed to prevent the project from overrunning. A project timetable and deadlines for each part of the work will be included in the design. A system specification is drawn up in sufficient detail for the programmers to implement the system.

Implementation

Implementation consists of a number of stages:

Hardware and software development

This is the stage when the system is produced by the development of programs and/or customisation of software packages. Programs are coded, tested and documented. In all but the smallest projects, a team of programmers will be involved. It is vital that the work is monitored very carefully and that time limits are adhered to. Files will need to be converted into a form suitable for the new system. Hardware must also be installed and thoroughly tested. Installation may require extensive cabling and alteration of buildings.

Testing

Testing is a crucial part of program development. Test data should test that all branches of the program perform to specification. Data should be used to test extreme cases. For example, if a temperature value can be any number in the range 0 to 25, the values 0 and 25 would be the extreme values. Testing should also include invalid data to ensure that it is rejected. (Temperature values of 26, –4 and 56 would be invalid.) When testing, it is crucial that the results produced by the program are compared with expected results. Any discrepancies should be investigated.

Changeover

The changeover to the new system takes place once all the programming is complete and follows a complete systems test. It is possible to test a system before full implementation by using historical data. The output from the new system is compared with that produced by the old system.

It is crucial that all users of the new system should be trained. They will need to have confidence in their ability to use it.

There are four commonly used methods of changeover: parallel running, direct conversion, phased conversion and pilot running. The choice of the appropriate method of implementation depends on a number of factors that will include the nature of the system and the type and size of the organisation.

Changeover methods

PARALLEL RUNNING

With parallel running, both old and new systems are run together for a certain time. When the new system is established and running smoothly, the old system can be dropped. This is a safe method of conversion as a backup to the new system is available in case problems arise. If any bugs arise in the new system, they can be corrected. Users can learn the new system at their own pace, without the fear that making mistakes would be disastrous.

However, parallel running can be very costly as extra time will be required to run both systems concurrently. It can also lead to confusion.

DIRECT CONVERSION

With a direct changeover, an existing system is replaced by the new system at a certain time and date. From then on, the old system is no longer used.

A direct changeover costs less than any other method of conversion, as at any time only one system is operational, so no time is wasted. However, there is no backup if things go wrong so there is a much higher risk than with parallel running. Staff will need to have received a high level of training prior to changeover so that they feel confident in using the new system. For some systems, direct changeover is the only possible method.

PHASED CONVERSION

Phased conversion allows the changeover to occur in stages. This is only appropriate for systems that can be broken down into separate sections that can be developed one after the other. In most systems this is not possible, as different sections of a system all interrelate.

PILOT RUNNING

The final method of conversion uses a pilot. This is where the system is implemented in one department or location in advance of the whole organisation. Bugs and running problems can be cleared up and users' reactions to the system taken into account before the whole system is implemented. Training can also be modified in the light of experience. Such a method is only possible in organisations that have discrete sections or branches. It may prove necessary for the pilot sites to run the old system in parallel.

Maintenance

Once a system is in full operation it is monitored to check that it has met the objectives set out in the original specification. Inevitably, changes will need to be made to the systems. These changes are known as **systems maintenance**. Most programming hours are spent on maintaining existing systems rather than in producing new systems.

Evaluation and review

When the implementation of a project is complete, it is necessary to evaluate the success of the project and review its effectiveness. Such evaluation will involve returning to the original objectives and performance criteria to assess how well they have been met.

Evaluation will involve discussions with management and users of the system some time after it has been installed to gather their opinions of the new system's effectiveness. Other, objective, tests of performance should be made, such as testing that the speed of carrying out difference tasks is within the requirement set. Surveys can be used to find out if information flows are correct and whether or not the information that is delivered is of a high quality (see Chapter 5 on Information).

Case Study 1

A new system at Nissan

Paperwork at Nissan's Sunderland plant had reached such proportions that labour costs were excessive and mailing costs high.

A feasibility study suggested that some of this paperwork could be carried out by computer using EDI (Electronic Data Interchange). This means sending documents such as orders and invoices to suppliers electronically via the telephone network rather than by post.

The analysis involved looking at the old manual system to see how it was carried out and what documents were involved.

A new system was designed cutting out the printed mailings. This saved time in communicating and removed the need for rekeying, thereby reducing errors.

After thorough testing implementation took place, originally with only a few suppliers. The system was then extended to more suppliers, cutting the mail to suppliers by over 90 per cent.

- Explain, in your own words, why the old system was replaced.

- What is EDI? Investigate its use by searching the Web.

- Which changeover method was used? Why?

Case Study 2

An electronic registration system

A sixth-form college in the south of England decided to install an electronic registration system for class attendance. Each teacher has an A4 wallet which holds a specialised computer device. Each device is battery run and linked to a central computer by radio, a receiver/transmitter being installed for each cluster of classrooms.

The new method of registration was chosen to replace the current, paper-based system. Transmitters were installed and wallets configured during the Easter holidays. For the first half of the summer term, the system was piloted by the Biology and English departments. Some bugs and operational problems were sorted out during this pilot run. The rest of the teachers were introduced to the system and trained in its use.

Figure 3.2 EARS register in use in the classroom

continued...

Case Study 2 *continued*

After the half-term break, the system went live throughout the college. However, to ensure that backup would be available in the case of failure, the paper-based system was continued in parallel. Gradually the staff bacame more confident users and fewer mistakes were made and less support needed. The following September the old paper-based system was abandoned.

○ Explore the effects that computer failure of the EARS system could have on the college attendance system.

○ Describe three other electronic means of collecting attendance data. Explain the advantages and disadvantages of each method.

○ Examine the aspects that would have been considered by the college when undertaking a feasibility study.

Summary

The system life cycle is the series of stages involved in replacing an old system with a new one. The stages are:

○ **Problem identification and preliminary study**.

○ **Feasibility study** – A preliminary investigation to find out whether the required new system is technically and economically possible. At the end of this stage the senior management will decide whether or not to give the go ahead.

○ **Analysis** – An investigation into the current system to find out how it works and what is required from a new system. Techniques used include:

   ○ interview
   ○ questionnaire
   ○ observation
   ○ detailed study of documents.

○ **Design** – All the elements of the new system are planned:

   ○ inputs
   ○ outputs
   ○ data storage
   ○ human–computer interface
   ○ test plan
   ○ clear timescales are needed and deadlines set.

○ **Implementation and testing** – The application is built using an appropriate programming language or software development tool. It is thoroughly tested, using a realistic volume of real data as well as extreme and invalid data. The current system is replaced with the new system. New files have to be created, hardware set up, users trained. Implementation can be:

   ○ parallel
   ○ direct
   ○ phased
   ○ piloted.

○ **Maintenance** – On-going changes are made to the system.

○ **Evaluation and review** – The effectiveness of the system is investigated.

Development and life cycle of an information system questions

1. Explain the purpose of a feasibility study. Include in your answer the areas that should be considered. (5)

2. Draw a diagram to illustrate the main phases of the traditional system life cycle. (5)

3. Describe the advantages of using prototyping in systems design. (6)

4. The management of a company wishes to introduce a computerised diary and scheduling package that is known to be compatible with the existing software base. With the aid of examples, give three factors that could influence the success or failure of this exercise. (6)
   NEAB 1997 Paper 3

5. Give, with justification, a suitable method of changeover for the following:

   a) a new electronic data entry system for a chain of retail clothing shops

   b) a computer-controlled traffic light management system

   c) a computerised loans system for a college library to replace the current card-based manual system

   d) an online seat booking system for a cinema, allowing seats to be booked from a number of outlets

   e) an electronic timekeeping system in a manufacturing company with ten factories throughout the UK

   f) a network-shared diary system for a large business. (6)

6. A systems analyst has been employed to produce a computer-based system to replace the current manual one in a lending library. Describe three methods of investigating the current system. For each method explain what information the analyst would expect to gather. (9)

Corporate information systems strategy

Business strategy

All organisations have objectives which determine the way in which they function. For many organisations an objective may be to make a profit whilst for others providing a service may be the main objective. Breaking even, survival, growth or maximising sales are all possible objectives.

Businesses need a strategy to help them to achieve these objectives. The strategy may define what the business will do to become or remain successful. For example the strategy might plan areas of expansion and anticipate areas of growth.

Information system strategy

The business strategy should include an information technology strategy. An IT strategy is concerned with the planning, introduction and use of IT resources for the benefit of the entire organisation. The strategy must be closely linked to the other strategies and plans of the organisation.

IT is not an end in itself. It is used to help the business perform better. Similarly the IT strategy is not an independent strategy but part of the whole business strategy.

Corporate thinking

It is important that there is a corporate approach in any IT strategy, that is, an approach that covers the whole organisation. It would not be a good idea for one department in a business to use one type of computer and another department to use another. Using similar equipment has several advantages:

- Purchases of hardware and software licences may be cheaper with economies of scale.

- Data files from one department may be used by another department.

- Departments can communicate easily – they may be on the same network.

- Training and technical support only needs to be offered for one type of computer.
- Staff can move from one department to another without the need for retraining.

Factors influencing an information system within an organisation

Every organisation is different and the information system must be developed to meet its needs. Among the factors influencing the choice and design of an information system are:

The objectives of the organisation

The information system is only a means to an end. It exists to support the organisation in pursuit of its objectives. A company manufacturing automotive parts will have different objectives from one selling insurance. This will affect the sort of system required.

The organisational structure of the organisation

The information system needs to provide information to the right person at the right level in the right detail. For example, an organisation which is managed geographically will have regional managers who require reports summarising the performance of all functions within that region. In an organisation that is structured functionally, a production manager would require summaries of the performance at all factories in the organisation.

Information flow within the organisation

The information system should enable good communication within the organisation. The design of the information system must take account of information flow. Who sends which information to whom? When is it sent? How often?

Hardware and software

Any information system must be able to read existing data files. New software must be compatible with old software. To change to another package could cause unnecessary anxiety and require further training. Hardware must be appropriate. In buying new hardware, it is essential that old software and data can be used easily. Continuity is important.

Legal issues

The information system must take account of legal requirements such as Health and Safety regulations, the Data Protection Act and financial audit requirements.

Personnel organisation

The system must take account of the personnel and their roles. It will differ depending on who has responsibility for the information system within the organisation, who is responsible for writing the IT strategy, who is responsible for implementing it and who purchases equipment?

Management organisation and decision making methods

The nature of the information system will depend on who makes the decisions in the company. It could be the Chief Executive or Managing Director or the Board of Directors. Some organisations make extensive use of committees for decision-making. Some delegate decisions to less senior staff.

The resources available (finance, staff and time)

The resources must be available to purchase and maintain the system.

Behavioural factors

In any organisation human behavioural issues will determine priorities. The personalities of the people who will use the system, their motivation and ability to adapt to change all have to be taken into account.

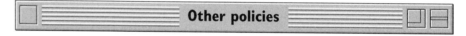

Other policies

Organisations will also need policies on the following:

- Information – what to store and for how long
- Security – keeping information secure
- Backup – how, when and what to backup
- Legal – how to comply with the Data Protection Act.

These policies are covered in Chapters 8, 9, 14 and 15.

Many public bodies publish their IT strategy on the Internet. For example, Essex University's policy can be found at: www2.essex.ac.uk/iss/policies/InformationSystemsStrategy/CurrentStrategy.htm.

Case Study 1

A local council's IT strategy

The following excerpts are from a local council's IT strategy. In recent years the council, like every other large business, has become increasingly dependent on computers for its administration.

Previously computers had been used simply as a means of handling large volumes of data and of carrying out calculations quickly. As such their use was mainly confined to the major financial systems and consisted of the processing of 'batches' of data leading to the production of large volumes of printed output. Examples were the payroll, rates bills and cheques for the payment of creditors.

continued ...

Case Study 1 *continued*

More recently, computer technology and software have developed rapidly. The development of online systems and associated elimination of paper records mean that whole areas of operation are now totally dependent on computers for both storage of data and for calculations. The government has set the council deadlines for introducing more and more service delivery electronically.

The need for a strategy

The whole installation has developed over a number of years as and when required. Generally, these developments have taken place either in response to a perceived need to increase efficiency, to provide an improved service to the public, or in response to legislation.

In spite of this fragmented approach to computer development, a high degree of compatibility between systems and departments has been maintained. However, a large part of the present installation is now technically obsolete and will need to be replaced within the next year. If the replacement is to be done in the most cost-effective way it needs to take place within an agreed strategy for information technology.

At present the council has no such formal plan and it is now time to adopt a broad strategy within which future acquisition of equipment and development of systems should take place.

Extract from the IT strategy of the council

1   The Council should continue to maintain automated office systems which permit the maximum possible transfer of data between users. All future system developments and acquisitions of equipment should be designed with this principle in mind.

2   The Council should be asked to approve each year a rolling programme for the development of new computer systems. This programme should be designed to take account of both legislative requirements and potential improvements in efficiency (whether internal initiatives or external audit recommendations).

   The programme should indicate the reason for the proposals and the level (if any) of cost savings which will result.

3   Whenever appropriate new computer systems are recommended in the rolling programme they should be capable of exchanging data with existing systems. Data common to more than one system should be held so far as possible in one place only.

4   As a gerneral rule the Council should aim to purchase commercially produced software whenever possible, unless a suitable product is not available or it can clearly be shown that in-house development is more economical. This strategy recognises that in some cases the purchase of stand-alone Personal Computers in order to run specific software might be the most cost-effective solution to a problem.

   Before such purchases are made, however, a proper technical appraisal of the options should be carried out by specialist computer staff within the Finance Department. This appraisal should take into account the compatibility of both the proposed hardware and software with that already being operated by the Council.

5   The Council's major financial systems should continue to operate on the existing mainframe computer until it is in need of replacement. At that time a full appraisal of the means by which these systems are to continue should be undertaken.

6   A full appraisal should be undertaken into the possible advantages of increased use of electronic data transfer, either by e-mail or alternative means. If increased use of this facility is recommended, formal procedures for such use should be drawn up.

7   This strategy should be reviewed periodically at intervals of not more than two years.

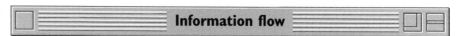

Information flow

Managers need information that is relevant to the task in hand. Good information helps them to plan, to control and to make the right decisions. The better the information, the greater their knowledge of the situation and the better the decision-making.

Information flows externally between the organisation and the outside world. For example, a customer might order items from the company. The company might respond by sending an acknowledgement to the customer. These are both examples of external information flow.

Information also flows internally within the organisation. Huge amounts of information can be generated as a result of day-to-day processes. An organisation must establish appropriate methods and routines for communicating information internally. For example, distribution lists will be kept with the names of all people who should receive a certain report when it is produced.

Within the same department, information usually flows up and down the chain of command. It is unusual for information to go up or down more than one level at a time. For example, the production line in a factory breaks down: the production line workers tell the foreman; the foreman tells the production supervisor; the production supervisor tells the production manager; the production manager tells the production director who may make the decision. This may mean that messages get distorted and decisions take a long time.

There are a number of different formal methods by which information flows, such as:

- Formal meetings are a common way of disseminating information.

- E-mail is an increasingly common way of communicating internally, particularly as e-mails can very easily be sent to a 'global' mailing list of every employee.

- Internal memos can be sent to individual employees or to a whole section or department.

- Notice boards in common work areas such as corridors, staff rooms or canteens. These are often used for legal requirements such as health and safety regulations and fire notices.

- Presentations to groups of employees to explain why something is going to happen.

Of course there are less formal methods of information flow which may be less reliable and less accurate, such as the office grapevine, stories in the local press and rumours. Informal data flow is an important element within an organisation.

Formal data flow

This is defined by the system with fully documented and agreed procedures stating stages of flow, control, exception handling and the network for distribution.

Informal data flow

This 'naturally arises' within the organisation via phone calls, personal conversation, meetings or observation.

When an employee requires some stationery he fills in a form that is sent to the Supplies Department where the data is entered into a system that produces a weekly list of requests. Goods are then distributed and a report sent to the Accounts Department detailing the amounts to be charged to the appropriate departments. This is the formal information flow. When a member of staff needs an item of stationery urgently she phones the Supplies Department with the request. This is an example of informal information flow.

A company information system must support the information flow of the company. For example, if the Marketing Department use information on last month's sales to plan their next campaign, the department manager will require accurate information quickly on which to make decisions.

Information flow and the organisational structure

It is crucial that information arrives at its destination in time to be used. For this to happen, it is vital that the data and information flows within an organisation are carefully planned. These flows will differ between organisations and are dependent upon a number of factors.

The size, type and structure of an organisation will all play a large part. Within a small business the close proximity of employees means that formal systems for sharing information are not necessary.

Within a large organisation, the flow of information needs to be carefully planned. As information normally flows up and down the chain of command, it often has to pass through many levels. This can lead to delays and distortions. If the organisational structure is poorly designed, one person may have to deal with more information that they can cope with. This creates a bottleneck and inevitably other people will be waiting for the information.

The amount of information will affect information flow. Obviously the more information, the longer it can take to process.

The nature of the data will have a major effect on information flow. How and where the data originates is a factor. It could be electronically generated, for example, through Point of Sale (POS) terminals and processed by powerful tools to produce information that is disseminated over a network to managers on their desktop computer. Alternatively, it could have originated from hand written notes and telephone conversations.

ICT, particularly e-mail, can make information flow more easily. Firstly, it is immediate. Secondly, it is easy to send to many recipients such as every employee and so can bypass the bottlenecks. Thirdly, it is easy to reply to or forward by clicking on one button. This may however lead to information overload. It is too easy to send the message to everybody even if it is not really relevant to them. Users in many organisations complain of e-mail overload where the indiscriminate copying and forwarding of messages has caused an unmanageable volume.

Many large organisations now provide information internally using an intranet enabling employees to share information.

> **Personnel**

The three different levels of an organisation (strategic, tactical and operational) have different information requirements and this will be reflected in the design of a company's information system. The dissemination and distribution of reports to the appropriate people at the appropriate time will be a crucial factor in a system's success. Reports must arrive at the right manager's desk at the time when a decision needs to be made, in a suitable format to be useable.

Operational

IT was first used at the operational level for data processing. It is still used extensively at this level. A supermarket checkout operator receives operational information, that is, the price of each product as it is barcode scanned and the total price of a customer's purchases.

Tactical (or implemetational)

When making decisions, a supermarket manager will not be interested in individual sales. However, she will be interested in sales trends and information on staff performance. Information may be aggregated using an MIS and the manager may have access to a range of graphical displays.

Strategic

The supermarket's chief executive will not be interested in individual staff within a store but will want to know which stores are performing well and which are performing badly, which products are no longer popular and which products are increasing in sales. This information will help decisions about future strategies.

> **Example of information flow**

- A mail order company takes a telephone order for a product (external source).

- The details must be recorded, either on paper or on a computer. The information must be sent to the dispatch department in the warehouse. This could be done on paper or by e-mail (internal operational information transfer).

- The dispatch department finds the goods and writes the dispatch note (external operational information transfer) to send with the goods. This could also be done on a computer. A copy is sent to the accounts department (internal operational information transfer). The goods are posted.

The accounts department prepares an invoice (external operational information transfer) to send out and records (on a computer) that the payment is due. The payment is awaited (external operational information transfer).

This is all common day-to-day operational information. If the dispatch department noticed that this particular item was out of stock, they may inform their manager (internal operational information transfer) who may need to make a tactical decision based on this and other information, to order more stock or to order from a different supplier or to find out if there are problems with the supplier (tactical information transfer).

If the supplier is unreliable, the manager may need to tell the managing director who may need to take the strategic decision not to buy from this supplier any more (strategic information transfer).

Summary

- Organisations should have policies on:
  - IT – A corporate approach to buying equipment ensuring current data can be used.
  - Upgrading – compatibility needs to be considered.
- Issues that affect the IT policy include organisational structure, decision making methods, legal requirements, information flow, hardware and software and behavioural factors.
- Information flow can be formal or informal.
- **Formal data flow** is defined by the system with fully documented and agreed procedures stating stages of flow, control, exception handling and the network for distribution.
- **Informal data flow** 'naturally arises' within the organisation via phone calls, personal conversation, meetings or observation.
- Information flow is affected by a number of factors. Delays can occur at all stages of flow. Factors include:
  - the structure of the organisation
  - the size of the organisation
  - the geographical structure of the organisation
  - how data originates within an organisation
  - the form of the information
  - the volume of data.
- E-mail and intranets can speed up access to information.
- Different levels of an organisation need different levels of information.

Corporate information systems strategy questions

1. 'If I need an IT system I buy whatever hardware and software I want without any regard to anyone.' This statement was made by a manager of a department in a company. Why is this an inappropriate approach in a large organisation? (6)

   NEAB Specimen Paper 5

2. 'I don't care which version of a word-processing package the rest of the company uses. As a senior company manager I intend to upgrade my department to the latest version.' Give four potential problems this attitude may cause for other IT users in the company. (4)

   NEAB 1998 Paper 5

3. Information flows through an organisation.
   a) State six factors which influence the flow of information and data within an organisation. (6)
   b) With the aid of examples, describe three techniques which could be used to review the current information flows. (6)

   NEAB 1997 Paper 4

4. A supermarket cashier scans a bar code on a product. The code is sent to the store's computer. The price and name of the product is sent to the till and printed on the receipt. Details of the sale are immediately stored in a transaction file. Every hour the transaction file is sent to the store's warehouse to update stock levels.

   a) What is the source document?
   b) What level of information is the code going into the computer?
   c) What level of information is contained in the transaction file going to the warehouse? (3)

5. For each of the following examples say if the communication is internal or external and if the information is strategic, tactical or operational.
   a) The managing director's diary for next week.
   b) Details of a car's former owners from the Police National Computer.
   c) Sales figures for a supermarket's 200 stores.
   d) News that George will be off sick today.
   e) 6000 widgets need to be delivered immediately. (10)

6. A customer of a bank wants to withdraw some money from a cash machine. Describe the information flow. (6)

7. A company with two office buildings 200 m apart is having problems with internal communications. They are considering internal e-mail to solve the problem. Explain three reasons why this may help and three reasons why it may not. (6)

8. In planning the information flow within a system, where are the delays likely to occur and why? (6)

   NEAB Specimen Paper 4

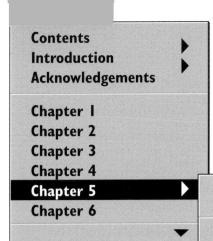

Information

The difference between data and information was explored as part of the AS course. Raw facts and figures are recorded as data. When data is given a structure and put into a context it becomes information. Information is a vital tool at all levels of an organisation. However, it is not just a matter of 'the more information the better' – too much information, particularly if much of it is irrelevant to the particular situation, can make it harder to pick out what is important.

The use of e-mail as a major medium of communication has led to problems in some organisations. Some managers can return to their desks after a few hours away to find dozens of e-mail messages awaiting them. Many have been sent to them unnecessarily, forwarded by colleagues. Many users click on the 'reply all' option rather than the 'reply' so sending their response to a message to everyone on the circulation list instead of just the originator of the message. Some e-mails contain trivial messages. Misuse of e-mail has got so bad in some organisations that management have imposed e-mail free afternoons when employees are banned from sending internal e-mails.

Internet users can often be frustrated when they find it hard to find the exact information they need. It is not unusual to go to a rail company web site to find out the time of trains to a particular destination only to be faced with details of special offers, timings of rail works and holiday ideas.

Managers in all kinds of organisations need information that is relevant to the task in hand. It is needed to help individuals to plan future actions, to control and to make decisions. The greater the relevance of the information the more the knowledge of the situation will be increased.

All managers need information to do their job effectively. However, the information that they need, and the form that it should be in, will be different in different situations. The type of information needed depends on a number of factors, including the level of the manager, the actual task being carried out and its urgency.

To help make sense of the huge variety in information it is useful to identify the characteristics of specific information needs. This information can be classified in many ways including:

- **By source:** for example, internal, external, primary, secondary.

- **By nature:** for example, quantitative, qualitative, formal, informal.

- **By level:** for example, strategic, tactical, operational.

- **By time:** for example, historical, present, future.

- **By frequency:** for example, continuous (real time), hourly, daily, monthly, annually.

- **By use:** for example, planning, control, decision-making.

- **By form:** for example, written, aural, visual, sensory.

- **By type:** for example, detailed, sampled, aggregated.

Sources of information

A **source document** is the original document bringing information into an organisation. When an electricity company calculates customers' electricity bills, the source document is the meter reading card storing details of the customer's meter reading. This is an **internal source of information**.

When a mail order company receives a written order from a customer, this is an **external source of information**.

Both these examples are filled in directly, they are **primary sources of information**. Sometimes the information has to be transferred on to another piece of paper or on to a computer file. This is a **secondary source of information**.

Internal sources of information

Internal information is generated from within the organisation. Its source is likely to be an information system or it may be produced as a by product of a data processing system. For a detailed study refer to Chapter 2.

External sources of information

External sources of information are those which are outside an organisation. Business people may use external surveys and annual reports from other organisations, as well as statistics and research reports. There are many information sources available: newspapers, magazines, radio, television, teletext, local authority departments and government agencies.

Many local authorities have advisory services which can provide help to people who want to set up small businesses. Any organisation which wishes to extend its buildings must consult the local Planning Office before building. Information will be needed from the

Department of Environmental Health about issues such as noise levels and waste disposal.

The public library contains a wide selection of business and commercial directories which can be a useful source of information. Information can also be purchased from outside sources, such as research houses and public opinion organisations like Gallup. Government websites provide a considerable amount of information that is useful for managers when planning and making decisions. The guidelines relating to IT legislation are an example of the kind of information available.

When a school or college analyses its A level results, comparisons will be made with the national figures for each subject. These national figures are an example of external information.

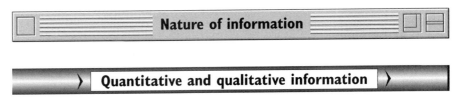

Nature of information

Quantitative and qualitative information

Information can be of two general types: **quantitative** and **qualitative**.

Quantitative information is that which can be measured numerically, for example, 3476 cars were sold last week and Mike German's net salary was £1243.44 last month. Quantitative information can easily be presented in numerical or graphical form. A balance sheet or a graph showing sales trends both contain quantitative information.

Qualitative information cannot be measured in numerical terms, for example, the different colours that a model of car can be produced in. Qualitative information may have come from data based on value judgements, that is data that is based on a person's opinion and so is often harder to present and interpret than quantitative data, but can be just as important to a manager.

Case Study 1

Ed Black

Ed Black runs his own business. He sets up management training courses for a wide range of organisations. For each course that he runs he gathers information that helps him to run his business. He records the number of people attending each course, if the course was full, the number he was unable to accommodate, the amount paid by each course member, client satisfaction and any comments on how the course could be improved.

- ◯ Explain how Ed would use each of the items of information he collects.

- ◯ Identify the qualitative and the quantitative information that Ed collects.

- ◯ Can you suggest any further internal information that would help Ed in the running of his business? Give your reasons.

- ◯ Can you suggest any external information that would help Ed in the running of his business? Give your reasons.

Formal and informal information

Formal information is created and disseminated as part of the predetermined information systems of the organisation where fully documented and agreed procedures define the flow and control of data and the way in which exceptions should be handled. The details of the distribution of reports, such as who receives a copy and how frequently, is defined. It can consist of reports of all types provided by a Management Information System. Examples could include an annual regional sales summary, a department's monthly expenses summary and a report of current stock levels.

Committee meeting minutes and agendas, and internal publications such as a company newsletter, are also examples of formal information.

Informal information naturally arises within the organisation and is communicated through personal conversations both by face-to-face contact or through telephone conversations. It can also be conveyed in memos or even scribbled notes written on a piece of paper. There is no clearly defined distribution network for informal information.

Level of information

Strategic information is that which is required at the highest levels to make decisions. A director or chief executive would use strategic information to decide on future policy, for example, the decision of a supermarket to offer a banking service. Strategic information is often in the form of a report where information from a number of sources and of a number of types has been brought together.

Tactical information is used by middle managers. For example, a sales manager may need information relating each product and its sales performance so that he can make appropriate decisions on future pricing and advertising plans.

Operational information is required for the day-to-day running of an organisation. An example of operational information is that used by a foreman in a factory to decide on the day's production and staff rotas.

Timing of information

Management information systems attempt to ensure that managers can obtain accurate, relevant information at the right times to improve their decision making. It should provide information on the past (**historic** information about production levels, and so on), the present (**current** production figures, markets, and so on) and the future (**projected** or **forecasted** profits, and so on).

Activity 1

A school or college will use both formal and informal information. Working in a group of three or four, identify examples of information used in your institution and then categorise each as formal or informal. Highlight those examples that are qualitative information.

An example of **historic information** could be last December's sales figures, needed for a toy shop just before Christmas to plan for this Christmas's stock levels. The information in a company's annual report for shareholders will be historic with summaries of sales, expenditure and development in different areas of the company.

Summaries of GCSE and A level results for all schools appear in national newspapers a few weeks after the results are received by the pupils. Such a report is historic information.

An example of **current information** could be information from time sheets for this week's wages which have to be paid on Thursday.

An example of **future information** could be projected sales figures and population details for an area, helping the store decide whether to open a new store or expand an existing store.

Frequency of information

The use to which information is put determines the frequency of its production.

Real time information is produced immediately transaction data is processed. When a shop assistant swipes a customer's credit card to check the credit ratings, she requires feedback from the credit card company's computer at once before carrying on with the sale. When booking a flight at a travel agency, information on availability and cost are needed straight away so that a decision can be made whether or not to book.

Other information is needed at **regular intervals**, perhaps hourly, daily, weekly or monthly. Percentage figures for student attendance in class can be obtained on a weekly basis from an electronic attendance registration system. The amount outstanding on a credit card account is calculated monthly, a statement and request for payment is then sent to the card holder.

Uses of information

Information helps managers in several ways.

Information is used by a manager to monitor and control the work done under his span of control. For example, a sales manager may use the monthly sales figures of different regions as the basis for making changes where individual performances are below target. In a factory producing plastic mouldings for car interiors, the foreman can make technical adjustments to the machinery on the basis of quality control information on faulty goods.

Information can be used for **planning**. For example, a marketing manager, planning the launch of a new product, would use historic sales information on other company products together with their projected sales. External information gathered from consumer surveys would also be valuable in deciding how to market the product, which market sectors it should be aimed at and what price to charge.

Information is a vital tool in the decision making process. For example, if a marketing manager has to decide whether or not to continue producing and selling a particular product, he will need a range of information on which to base his decision. Such information would include the level of sales over a period, the profit from the sales, the projected sales for the future and performance of similar products.

Decision making takes up a large part of the work of a manager. The appropriate information helps the manager make good decisions. It is a management cliché that 'a decision is only as good as the quality of information it is built on'. What makes good information is discussed in detail later in the chapter.

Form of information

Information can be presented in a variety of forms. The intended audience may determine the from that the information takes.

Much business information is **written** in the form of reports, memos or tables. Most of these will be computer produced.

However, for many purposes, a more **visual** representation can convey the same information with more impact; charts, graphs and pictures are often used to convey information more clearly.

Some information is received aurally (by ear) in casual conversations, at meetings or over the telephone. Information can also be obtained through other senses such as touch.

Type of information

Detailed information, such as an inventory list showing the stock level of every item held, is most often used at the operational level.

Aggregated information consists of totals created when detailed information is summed together. For example, the details of all purchases from all the customers added together would be aggregated data. Figure 5.2 shows the total number of each type of hat sold by a manufacturer for each three month period during 2002. This information would be used to spot trends in sales of particular hat styles as well as highlighting the most popular models. Detailed information, which might itemise every sale, would not be useful in this way.

Activity 2

The case study on page 35 referred to Ed Black who runs his own management training business. Describe what information Ed would need to enable him to plan his next series of courses.

Actvity 3

Find five examples of bad decisions that were made because of inadequate information being available at the time the decision was made.

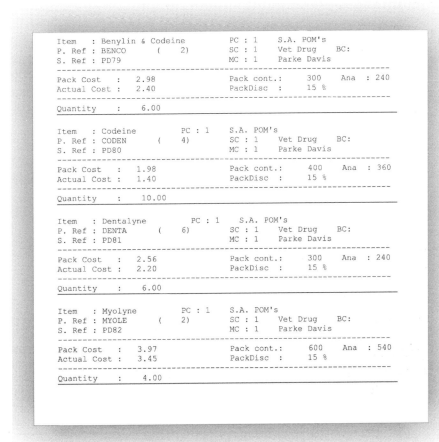

```
Item   : Benylin & Codeine      PC : 1    S.A. POM's
P. Ref : BENCO        (    2)    SC : 1    Vet Drug     BC:
S. Ref : PD79                    MC : 1    Parke Davis
-------------------------------------------------------------
Pack Cost    :    2.98          Pack cont.:     300    Ana  : 240
Actual Cost  :    2.40          PackDisc  :      15 %
-------------------------------------------------------------
Quantity     :    6.00

Item   : Codeine              PC : 1    S.A. POM's
P. Ref : CODEN        (    4)    SC : 1    Vet Drug     BC:
S. Ref : PD80                    MC : 1    Parke Davis
-------------------------------------------------------------
Pack Cost    :    1.98          Pack cont.:     400    Ana  : 360
Actual Cost  :    1.40          PackDisc  :      15 %
-------------------------------------------------------------
Quantity     :   10.00

Item   : Dentalyne            PC : 1    S.A. POM's
P. Ref : DENTA        (    6)    SC : 1    Vet Drug     BC:
S. Ref : PD81                    MC : 1    Parke Davis
-------------------------------------------------------------
Pack Cost    :    2.56          Pack cont.:     300    Ana  : 240
Actual Cost  :    2.20          PackDisc  :      15 %
-------------------------------------------------------------
Quantity     :    6.00

Item   : Myolyne              PC : 1    S.A. POM's
P. Ref : MYOLE        (    2)    SC : 1    Vet Drug     BC:
S. Ref : PD82                    MC : 1    Parke Davis
-------------------------------------------------------------
Pack Cost    :    3.97          Pack cont.:     600    Ana  : 540
Actual Cost  :    3.45          PackDisc  :      15 %
-------------------------------------------------------------
Quantity     :    4.00
```

Figure 5.1 Report showing detailed information

Sampled information refers only to selected records, for example, details from just a few of the customers. Reports of this type are often called exception reports. The report shown in Figure 5.3 could be used to highlight major customers who may be sent a special offer.

Good decisions require good information. The characteristics of good information are given below.

Internal and external information requirements – An organisation has to produce information for a number of reasons. Most information is used internally within the organisation, but there are certain needs external to the organisation. Examples of these would be company reports to shareholders and product information for customers.

A sixth-form college has an MIS system that produces a wide range of information including details of student attendance and performance, exam entries and results. Many internal reports are produced for different personnel within the college that are relevant to their particular roles.

Information is also needed for external use. Together with a prospectus with details of courses, prospective students and their parents often require a summary of the exam results of the previous year giving the number of passes in each grade band for each subject.

HATHERLEY HATS UK SALES - 2003							
	Trilby	Boater	Bonnet	Topper	Bowler	Cap	Total
1st Quarter	234	1245	345	734	3456	2421	8435
2nd Quarter	245	1078	356	722	7894	2567	12862
3rd Quarter	256	1076	376	678	5567	2789	10742
4th Quarter	287	1098	386	456	5237	2599	10063
Quarterly Average	255.5	1124.25	365.75	647.5	5538.5	2594	10525.5
Quarterly Total	1022	4497	1463	2590	22154	10376	42102
% of Total Sales	2.43%	10.68%	3.47%	6.15%	52.62%	24.64%	100.00%

Figure 5.2 Report showing aggregated information

Orders over £1000 in value				
Order Number	Order Date	Co. Ref	Co. Name	Value
21403	11-Mar	1289	Bradshaw & Son Transport	£4,456.06
21409	12-Mar	1289	Bradshaw & Son Transport	£1,652.00
21405	09-Mar	1414	Garvey Linguistic Services	£1,466.23
21406	11-Mar	2561	ADS	£1,654.56
21410	12-Mar	1414	Carr Associates	£2,489.57
21407	10-Mar	1451	Green Cosmetics	£2,389.89
21408	11-Mar	1290	Joslin International	£1,495.23

Figure 5.3 Report showing sampled data

Detailed tables of information on all student enrolments and achievements together with a range of other statistics are required by the Local Skills Council (LSC) for funding purposes. The information is transmitted electronically.

The college governors require an annual report that summarises the number of students and the achievements of different subjects in examinations.

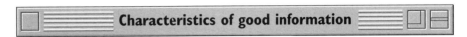
Characteristics of good information

Good information is that which is used and which creates value. Experience and research show that good information has numerous qualities.

Good information is:

1   **relevant** for its purpose
2   **complete** enough for the problem
3   **reliable** – from a source in which the user has confidence
4   sufficiently **accurate** for its purpose
5   communicated to the **right person**
6   communicated in **time** for its purpose
7   that which contains the **right level of detail**
8   that which is **understandable** by the user
9   communicated by an appropriate **channel of communication.**

Relevance

What is relevant for one manager may not be relevant for another. The user will become frustrated if information in any way contains parts that are irrelevant to the task in hand. A stock report would not be relevant to a human resources manager who is concerned with employees.

Completeness

If a marketing manager was deciding whether the sale of a particular product should be discontinued, his decision could be impaired if he did not have figures for overseas sales. Ideally all the information needed for a particular decision should be available. However, this rarely happens. In reality, good information is incomplete, but complete enough to meet the needs of the situation.

Confidence in the source

There is no point in producing information if it is not going to be used. Managers will not use information if they do not have confidence that it is likely to be good information. If the source has always been reliable in the past the user is likely to use it.

Accuracy

Information needs to be accurate enough for the use it is going to be put. To obtain information that is 100 per cent accurate is usually unrealistic as it is likely to be too expensive to produce on time. The degree of accuracy required depends upon the circumstances. At operational levels information may need to be accurate to the nearest penny, pound, kilogram or minute. A supermarket till receipt, for example, will need to be accurate to the penny. A Regional Manager comparing the performance of difference stores at the end of a month would find information rounded to the nearest £100 most appropriate.

Communication to the right person

Each manager has a particular area of work within the organisation and needs to be provided with the necessary information to help him do his job. A retail organisation's Managing Director does not need detailed information on current stock levels at a particular warehouse but the Warehouse Manager does.

Timing

Good information is communicated in time to be used. If information arrives too late or is out of date by the time it does arrive, then the manager cannot use it when decisions are made. For example, a Marketing Manager decides to stop selling a particular product whose sales have been dropping over the last few months. When he makes his decision he had not received the last month's figures showing a sudden, large growth in sales.

The frequency of which information is produced is important and needs to be driven by the needs of the manager who is using it. A factory manager organising shifts will need daily information on personnel absence. The company's Personnel Manager will need summary information on absence on a monthly or annual basis.

Detail

The amount of detail needed in information should be determined by the purpose to which it will be put. More detail than is necessary will confuse the recipient. Too little detail will provide an incomplete picture of the situation. When a Regional Sales Manager is checking the monthly expense claims of salespersons within his region he will require a summary report of monthly totals for each person. The Team Leaders who check the claims will need a detailed, itemised report of all claims made.

Understandability

Understandability, or putting into context, is what changes data into information. If the information is not understood then it has no meaning and cannot be used. The method and style of the presentation of the information will affect its understandability, for example, the appropriate use of charts and graph can make complex numerical information more understandable.

Activity 4

Characteristics of good information

Copy the table given below. For each of the characteristics of good information, give a suitable example that is different from those given in this book.

Relevance

Accuracy

Completeness

Reliability

Communicated to the right person

Timing

Detail

Understandability

Activity 5

Prepare an interview for a manager in a local organisation to find out the information needed for her job.

After you have carried out the interview, list the information categories that are needed and classify each category using the classifications given earlier in the chapter.

Activity 6

For each of the following, choose the best method of presentation from the options given. Explain carefully why you made the choice and why you feel the other options are not appropriate. If you feel an alternative method would be better than the options given, state your reasons.

Information need: A level results:

○ for class teacher

○ for head teacher

○ for the govenors' report

○ for the parents of prospective students

Figure 5.4 Characteristics of good information

Case Study 2

'Lennon provides a Ticket to Ride' adapted from article in Computing 2002

Train services are provided by a number of operators, but ticket sales are made through one system. If you purchase a ticket for a long distance journey that involves several different trains, run by different operators, you do not have to make separate payments for the different stages of the journey, each to a different operator. The allocation of ticket sales and revenue is made by a computer system. A new such rail settlement system, called Lennon, is being installed. The system is designed to allocate revenue generated from ticket sales to the appropriate train operators, as well as providing detailed information about how, when and to whom the tickets were sold.

Lennon will replace a 15-year old system and will process about 700,000 ticket sales every day. The train companies will be notified of their revenue and presented with sales information the following day. The current system takes up to six weeks and does not have the data analysis facility.

The new system will deliver information that will be used in marketing and promotional activities. It will aid the train companies in their decisions to introduce new ticket types and allow them better understanding of their customer requirements.

○ In which ways will Lennon provide better information than the old system?

○ What is the purpose of the information produced by the system?

○ How could information be used in marketing and promotional activities?

Activity 6 continued

Option 1: A table showing the number of each grade in each subject.

Option 2: A text report in an alphabetic list for all students in all subjects.

Option 3: A text report of student results ordered by subject.

Option 4: A table showing the percentage of each grade in each subject.

Option 5: A pie chart showing the percentage of each grade in each subject.

Effective presentation of information

For information to be of greatest use it must be presented in a style and form that allows the person for whom it is intended, the audience, to understand it best.

The variety of ways that information can be represented was discussed in ICT for AS level Chapter 17. Great care must be taken over the correct choice of presentation method and style, otherwise the correct message may not be given.

A detailed list of sales, in date order, would not be appropriate for a regional sales manager wishing to review the performance of each salespersons over the last month. For him, a summary report showing the total number and total value for each salesperson would be most appropriate.

The breakdown of the annual expenditure of a company, to be included in the annual report for shareholders, would best be presented as a pie chart.

Summary

- Information is necessary to make good decisions.
- Information can be classified in a number of ways:
  - **By source**: for example internal, external, primary, secondary.
  - **By nature**: for example quantitative, qualitative, formal, informal.
  - **By level**: for example strategic, tactical, operational.
  - **By time**: for example historical, present, future.
  - **By frequency**: for example continuous (real time), hourly, daily, monthly, annually.
  - **By use**: for example planning, control, decision-making.
  - **By form**: for example written, aural, visual, sensory.
  - **By type**: for example detailed, sampled, aggregated.
- Information is important in aiding the decision-making process.
- Good information has the following characteristics:
  - relevancy
  - accuracy
  - completeness
  - reliability
  - in time
  - right level of detail
  - disseminated by an appropriate channel of communication
  - understandability.

Information questions

1. 'BettaShu' is a small, retail chain which specialises in the sale of high quality shoes. The company is currently investigating the feasibility of replacing their current information system. It is important that all information needs are considered. Can you suggest examples of:
   - information that is needed in real time?
   - information that is needed daily?
   - information that is needed monthly?
   - information that is needed annually?

   For each, identify who would use the information (include level) and why they would need it (include use).

2. Plumper Pets plc has traditionally produced a range of cheap and medium priced cat and dog tinned food brands. It has recently launched a new, luxury brand for dogs, and is now considering launching a similar brand for cats which they intend to call 'Kat-i-dins'. Describe the range of information that Plumper Pets would need to enable them to make their decision. Explain where they would obtain the different information (distinguish between internal and external).

3. A company keeps records of its sales and uses a Management Information System to produce reports for its sales personnel and for its shareholders.
   a) Describe **two** differences between the information needed by sales personnel in their day-to-day work and by shareholders reading the annual report. *(4)*
   b) Describe, with the aid of an example, one characteristic of good quality information that might be produced by this system. *(3)*

4. For each of the following examples say if the communication is internal or external and if the information is strategic, tactical or operational and historic, current or future.
   a) the managing director's diary for next week
   b) details of a car's former owners from the Police National Computer
   c) a delivery note when a washing machine is delivered to a customer
   d) news that George will be off sick today
   e) 6000 need to be delivered immediately. *(15)*

5. Give two examples each of strategic information, tactical information and operational information in a school or college. *(6)*

6. An IT department uses a computer program written in-house which cannot draw graphs but can export to a spreadsheet. The IT manager then uses the spreadsheet to draw the necessary graphs. This takes three days. On presenting his report, the IT manager is told that the figures appear to be out of date. How did the problem arise and how could it be overcome? *(5)*

7. A company has decided to open a computerised distribution warehouse in the Midlands to handle deliveries for the whole country. Give an example of strategic information, tactical information and operational information needed in setting up the warehouse. *(6)*

8. 'The quality of management information is directly related to its timing.'
   Discuss this statement paying particular reference to:
   - the different purposes for which the information may be required
   - the relative merits of speed versus accuracy. *(6)*

   NEAB Specimen Paper 4

9. The manager of a company complains that the Management Information System (MIS) continually fails to produce the appropriate information at the right time. The person responsible for the MIS responds by stating that there are inadequate data and information flows within the company and that others fail to realise the significance of information handling.
   a) State six factors which influence the flow of information and data within an organisation. *(6)*
   b) With the aid of examples, describe two techniques which could be used to review current information flows within an organisation. *(4)*

   AQA June 2001 Paper 4

10. A sales manager claims that he is always provided with 'quality' management information from his Management Information System. With the aid of examples where appropriate, describe five characteristics of good information. *(10)*

    NEAB 1998 Paper 4

11. A local education authority wishes to analyse university applications and entries for the last four years. The Director of Education has arranged the collection of the relevant data from all schools and colleges in the area. This took place in February. An example is show below:

School Name: My High School	Sept 2000	Sept 1999	Sept 1998	Sept 1997	Sept 1996
Number of University Applications	73	76	84	90	94
Number of University Entries	N/A	64	72	83	84

N/A = not yet available

In addition, each institution has been asked to submit a list of the names of universities for which September 2000 applications have been made and the number of applicants to each one.

The Director has asked you to collate the data into meaningful information, which can be used by three different groups:

- A group of fellow students in your school/college.
- A group of head teachers and principals.
- The Director of Education and local officials.

For **each** of these groups select an appropriate, but different, method of displaying the information. Describe the format and content of the information, stating clearly the reason for your selection. *(9)*

AQA June 2000 Paper 4

12. A college is planning to introduce a computer-based attendance system. A register will be taken at each class attended by students. The purpose of the system is to provide attendance records to enable students to claim a weekly grant for attending college. Students who fail to satisfy a certain minimum attendance level will have their grant suspended.

a) Describe three alternative methods of collecting the attendance data for the system. *(6)*

A student is told that she has failed to satisfy the minimum attendance level and that her grant has been suspended.

b) Describe **three** examples of different reports the system could produce to justify this action. *(6)*

AQA June 2000 Paper 4

13. A college is planning the introduction of a computer-based, end of term performance review system for sixth form students. The purpose of the system is to produce information for the following end-users.

- Personal tutors
- Heads of subject
- Senior Managers

For each pupil, the following data will be collected for each course studied.

- Percentage attendance
- A predicted target grade and the grade achieved
- An effort grade

a) Describe two alternative methods of collecting the data for this system. *(4)*

b) The data is collected from a number of sources. For each of the data items, suggest one guideline or criterion which is required to enable consistent information to be produced. *(3)*

For each of the different end-users describe, with the aid of examples, information that the system might produce in relation to their requirements. *(6)*

AQA June 2001 Paper 4

14. The owner of an independent driving school, which employs six instructors, decides to get a local software house to write a bespoke package to manage client information, including the booking of lessons, the tracking of progress and the recording of payments.

a) Identify **two** different potential users of this system. *(2)*

b) With the aid of examples, describe the different levels of information that each of these two users might require. *(6)*

AQA Jan 2003 Paper 4

Data

As part of the AS course, the different ways in which data can arise was studied. Sometimes this can occur as an automatic by-product of a routine data processing operation. In a supermarket, Point of Sale (POS) terminals are used with bar code scanners to capture data on goods purchased. An itemised bill is produced with a calculated total for the customer. The data collected can also be used, both in the stock control and reordering system for marketing decisions as trends of product sales can be analysed, and for personnel tracking as the rate of working of POS operators can be calculated.

Data is very often typed in on a keyboard but it can be collected by other means such as by using computer readable documents (using OCR, OMR or MICR), voice recognition or sensors (for example, under the road at traffic lights, PIR sensors in burglar alarms).

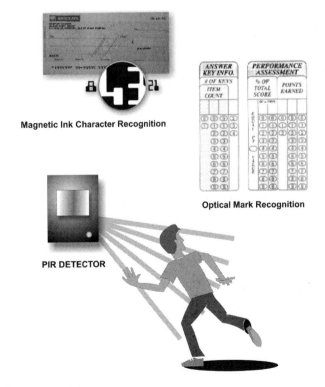

Magnetic Ink Character Recognition

Optical Mark Recognition

PIR DETECTOR

Figure 6.1 Types of data capture

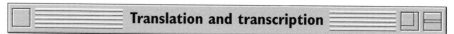

Translation and transcription

If data is not captured automatically, it may require translation or transcription before entry into the system.

Translation involves taking data that is in one form and turning it into another form that is suitable for data entry into a computer system. Translation may involve the coding of data. For example, an order processing clerk for a clothing mail order company might receive an order for a pink T-shirt, size 12. This would need to be translated into the product code (say C72-543-12) for entry into the online order system.

Transcription is the copying of data. When data originates in paper form the details are entered into a computer system by copying the written data through the use of a keyboard.

Translation and transcription can affect the accuracy of the data as human error can cause mistakes to be made. For example, the order processing clerk could mistype the order as C72-453-12, thus creating an order for a completely different garment.

A series of data controls need to be put in place in order to ensure that the quality of the data is maintained. Such controls are designed to highlight when errors are made so that they can be corrected.

Data can get lost before it is even input, or it might contain errors. The likelihood of errors will depend on the method of processing input data. Any form of human involvement will open up the possibility of error.

When data is being written down or keyed in, a number of categories of potential error can be identified. It is common to get the order of characters (especially numbers) wrong. For example, keying in an account number of 58762 instead of 57862. Here the operator has swapped around the 7 and the 8. This is called a **transpositional** error as the position of the characters has been misread. **Spelling mistakes** are common, especially with data such as a customer's name. Other, less common, mistakes can occur when measurements are being made (for example, reading the current value from an electricity meter dial) or incorrectly coding information from a source document.

In fact, any form of human copying of data, called **transcribing**, is liable to cause mistakes. If the source document is handwritten, it may not be easy to read the handwriting. Whenever data needs to be transcribed or translated into another format before entry into the system there is a risk that the accuracy of the data will be reduced.

Choosing appropriate method of data entry

A number of factors will be taken into account when a systems analyst is designing the most appropriate method of data capture for a particular system. These will include the nature of the data itself and how it arises, the current state of technological development and the quantity of the data to be collected.

Activity 1

On-line shopping

Using an Internet site such as www.amazon.co.uk or www.tesco.co.uk go through the stages of ordering some goods on-line. (Don't actually carry out the transaction!)

- Produce a simple user guide using DTP software to guide a first time user through the process of ordering goods. Include screen shots as well as text.

- Describe the ways that in which you could pay for the goods you wish to purchase.

- What information needs does such a system demand?

The method of data capture chosen will have an impact on both the quantity and quality of the data that can be captured.

When the sale of goods is recorded in a supermarket, the use of keyboard entry would prove slow and could generate many mistakes if the wrong prices were entered. Only the prices are likely to be recorded, so little use could be made of the data other than for producing the customer's bill. The use of a barcode scanner, which reads a code identifying the individual product, would allow a greater quantity of data to be entered in a given time. The data would also be of greater quality: it would be more accurate, as the scope for human mistyping error would not be present and the data could be used for a stock control system as the individual products would be itemised.

When a new car is sold a barcode scanner would not be used to enter data of the sale. The quantity of cars sold in a day is very low compared to the number of items sold in a supermarket! Also considerable detail relating to both the car and the purchaser will need to be recorded. Entry of this data is likely to be made by keyboard.

A range of different methods can be used for payment of goods or services and each may involve a different method of data capture. When payment is made in cash, the operator keys in the amount tendered into the POS terminal. The amount of change is calculated and, in some systems, the appropriate coins are delivered. When a purchase is made using a debit (for example Switch) or credit card (for example Visa or a store card) the details of the account are read from the magnetic strip when the card is 'swiped' through the reader. Payment can also be made by cheque. All the cheques given in a store will be collected together and deposited in a bank where the data will be read using MICR (magnetic ink character recognition) in batch mode.

Controls over data capture

Methods of controlling and checking the accuracy of data are discussed in detail in ICT for AS Chapter 12. **Verification** is used to check that data is entered correctly. The most common method of verification involves typing data into the computer twice. **Validation** is computerised checking that detects any data that is not reasonable or is incomplete.

Control mechanisms

When data is transcribed into a computer system, a number of control mechanisms need to be put in place to ensure that no transaction is missed or lost. When the mode of operation is batch processing, controls are needed to ensure that every batch of data reaches the data entry department and that every transaction within the batch is entered into the system.

Each batch of paper documents is grouped together in a batch and an extra document, the batch header is included. This will contain a field, called the **batch total**, for the number of documents in the batch as well as other control totals.

Details of a batch, such as its source, date and time, and an identifying, unique, batch number would be recorded, together with the numbers of transactions in the batch, in a log book at the source of data.

An example of a **control total** for a batch of product sales transactions could be the total value of all the transactions in the batch. The total would have to be worked out manually and added to the batch header before the data is entered. As the transactions are entered the computer program keeps a running total of the value fields from each transaction. When all the transactions in the batch have been entered this total is compared with the one entered on the batch header. If the two values are not the same, an error is reported.

A **hash total** is a particular kind of control total where the sum total has no particular meaning, and is purely carried out for control purposes. An example field that could be used for a hash total is an identity number.

As seen in Chapter 8, an audit trail can provide a history of transactions made. A company selling goods on-line can make good use of such a trail of transactions. A regular customer can be shown a list of previously chosen goods to make their selection quicker and easier. Amazon provides regular customers with a list of titles of books that might interest them, based on previous purchases.

Audit mechanisms

When data originates in paper form the documents should be kept as they provide a vital source of information for auditors. An auditor attempts to check that all the recorded transactions are real, that all the transactions that have taken place are recorded and that the correct values are given (see Chapter 8).

When data is captured in other ways then it is important that mechanisms are in place that allow auditors to track the effects of a transaction through a system.

Different types of control mechanisms are required when making on-line transactions. This is particularly apparent when goods are purchased on-line using credit or debit cards. There is a high risk that orders will be placed using stolen or fake credit cards. A number of controls need to be in place to protect against this. A user is often required to register on-line, giving personal details including their e-mail address and credit card details before they are able to order goods. They are then e-mailed a code which will enable them to place an order. The confirmation of any order made can be e-mailed to the given address; a customer will instantly be alerted if someone is wrongly ordering goods in their name.

Summary

- Data may require **translation** or **transcription** prior to entry into a system. This can affect the accuracy of the data.

- The most appropriate method of data capture for a particular system will depend on:
  - the nature of the data and how it arises
  - the current state of technological development
  - the quantity of the data to be collected.

- The method of data capture chosen will have an impact on both the quantity and quality of the data.

- **Verification** is used to check that data is entered correctly.

- **Validation** is computerised checking that detects any data that is not reasonable or is incomplete.

- **Control mechanisms** are used to ensure that no transaction is missed or lost. Examples of control mechanisms include:
  - batch totals
  - control totals
  - hash totals.

- **Audit mechanisms** are needed to keep track of data movement as they provide a vital source of information for auditors.

Data questions

1. A new anti-hooligan football smart card scheme has been introduced in Belgium. At first, some clubs refused to take part, but, after pressure was put on them by the Belgian Interior Ministry, which included clubs having to pay for extra police for certain games and being fined if there was trouble at matches, all clubs are now committed to the scheme.

A smart card is a small, wallet-sized piece of plastic which contains a microchip. Data can be both read from, and stored in, the card. The Belgian smart card contains 1 Kbyte of memory and can be used as an electronic purse and a loyalty card. An agreement has been made with the oil firm, Fina Belgium, to accept it at their petrol stations. The smart card also acts as an ID card. Once it is used to purchase a ticket the fan must use the smart card to gain entry to the match. Trouble-making fans can have their card deactivated so that further tickets cannot be bought. A controversial issue which worries civil liberty groups is that police have access to the networked smart card computer scheme which is connected to servers at all clubs. This gives police advance access to the identities of all those who will be attending a game.

a) Name and describe two other data capture methods that could be used for an identity card to allow entry into a sports ground instead of a smart card. *(6)*

b) Explain why civil liberty groups might be concerned about the introduction of these cards. *(8)*

c) Describe two other situations when the use of a smart card would be appropriate. *(4)*

2. The questionnaire shown in Figure 6.2 was given to all students studying AS level ICT in a particular school.

a) If data entry were to be made by copying the data from the forms using a keyboard, a number of errors could be made. Describe how these could occur. *(4)*

b) Suggest a more suitable method for data capture. Justify your choice. *(2)*

c) Describe validation checks that you would use. *(6)*

d) Explain why all data errors cannot be picked up by data validation. *(2)*

e) Explain who would use the different information that could be produced from the analysis of the questionnaires and why the information would be useful for them. *(6)*

AS ICT COURSE EVALUATION

Did you attend the induction course? Y/N ☐

Did you study ICT at GCSE? Y/N ☐

If yes, what grade did you get? ☐

Please select the type of computer you have at home.

486 ☐ Mac ☐ Pentium ☐

Pentium II ☐ Pentium II ☐ Pentium IV ☐

I find the turnaround time for homework marking satisfactory

Agree 1 2 3 4 5 Disagree

Please write below any comments or suggestions concerning homework.

☐

Figure 6.2 Questionnaire to ICT students

3. Puregreens, a retailer of organic vegetables, has recently launched a marketing website. The e-mail response from the 'contact us' button has been overwhelming, so they are thinking of expanding into selling online.

Discuss the implications of this, paying particular attention to the following:

- methods of data capture that will be available for online or off-line payment
- the control and audit issues associated with this method of selling
- the information needs of the management of this system
- the additional information that might be generated.

The quality of written communication will be assessed in your answer. (20)

AQA Jan 2003 Paper 4

Management of change

Change is necessary in life, often due to biological factors such as ageing or parenthood. Organisations change too, often due to external economic circumstances. The introduction or development of an information system within an organisation must lead to change.

Organisations will cope best with change if they plan ahead so that all the aspects of change that are likely to result from the implementation of the new information system are thought of in advance and suitable strategies are put in place to ensure that potential problems are avoided. The changes resulting from the implementation of a major new system can be wide-ranging and, if problems are to be avoided, the transition to the new system must be carefully managed.

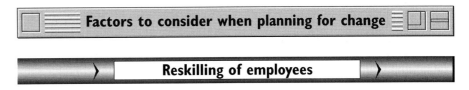

Factors to consider when planning for change

Reskilling of employees

The introduction of a new information system is likely to change the nature and content of many jobs associated with the system. Many old skills may become redundant and employees will need to be taught new skills. In some cases these changes could be relatively minor and simply require a few hours of training. In other cases the changes to the job might be more radical and much training and reassurance will be needed when reskilling staff.

The introduction of information systems can cause a shift from jobs which require basic, manual skills to those that contain a greater component of problem solving. The introduction of networked PCs has resulted in one person performing a much greater range of tasks. The role of many telephonists has been enhanced. Instead of having to pass callers on for help, the telephonist is empowered to answer many questions, for example, concerning availability of stock or product lines, by having access to an online database.

Many information systems are designed to be used directly by middle managers who in the past made no use of a computer directly, but would be provided with printed listings appropriate to their needs. For example, when a new information system is introduced, a regional sales manager, who has been sent weekly printouts of the performance of his salespersons, has to learn to access the same information for himself using a networked desktop PC. If he has not made use of a computer before, he may need considerable training.

Attitudes of employees

The change to a new system of working can provoke fear and resistance from employees. There is likely to be a fear of the unknown or an employee may feel unable to operate the new system.

Many employees feel that an information system will reduce their status within the organisation. They fear that their importance will be diminished as many of the tasks that are most important in their present role will be taken over by the information system, leaving them with less crucial and more mundane tasks. The introduction of a new database system often brings data together into a central system that was stored in separate departments. Managers are likely to have access directly to much more information without needing to contact other departments directly.

The tasks required by the new system might even result in job regrading which could pose a threat to an employee's ambitions.

Job satisfaction, an important motivational factor for an employee, can depend on many factors that can be affected by the introduction of a new system. The new system might reduce the range and variety of tasks to be carried out, reduce an employee's interactions with other employees making them more desk-bound, reduce the level of decision-making and judgement required or involve an employee with only carrying out part of an operation when before they were involved in all stages. Satisfaction can be reduced when aspects of a job are taken over by an information system, leaving the employee with less interesting, routine tasks to perform.

Organisational structure

The introduction of new information systems can result in major changes within an organisation. Changes in the work done may result in the need to modify the organisational structure. There has been a shift towards flatter, leaner structures as middle management jobs have been eroded. An MIS makes it easier for strategic management to monitor operations more directly. Some decisions, previously taken by middle management can be performed automatically by new systems. An example of such a decision could be the reordering of stock. The clear division between different departments may become reduced as information becomes more widely available.

Major operational changes can result from the adoption of a new system. As POS terminals are installed in shops, stock control, ordering and sales analysis can all be computerised. These changes can result in the need for changes in the organisation's structure as the traditional structure is no longer appropriate for the new information flow.

Employment pattern and conditions

Some jobs may disappear entirely when a new information system is introduced, leading perhaps to redundancy. Very often the jobs lost are those that require the least skills.

The working hours or the location of work may need to change for some employees. Many computer systems run 24 hours a day and staff are needed to operate and maintain the computers. Shift work may become a necessity.

The development of communications and IT has led to a growth in teleworking, where employees work from home accessing the company's computer system via a network.

Internal procedures

A new information system can lead to changes in the internal procedures of an organisation. The nature of the new system may force the way that things are done to be changed.

Case Study 1

Selfridges to automate stock reordering

Selfridges is piloting software that reorders stock automatically. It is the first retailer in Europe to do so.

At present reordering and delivery is controlled by a manual data entry process that is prone to error and is time-consuming. The new system will use an electronic catalogue that holds suppliers' details and will link with the merchandising (selling) system reducing the time taken in reordering by 60 per cent.

'Automating will allow employees to move from a wholly clerical function to work that is more exciting and engaging for them.'

- What problems could arise from this change in working practice at Selfridges?

- What measures should be taken to ensure that the change is made smoothly and effectively?

Managing change

If change is to be introduced with the minimum of distrust and upheaval, it must be managed. Careful plans need to be worked out well in advance of the implementation of any system. Current work practices and roles should be carefully reviewed. The possibility of redundancy, deskilling or loss of job satisfaction can all lead to resistance. Management should set out to involve personnel and, where appropriate, the trade unions, from the start and communicate fully and frankly with all those who are likely to be affected by changes.

The management style of the organisation will have an impact on the ease in which change can effectively be introduced. An organisation with an open management style, where employees are used to being consulted and having their views taken into account, may encounter fewer problems. Whatever the style, the people who are managing the change must ensure that they inform the workforce of the coming changes throughout the development of the project, including them as much as possible in decisions and allaying their fears.

The possibility of redundancy, deskilling or loss of job satisfaction can all lead to resistance. However, it is often possible to achieve necessary staff reduction through natural wastage over a period of time without the need for enforced redundancies.

Training and retraining schemes should be set up and personnel should be shown that routine, boring work can be eliminated and job satisfaction maintained or even enhanced. If employees can be convinced that the changes brought about by the new information system will be advantageous to them they are unlikely to oppose or resist the changes.

There are a number of factors that influence how successfully change is managed within an organisation. The structure of the organisation and the key roles are crucial. Change may bring about a restructuring which may require the loss of some jobs and substantial changes in others. The conditions of service under which the workforce are employed will be an important factor in determining the ease with which change can be undertaken. The attitude of both management and the workforce will be influential as well as the overall organisational culture. An organisation whose management has an open style, where there is mutual trust and support, is less likely to fear or resent change. If the skills needed far outstrip the current skills level of the workforce change will be difficult to bring about.

To manage change successfully, it is necessary to:
- Plan ahead
- Consult widely to find out what to do – for example, get expert advice and talk to trade unions.
- Be open about plans – otherwise rumours will spread
- Explain the reasons for decisions
- Train staff for their new roles.

Case Study 2

Changes in a college library

A traditional college library consisted of stacks of books organised in order according to the Dewey decimal system. Card indexes of books stocked were maintained in cabinets, one in author order and the other in Dewey decimal order. Borrowers were issued with tickets and each book held a tag which, when the book was on loan, was stored in a card file together with the borrower's ticket. Information on other books, not held by the library, was available on microfiche.

The modern librarian needs many new IT skills to cope with the new computerised systems that are in use. Books are likely to be bar-coded and all loans will be held on a computer-based system. Library users are able to search remote databases online to find details of books relevant to their studies. The library facilities are likely to have been extended to include access to CD-ROMs and the Internet, both of which provide the student with alternative ways of gathering information.

- Describe what you imagine the library of the future to look like.

- Do you think that any books will remain? Justify your answer.

- What skills does the new type of librarian need?

Summary

- The introduction or development of an information system will result in change which must be managed.

- Factors to consider when planning for change:

- Reskilling of employees

- Attitudes of employees

- Organisational structure

- Employment pattern and conditions

- Internal procedures

Management of change questions

1. Hopkins, Morgan and Hopkins is a firm of surveyors. There are nine surveyors in the firm and four secretaries whose jobs include the maintenance of records of all clients and surveys carried out, typing letters, reports and memos and keeping track of appointments. Each secretary has a stand-alone PC with a word-processor installed. An office junior/receptionist is employed to act as a runner, to carry out filing and answer the telephone, often taking messages for the surveyors when they are busy.

A new, networked system is to be installed which will provide every employee with a workstation. A record system will be installed, together with a range of drawing and financial packages, e-mail and a diary system.

a) Describe how the new system will affect the jobs of the:
  - surveyors
  - secretaries
  - office junior. *(9)*

b) In what ways and for what reasons might any of the above personnel be unhappy with the changes? *(8)*

c) Describe the steps that should be taken to ensure that the organisation runs successfully with the new system in place. *(6)*

2. An information system was introduced into an organisation and was considered a failure. The failure was due to the inability of the organisation to manage the change rather than for technical reasons.

With the aid of examples describe three factors which influence the management of change within an organisation. *(6)*

NEAB 1997 Paper 4

3. A multi-site college is considering the introduction of an IT-based system to log visitors. The current system is based on a manual log at reception. The new system will capture visual images of visitors together with details of their visit. The introduction of this system will cause considerable change for staff and visitors.

In the context of this example describe four factors that the management should consider when introducing this change. *(8)*

NEAB 1998 Paper 4

4. New information and communication technologies are frequently introduced into companies as a result of outdated existing systems, market pressure, new legislation and other factors. Companies have to adapt quickly or face going out of business.

Discuss the factors that need to be considered to manage such changes successfully within an organisation. Particular attention should be given to:
- organisation structure and information needs
- management and staffing issues
- internal procedures, external procedures and the customer interface.

Illustrate your answer with specific examples.

The quality of written communication will be assessed in your answer. (20)

AQA June 2002 Paper 4

5. A parcel warehouse distribution centre has introduced a new information system. Six months after its introduction the system is considered a failure. The management of the centre consider that the failure was due to their inability to manage the change, rather than for technical reasons.

With the aid of examples, describe **three** factors which could influence the management of change within an organisation. *(6)*

AQA June 2000 Paper 4

6. An information system was introduced into an organisation and was considered a failure. This was due to the inability of the organisation to manage the change.

With the aid of examples describe three factors, other than technical ones, which could have caused this failure. *(6)*

AQA June 2001 Paper 4

7. Company management sometimes introduce new information and communication systems giving little advance notice to their staff. This may contribute to the failure of these systems and cause other problems for their staff.

a) State **six** factors that may cause the failure of a system that has been introduced too quickly. *(6)*

b) Describe **three** problems that staff might encounter in this situation. *(6)*

AQA Jan 2003 Paper 4

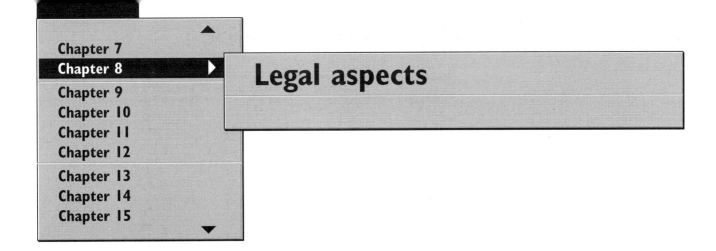

Legal aspects

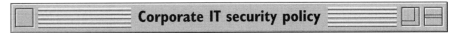

Corporate IT security policy

Adequate security is crucial to successful operations. Potential threats exist to hardware, software and data and such threats can occur from within and outside an organisation (see Chapter 9).

A company's knowledge and data are probably the most important assets of any organisation. Companies must make sure that the confidentiality, integrity and availability of their data is maintained at all times.

Three key security questions:

- Who sees the data?
- Has the data been corrupted?
- Can I access the server or data when I need it?

Although there are certainly many external threats to security, such as viruses or illegal access to systems by hackers, many experts think that the greatest security threat to IT systems comes from people working within an organisation itself. Breaches of security can be caused through incompetence (for example, a failure to encrypt data sent over public networks), networks that are poorly implemented and protected only by simple passwords that are easy to crack, or a firewall that stops nothing or protection software that is never updated.

On the other hand, breaches in security could be made on purpose by an employee perhaps because they are unhappy with their job or their boss. Such situations sometimes result in the destruction of vital information. There could be an intent to steal information, either for personal use or for selling to others, perhaps a competitor.

Many companies have a formal IT security policy which they publish and give to all staff. An effective security policy should not stay the same. It is a document that should change as corporate needs change.

The role of a corporate IT security policy

The role of a corporate IT security policy is to lay down the procedures, guidelines and practices necessary to keep hardware, software and data safe from theft, misuse and unauthorised access. An organisation has a responsibility to maintain security measures to ensure that the requirements of the laws relating to IT are not broken. An IT security policy is established so that misuse can be prevented, with methods of detection and investigation being put in place. Disciplinary procedures that will be used if staff are found to be breaking the rules laid down in the policy will be explained. By enforcing the corporate security policy, organisations can minimise their risks.

Companies storing personal data are obliged to abide by the Data Protection Act which states that personal information must be kept secret. The company is responsible for ensuring that this data is not divulged and that company staff are aware of the legal requirements.

A corporate IT security policy aims to:

- Prevent misuse

- Detect misuse through regular checking

- Investigate misuse through the use of monitoring software and audit trails

- Prevent unauthorised access

- Establish procedures for keeping data, for example, backing up data and maintaining passwords to limit access to files

- Lay down disciplinary procedures for breaches of security.

A corporate security policy will need to be frequently modified as new systems are introduced and old ones altered. For example, when insurance sellers are issued with laptops for the first time, to take with them when they visit clients, the company's security policy will have to be extended to contain rules to protect the data, the hardware and the software.

The content of a corporate IT security policy

The introduction of one company's IT security booklet states: 'The company is in a highly competitive industry in which the loss or unauthorised disclosure of sensitive information could be extremely detrimental to the company. These guidelines have been prepared to ensure that all staff understand the importance of safeguarding company information and the protective measures that need to be taken.'

A security policy is likely to first state the **purpose of the policy** so that employees reading the policy are aware of why it is needed and the threats to security that could arise.

Staff responsibilities should be drawn up and disciplinary procedures agreed so that any misuse is dealt with. A staff IT security document is likely to specify who can use company computer systems and to set out the password policy. It will lay down the steps that should be taken to provide protection against viruses and the physical security of computer systems. Rules will be provided to ensure that all computer use is within the law.

Activity 1

A template for a corporate IT security policy

The following document outlines guidelines for use of the computing systems and facilities located at or operated by [COMPANY NAME].

Use of the computer facilities includes the use of data and/or programs stored on [COMPANY NAME] computing systems, data and/or programs stored on magnetic tape, floppy disk, CD-ROM, or any storage media that is owned and maintained by [COMPANY NAME].

The purpose of these guidelines is to ensure that all [COMPANY NAME] users (business users, support personnel, technical users, and management) use the [COMPANY NAME] computing facilities in an effective, efficient, ethical and lawful manner.

[COMPANY NAME] accounts are to be used only for the purpose for which they are authorised and are not to be used for non [COMPANY NAME] related activities.

Users are responsible for protecting any information used and/or stored on and/or in their [COMPANY NAME] accounts. Consult the [COMPANY NAME] User Guide for guidelines on protecting your account and information using the standard system protection mechanisms.

Users are requested to report any weaknesses in [COMPANY NAME] computer security, any incidents of possible misuse, or any violation of this agreement to the proper authorities by contacting [COMPANY NAME] User Services or by sending electronic mail to [security@companyname.com].

Users shall not attempt to access any data, projects and/or programs contained on [COMPANY NAME] systems for which they do not have authorisation or explicit consent of the owner of the data, project and/or program.

Users shall not divulge Dialup modem phone numbers to anyone.

Users shall not share their [COMPANY NAME] account(s) with anyone. This includes sharing the password to the account or other means of sharing.

Users shall not make unauthorised copies of copyrighted software, except as permitted by law or by the owner of the copyright.

continued ...

Activity 1 *continued*

Users shall not make copies of system configuration files for their own, unauthorised personal use or to provide to other people and/or users for unauthorised uses.

Users shall not purposely engage in activities with the intent to: harass other users; degrade the performance of systems; deprive an authorised [COMPANY NAME] user access to a [COMPANY NAME] resource; obtain extra resources beyond those allocated; circumvent [COMPANY NAME] computer security measures or gain access to a [COMPANY NAME] system for which proper authorisation has not been given.

Electronic communication facilities (such as e-mail or Newsgroups) are for authorised [COMPANY NAME] use only. Fraudulent, harassing or obscene messages and/or materials shall not be sent from, to or stored on [COMPANY NAME] systems.

Users shall not download, install or run security programs or utilities that could potentially reveal weaknesses in the security of a system. For example, [COMPANY NAME] users shall not run password cracking, key logging, or any other potentially malicious programs on [COMPANY NAME] computing systems.

Any non-compliance with these requirements will constitute a security violation and will be reported to the management of the [COMPANY NAME] user and will result in short-term or permanent loss of access to [COMPANY NAME] computing systems. Serious violations may result in civil or criminal prosecution.

I have read and understand the [COMPANY NAME] security policy and agree to abide by it.

Signature: Date:

○ List, in your own words, the rules laid down in this policy document.

○ What sanctions for breaking the rules have been included? Can you include any other possible sanctions?

○ State what you would put into the User Guide for guidelines on protecting your account referred to in the policy.

For a security policy to be effective the staff must be fully aware of its contents and it must be enforced. All users, including the most senior employees, must be seen to be keeping to the policy.

Induction training

Many organisations ensure that staff receive a lecture on security when they join the organisation as part of an induction training programme for all new employees. Every new employee will be expected to sign a copy of the corporate IT security policy.

Staff access to guidance

However, an introduction to the policy on induction day is unlikely to be enough. Guidance on the policy should be available to staff when it is required, perhaps through an intranet or via the help desk. In some organisations a new recruit is not allowed near a terminal until they have been successfully tested on the security matters relating to the tasks in their job.

Interactive training

In the USA a new interactive training tool has been developed that tests employees understanding of the organisation's corporate IT security policy through the use of multiple choice tests. The new employee can only sign the policy when he passes the test.

Marketing security

The Prudential Assurance Company has introduced an education scheme throughout the company to improve its IT security. Their Head of Information Risk is reported to have said that companies are often too reliant on the technology of firewalls, antivirus software and intrusion detection systems, focusing too much on the technology and not enough on the people issues. 'It is not that the technology isn't working, but it can't legislate for stupidity,' he said.

Different approaches need to be taken to ensure the board and the staff take security seriously. The executives have direct legal responsibilities. If they are forcibly made aware of these they are likely to support security measures to remove any risk of being sent to prison.

The Prudential's computer-based training programme is re-enforced through posters and beer mats. It is important to use a variety of ways to educate staff; once a year is not sufficient, a more regular approach is more effective.

Case Study 1

Employees need training in security

A security company claims that businesses could cut external hacking attacks by 80 per cent by more effective enforcement of security policies among staff. They demonstrated how weak security can be when they carried out a spot survey of 150 people at Victoria Station in London that prompted two-thirds to reveal their network passwords.

Another recent survey found that 75 per cent of staff in the UK have not received any training on the security issues of using e-mail and accessing the Internet at work. Although most were aware of the risk from viruses, few were able to identify or deal with potential threats.

- What are the dangers that come from SPAM (the junk mail of the Internet) and the jokes and other such mail being forwarded by friends?

- Identify other common practices by members of staff that can lead to an IT security risk.

- Produce a plan for making and keeping the staff at your school or college aware of the IT security policy.

Disciplinary measures

If an employee is discovered to have broken a rule in the corporate IT security policy, for example, by installing unauthorised software on the organisation's network, they are likely to be subject to one of a number of sanctions. They may be given a verbal or a formal written warning. If the offence were of a serious nature, it could lead to suspension or even termination of employment. The employee could face action under the Computer Misuse Act, is likely to have network usage monitored very carefully and access rights restricted.

Case Study 2

MI5 laptop snatched at Paddington

A desperate search is under way for a computer belonging to MI5, which was stolen from an agent at Paddington station. The laptop is believed to contain sensitive information relating to Northern Ireland.

The £2000 machine was snatched on the main concourse when the agent left it for a moment to help a group of youths. It is understood the security worker chased the thief but lost him in the station crowds.

The Home Office says the information is highly encrypted and the theft does not pose a risk to national security.

- Explain what is meant by encryption.

- What other security measures could have prevented the thief from accessing vital information?

- What disciplinary measure is likely to have been taken on the agent?

Case Study 3

The threat from within

A report from the Institute of Directors (IOD) states that employees are as great a threat to data security as hackers and viruses. Firewalls, facing outside the organisation, are important but to combat internal security attacks, security controls must be imposed on every piece of data within an organisation. The IOD recommends a system that labels every item of data with the people allowed to see it, as it is being created.

The figures on the number of insider-job security breaches is likely to be much lower than the real figure as organisations often keep the occurrences of such breaches to themselves.

- What is meant by the term 'security breach'?

- Why would an organisation be reluctant to make public the rate of insider job security breaches?

- What other measures could be taken to protect against a security threat from employees?

Audit requirements

Company accounts have to be audited by law. An auditor is attempting to check that all transactions that are recorded are real, that all transactions that have taken place are recorded and that the correct values are given. Internal auditors will be checking for detail. External auditors are more concerned to check that the correct systems and procedures are in place to ensure that errors or fraud will be detected.

Role of an auditor

An auditor's task is to check that no financial mistakes have been made and that no fraud has taken place. The auditor needs to be able to access all relevant records within the organisation, for example, records of customer transactions, orders, payroll details, as well as the overall end of year statement of accounts. Most companies use IT systems to record financial information. Only very small companies record customer orders in a paper-based system these days. The computer-based applications are subject to audit in the same way as paper-based systems. However, the auditor will need to have a knowledge of IT and the particular risks of fraud and error associated with computer-based systems. It is likely that an IT-based financial information system will store much more data than a paper-based system. Auditing such systems is therefore a considerably more complex operation.

The auditor needs to have a sound knowledge of the organisation and responsibilities of the data processing staff and the methods of control of systems development, programming and operations. An understanding of the data collection and validation techniques, file organisation and processing techniques and systems controls used in the systems are all needed.

Impact of audit on data and information control

To carry out an audit, an auditor will need to examine the data files. However, files on magnetic media such as disk or tape cannot be read as easily as traditional paper ledgers. Old files are not normally kept for more than a few days before a tape is reused. The sorting of data from source documents is performed by the computer, therefore these documents, if they are kept, are not filed in order and so are difficult to retrieve. The sheer volume of work means that it is not possible for the auditor to check every transaction. The auditor will therefore probably only check a sample of transactions.

The types of error occurring in clerical ledgers were mainly mistakes in arithmetic and copying. Such errors are almost unknown in computer systems. The hardware and software errors which may occur in computer systems are very difficult to find. The auditor must be satisfied that the hardware and software has been fully tested and is bug-free. This is why an auditor should be involved with systems development, including the design stage of a new system. The system must be designed with the work of the auditor in mind, so that auditing is an integral part of the system. The auditor should supply a set of test data which includes deliberate errors. These are then processed by the computer and the auditor examines the output and compares it with the expected results. This will check the processing method.

It is then possible for the auditor to concentrate on the inputs and outputs of the computer and ignore the processing involved. Doing this should give sufficient information for the audit and the auditor would not need a detailed knowledge of the processing methods used. This is known as 'auditing around the computer'.

Test packs are used to test a system before it goes live. These test a system after it has been amended and test a system to make sure no unauthorised amendments have been made.

Audit package

A range of auditing software packages can now be bought which save the auditor a lot of routine work. They enable the auditor to check computer files.

The main facilities of an audit package are:

- verification of file control totals (these are validation totals stored in the file)

- verification of individual balances in records

- verification that all data is present in records

- selection of records for checking, for example, random records, overdue accounts, non-active accounts, payments over a certain value (these values are selected by the auditor)

- analysis of file contents, for example, debts by age, payments by size, stock by value

- comparisons of two files to show up any differences.

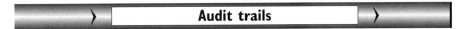

Audit trails

An **audit trail** is an automatic record made of any transactions carried out by a computer system (for example, all updates of files). This may be needed for legal reasons so that auditors can check that the company accounts are accurate.

An audit trail is a means of tracing all activities relating to a piece of information from the time it enters a system to the time that it leaves. An audit trail should provide sufficient information to establish or verify the sequence of events. It enables the effects of any errors in the accounting information to be traced and the causes determined.

Audit trails may be used primarily because they are legal requirements. They also can be used to protect staff from accusations of fraud as they can provide proof that no unauthorised transactions have been carried out on the data. They are also a useful tool in the prevention of fraud as the potential fraudster will know that a trail of their actions will be left and that illegal acts can be detected and traced to them.

Traditional audit trails follow transactions through a written ledger. This will include handwritten details of ordering, payments, sales, and so on, initialled by the clerk. This is not so easy on electronic media. It is possible to print out data during processing but this is not much help in trying to find the history of some transaction.

The systems designer may be asked to design a system to provide special audit trails on demand. This is a mechanism built into the software to allow the auditor to trace a transaction from input through to output. By typing in the record details, the auditor can find out all about the transaction and check it. An auditing log would also record who has been using the computer, when, how long for and what they did with the data.

An example of an audit trail in use is the Police National Computer. This is used to trace the history of owners of a motor vehicle. Before computerisation, every car was issued with a paper log book which had to kept by the car owner. The log book had details of all the previous owners of the car recorded in it. The current computer system has been designed to hold the same information so that the names of all past owners can be found on request.

An audit trail keeps track of:

- what has happened in a system

- who has been using it

- for how long thay have been using it

- what person did what with what data.

Problems with online systems

Online systems provide problems for the auditor for a number of reasons. Transaction details can be entered at many points on a WAN. Source documents may not exist; this could occur if an order was made by phone. Controls such as validation and verification may not be used as they may waste time in a time critical system. Very often, immediate processing may make an audit trail impossible.

The auditor must check the software thoroughly. In particular he or she must pay attention to the validation checks made on input data. Careful checks should be made that protection against unauthorised inspection of files is maintained, that passwords are used properly and that any suspicious transactions are reported. Operating system software can keep a record of all activities at network stations. The auditor can check this and make unannounced visits to terminal locations.

Overheads of maintaining an audit trail

The maintenance of audit trails does not come without a price. Additional storage will be needed to hold the extra data of the trail. The need to record data in an audit trail may well slow down transaction processing.

Joanna took her car to the local garage for a service. When she collected her car, she was told that the brakes were worn and that two pads had been replaced. Joanna was convinced that there was something seriously wrong with her car's braking system as she could remember paying out to have them repaired on several occasions. She talked to the manager who was able to view the trail of past transactions relating to Joanna's car and the specific repairs that had been carried out. With this information he was able to assess whether or not there had been an underlying problem with the braking system.

Auditing at an FE college

FE Colleges are funded by the Learning and Skills Council (LSC). Colleges receive funds on the basis of units of activity achieved. Units of activity are awarded for such events as a student attending an induction course, a student having enrolled on a course at a certain date, a student completing a course and a student gaining the qualification which was the aim of the course. Careful and accurate records have to be kept of all such events within a college.

Activity 2

Audit trails

When carrying out an audit trail it is necessary to examine all documents that relate to the particular system being examined.

The documents that might make up an audit trail to be examined when checking the accounts kept for a school trip to a theme park are given below.

Document required	Purpose
List of students on trip	To be able to work out total income; should match with total of student payment receipts and summary total of income received.
Receipt(s) for each student payment	
Receipt for coach payment	
Receipt for theme park tickets	
Summary of incidental cash payments	
Receipts from restaurant	
Notification of refund made to absent student	
Summary of payments made and income received	

Fill in the purpose of each document that is requested. Why might it be necessary to carry out such an audit?

Every student must have signed a formal document called a 'Learner's Agreement'. This lays out exactly which course or courses the student is studying. Any changes to this agreement must be carefully recorded and dated.

The auditors will scrutinise many records including those relating to enrolment, exam entry and the results obtained. It is likely that they will pick several students at random and check through every record relating to them. Class attendance records will be examined to cross check that claims for course completion are correct.

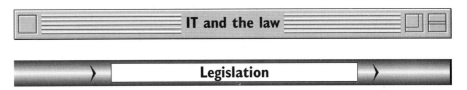

IT and the law

Legislation

Laws are a major influence constraining the operations of businesses. Laws come from three sources – common law (developed over hundreds of years' custom and practice), statute law (passed by Parliament) and the European Union. The procedures within a company must reflect the requirements of the legislation to ensure that all laws are being adhered to. When new legislation is passed, an organisation will need to look at current practice to check that new requirements are being met and, if necessary, modify procedures accordingly.

If a company employee breaks the law while at work, the company is legally responsible as well as the individual, unless it can be proved that the company has done everything reasonable to prevent the employee breaking the law. For example, if an employee discloses personal information and unwittingly breaks the Data Protection Act, the company can be prosecuted.

Several companies have ended up in court because of the actions of their employees. As well as the possiblitiy of a large fine, the company is likely to suffer through bad publicity. Companies must ensure that employees are aware of:

- the law
- what the employee must and must not do
- sanctions against the employee if they are found to have broken the law.

The requirement of an organisation in ensuring that all its employees are aware of their legal responsibilities includes those laws that relate to IT, which are the Data Protection Acts of 1984 and 1998, the Computer Misuse Act 1990, the Copyright Designs and Patent Act 1988, the Health and Safety at Work Act 1974 and the EU Health and Safety Directive 87/391. (For details of the Acts see ICT for AS Level

Managers in a company can claim expenses for trips made as part of their work. They fill in a monthly claim form which is checked by their line manager. Train and air fares, hotel and meal costs can be claimed as well as a mileage allowance when appropriate. Hotel costs and meals are paid within a certain allowance band.

List the documents you would expect to examine when undertaking an audit of the expense claims for a department over the last year.

Chapters 8–10). An organisation might need to alter many of its procedures to ensure that the laws are kept. For example, it might be necessary to prevent individual users from purchasing and installing their own software, instead centralising all such purchases with the IT support department so that careful records can be kept to ensure that the correct licences are held for all the software installed on the organisation's computers.

New employees usually undergo an induction course which provides them with a background to the organisation as well as giving specific training about the job. This course should include a discussion of the legal requirements of the post. All employees should be given a handbook which lays out their legal responsibilities. It is useful to provide a list of 'dos and don'ts'.

It is vital that managers take an active role to ensure that legislation is enforced within an organisation. Employees should be reminded of the law through individual memos, public notices posted on walls, and the organisation's intranet. Employees should be expected to sign an agreement that lists the rules and procedures that apply to ensure that the requirements of all relevant legislation is met.

Methods of enforcing and controlling data protection legislation

The Data Protection Act was created to provide individuals with rights that protect them against the misuse of personal data held about them. The main aspects of the DPA are that all personal data held should be secure, accurate and should only be used for the purpose for which it was gathered. Individuals have the right to see data kept about them and can demand that errors in the data be corrected.

Every organisation must ensure that they register all data stores that fall under the Data Protection Act with the Data Protection Commissioner. It should be clearly stated how the data is to be used and to whom it is to be passed on. Enquiries should be made to the Commissioner in any cases of doubt about the need to register personal data. The organisation should draw up a written data protection policy which should make clear what data can be kept and for how long. In large organisations, a Data Protection Officer should be appointed who is responsible for monitoring practices and making sure they are following the requirements of the Act.

The person whose personal data is being stored is referred to as the Data Subject in the Data Protection Act. An organisation should make public its privacy policy and the rights of data subjects. They should be made aware of the use to which their personal data is to be put and no unnecessary data should be collected.

No data can be sold to other organisations without the data subject's consent. This is often obtained by adding an opt-out tick box to the form on which the data is being collected – if the subject does not tick the box it is assumed that personal data can be given or sold to other organisations.

Data collection methods should be designed to ensure that the data stored is accurate and methods need to be put in place to ensure that accuracy is maintained. Systems often fall down in this respect: the initial data collection is accurate but subsequent changes to the data are not recorded systematically. It is most important that a systems analyst takes data protection requirements fully into account at the design stage of any new system. The intended 'life' of data should be established and procedures put in place to ensure that the data is destroyed when this time has expired.

Procedures need to be in place within the organisation to allow the data subject to access the information stored about them. The facilities to make corrections if errors are found must be in place.

It is important that all employees are aware of rulings of the Act and of their responsibilities. An organisation must use a variety of methods to remind all staff of their responsibilities in keeping data private. Matters of data protection should be included in the organisation's security policy where the responsibilities and liabilities of employees should be highlighted. Every employee should be expected to sign a copy of the policy on joining the organisation.

An individual should be responsible within a work area for ensuring that data security and privacy is maintained: this could be the Data Protection Officer himself, or it could be delegated to another manager. Spot checks could be made to ensure that the Act is being complied with and staff should be reminded of the need for care and compliance on a regular basis.

Employees need to know that they should not create their own individual databases, perhaps on their own workstation, that contain personal data without telling the organisation's Data Protection Officer who will register the database with the Commissioner.

Careful operational procedures need to be set up to ensure that personal data is not disclosed to unauthorised people. It is not sufficient to ensure that the data is safe while stored in the computer, through the use of password protection and other security methods. Employees need to be trained not to disclose personal information, either in person or over the telephone, without carrying out careful checks that the person they are speaking to is permitted to be given the information. Paper copies of data that have been printed out must always be stored in a secure place out of sight of prying eyes.

Case Study 4

M&S admits to being in breach of Data Protection Act for 15 years

Based on article by Sylvia Pennington

In 1999 Marks & Spencer was forced to tighten its procedures for dealing with its charge card holders after learning it had been acting in breach of the Data Protection Act for almost 15 years.

The company will now only disclose information relating to charge card accounts to the primary account holder, who is legally liable for paying the bill. In the past, supplementary card holders who are authorised to charge goods to another person's account but are not responsible for paying the bill, were given access to this data and were allowed to alter personal details, such as mailing addresses.

This could constitute a breach of the eighth data protection principle, which calls for organisations to take steps to prevent unauthorised access to personal data.

A Marks & Spencer spokesman stated that the retailer had been acting in breach of the original DPA since it was passed in 1984, but added that it was unlikely to be alone in this regard.

Marks & Spencer had always sought to both comply with legislation and meet customers' requirements, a second spokesman added. An account holder whose details were altered by a supplementary card holder could allege that the store was in breach of this principle if problems arose afterwards, the spokesman said. Stores needed to juggle their desire to be customer friendly with the requirement to protect customers' personal data, the spokesman added.

- What steps would M&S have to take to keep within the DPA?

Activity 3

- Prepare a slide show to present to employees in an organisation showing how the Data Protection Act affects them. You should include all the measures that they should be taking to ensure that they comply with the DPA in their work.

- Find three examples of data collection where personal data is collected. For each example describe how the Data Subject is informed of their rights under the Data Protection Act.

- Explore the website www.dataprotection.gov.uk

Methods of enforcing and controlling the Computer Misuse Act

This act aims to protect computer users against malicious vandalism and information theft. Hacking and knowingly spreading computer viruses were made crimes under the Act which aims to secure computer material against unauthorised access and modification.

An organisation needs to make its employees aware of the Act and to establish procedures that will make it difficult for employees to break the law.

Employees should be banned from using external disks on the organisation's computers and should not be allowed to install any software of their own on to their workstation. It is important that software downloaded from the Internet is included in this ban. Such a rule can be enforced by spot checks of the hard disks of employees and backed up with appropriate disciplinary action if an employee is found to have broken the rules.

Dividing up a job so that no one individual has access to all parts of the system is necessary so that no employee is put in a position where they can carry out a fraud. Some banks insist that key staff take a minimum of two weeks of their annual leave at one time to make it harder for them to sustain a fraud.

Copyright laws protect the intellectual rights of authors, composers and artists. They also apply to computer software. When you buy software you do not buy the program, only the right to use it under the terms of the licence. It is illegal to copy or use software without having obtained the appropriate licence.

Every organisation needs to take positive steps to establish procedures that will ensure that the Copyright Designs and Patent Act is not being broken. No software should be used without the appropriate licences being in place. Particular care needs to be taken when LANs are used as sufficient licences for the number of users must have been obtained. The use of software should be monitored; it is possible to buy network software that will keep track of the number of users of a particular piece of software and limit the number of concurrent users to the number of licences held. Once the licenced number of users are accessing a piece of software, other users will be denied access to the software.

Software should only be installed with permission: spot checks can be made to check that employees have not installed programs illegally. If unauthorised software is found on a user's workstation it should be removed immediately and appropriate disciplinary measures taken. Laptop computers should be collected in by the IT department on a regular basis and checks made to ensure that the software installed has been correctly authorised.

What is unauthorised software in an organisation?

It could be:

- Software that has been installed without the permission of the network manager.
- Software that does not have the necessary licence.
- Software that **is** authorised, but has had its source code changed without permission.
- Software personally owned by the employee.
- Software that is not standard within the organisation.
- Software downloaded from the Internet.
- Pirated software.
- Software that might affect the network security.

Software purchasing and control should be centralised: all requests for software should be made to one person or team who has the responsibility for ordering and overseeing the installation of the software. They will be able to ensure that all installed software is correctly licenced. An inventory should be kept that holds details of all software that is installed on computers within the organisation and the licences that are held. Such centralisation also allows reliable, known suppliers to be used and makes the checking that no unauthorised software has been installed a relatively straightforward matter.

Regular and systematic audits should be taken to ensure that the central inventory holds a correct record of software installation.

Software theft

Software theft can be divided into two categories: piracy and counterfeiting. Piracy occurs when more copies of software are made than the number of licences purchased. Many users do not realise that it is illegal and can sometimes do this. Counterfeiting is when software is illegally copied for sale to other users. Often counterfeit software comes without manuals, user guides or tutorials. The software cannot be registered, so there is no technical support or upgrade service available. An added problem for users is that such software carries a high risk of carrying a virus.

BSA

The Business Software Alliance (BSA) is an organisation set up to combat software piracy by trying to promote the use of licensed software. The BSA is an international organisation which represents leading software companies. It works in conjunction with software sellers, governments, law enforcement bodies, and users. The BSA attacks the costly problem of software piracy in three ways.

Firstly, it aims to educate users. Its educational programme concentrates on making end users and IT managers aware of the legal implications of software theft and highlighting the importance of correct software licensing.

Secondly, the BSA aims to enforce current legislation through software audits, raids on premises and legal action against software thieves. So far over 600 legal actions have taken place as a result of the BSA's work. Sentences imposed have ranged from heavy fines to imprisonment.

Finally the BSA lobbies governments at both national and European level to introduce legislation to protect software copyright.

Five software licensing tips from the BSA:

1 Define a software management policy and create a role with responsibility for administering it and purchasing software.

2 Carry out a software audit to reconcile what you have with what you think you have.

3 Carry out regular audits to take changes and oversights into account.

4 Do not allow employees to buy software directly or charge it to expense accounts.

5 Ensure that staff cannot download software from the Internet without approval.

○ For each of the points listed, explain why it is necessary and how it would be carried out.

Organisations must maintain a healthy and safe environment for work. The role of safety officer, who checks that the appropriate laws are complied with, must be established. The safety officer should review health and safety issues on a regular basis. A safety committee, with representatives from all parts of the organisation, should discuss safety matters on a regular basis. Management should encourage and give recognition to a trade union health and safety representative who could act on and report the concerns of colleagues. Such representatives should be given a very thorough training.

It is the management's responsibility to ensure that risk assessments are carried out on a regular basis.

All staff need to be reminded of the importance of health and safety issues on a regular basis. Posters can be displayed which show potential hazards and precautions to be taken. A health and safety policy should be produced and a copy given to all staff. Regular training should be undertaken to inform and remind employees of potential health and safety hazards and their responsibilities in preventing them.

Figure 8.1 Health and safety posters

In workplaces where mistakes can be life threatening, such as oil refineries, safety incentive schemes are often introduced. In one such scheme, the team or location with the best safety record each year is rewarded with a bonus payment.

A number of health issues relate to the use of computers in the work place. It is important that computer-related matters regularly occur on the safety committee agenda.

The dangers to health and safety that could be caused by computers were covered in Chapter 10 of ICT for AS level. It is important that these dangers are taken into account by employers and employees alike.

When installing a new computer or designing the layout for a new office it is important that space guidelines are complied with. Care should be taken to make sure that equipment and furniture are used that are ergonomically designed for the required use.

For employees who are using a computer for most of their working day, there needs to be a clear understanding that appropriate breaks are built in and facilities for refreshment and relaxation away from the computer should be provided.

An organisation should establish a policy that specifies the human–computer interface (HCI) requirements for software design that should be adhered to whenever new systems are developed.

Case Study 5

Computer–based training for health and safety

A large multi-national retail company had problems keeping its in-store employees up to date with health and safety issues. The company did not employ dedicated trainers for its stores; the responsibility for keeping staff up to date fell on the store managers.

Most employees were given a thorough and appropriate induction training programme when they first joined the store, but ongoing and refresher training was more haphazard.

To get around this problem, an online computer-based training package was devised that staff could use at times convenient to them. A log of employee use was maintained centrally that recorded both access to the system by individuals together with details of their performance while working through the material. In this way employees could be reminded when they needed a refresher.

- In what ways would the computer-based training ensure that the company met its obligations for staff training in health and safety?

Summary

- An organisation needs to have a corporate IT security policy. Its aim would be:
  - to prevent misuse from occurring
  - to enable any misuse that did occur to be detected and investigated
  - to lay down procedures that should prevent misuse
  - to establish disciplinary procedures to be used when an employee has been found committing an act of misuse.

- Many IT applications are subject to audit. The auditor needs to be familiar with data-processing techniques.

- Audit packages are computer programs to help the auditor.

- An audit trail is an automatic record made of any transactions carried out by a computer system (for example, all updates of files). This may be needed for legal reasons so that auditors can check that the company accounts are accurate.

- An organisation has a responsibility to ensure that all its employees are aware of laws relating to IT and their responsibilities under these laws, which in particular are:
  - Data Protection Acts 1984 and 1998
  - Computer Misuse Act 1990
  - Copyright Designs and Patent Act 1988
  - Health and Safety at Work Act 1974
  - EU Health and Safety Directive 87/391.

- To comply with the Data Protection Act an employer should:
  - register with the Data Protection Registrar
  - appoint a Data Protection Officer to monitor systems
  - ensure all new systems take data protection into account at the design stage
  - use a variety of methods to remind all staff of their responsibilities in keeping data private

  - include matters of Data Protection in the organisation's security policy
  - put measures in place to make it easy for customers or clients to obtain their rights.

- To comply with the Computer Misuse Act an employer should:
  - make employees aware of the Act
  - ban employees from installing their own software
  - carry out spot checks
  - take disciplinary action as appropriate.

- To comply with the Copyright Designs and Patent Act 1988 an employer should:
  - centralise the purchase of software
  - carry out spot checks as well as regular audits to ensure that no unauthorised software is stored on individual computers
  - remove all illegal software as soon as it is found
  - maintain records of all licences held
  - discipline employees who break the rules.

- To comply with the health and safety legislation employers should:
  - establish a safety committee and ensure that computer-related matters regularly occur on the agenda
  - follow space guidelines when designing office layouts
  - carry out risk assessments on a regular basis
  - make sure that the correct equipment and furniture is used
  - inform all staff of likely hazards using a variety of methods
  - establish a health and safety policy and ensure that all staff are familiar with it
  - appoint a safety officer.

Legal aspects questions

1. An insurance broker is introducing computers so that all members of staff have access to a new computer database. What advice would you give to the owner of the business about:
a) Legal requirements relating to the keeping of customer information on computer file. *(2)*
b) How to ensure that members of staff are aware of these requirements. *(2)*
c) Regulations governing the working conditions of staff. *(2)*

2. A particular college uses a computer network for storing details of its staff and students and for managing its finances. Network stations are provided for the Principal, Vice-Principal, Finance Officer, clerical staff and teaching staff. Only certain designated staff have authority to change data or to authorise payments.
a) What are the legal implications of storing personal data on the computer system? *(4)*
b) What measures should be taken to ensure that the staff understand the legal implications? *(3)*

NEAB Specimen Paper 4

3. Many retail organisations have developed large databases of customer information by buying data from each other.
a) Describe two possible uses these organisations could make of the data they purchase. *(4)*
b) Some customers may object to data held on them by one organisation being sold to another organisation. Describe some of the arguments which either of these retail organisations may use to justify this practice. *(4)*

NEAB Specimen Paper 4

4. 'Legislation will have an impact on the procedures used within any organisation.'
Discuss this statement. Particular attention should be given to:
- the different aspects of IT-related legislation which affect organisations
- the types of formal procedures which are used to enforce legislation
- the potential differences between legislation and company policy.

Illustrate your answer with specific examples. *(20)*

NEAB 1999 Paper 4

5. Explain why auditors have had to change their practices in recent years. *(6)*
Using an example, explain what is meant by an audit trail. Describe what would be found in it. *(5)*

6. Some software packages can be set up to monitor and record their use. This is often stored in an access log. Name four items you would expect to be stored in such a log. *(4)*

NEAB Specimen Paper 4

7. Many accounts packages have an audit trail facility. Explain why such a facility is necessary, what data is logged and how this information can be used. *(6)*

NEAB Specimen Paper 4

8. Some IT applications use software which maintains an audit trail. Name one such application and state why this facility is necessary. *(3)*

NEAB 1998 Paper 4

9. A particular organization uses a financial accounting software system which supports an audit trail.

a) Describe the functionality which should have been built into the audit trail. *(2)*

b) Explain why this functionality is required. *(2)*

c) State **two** potential system overheads caused by the operation of this functionality. *(2)*

AQA June 2000 Paper 4

10. IT managers have to be aware of certain legislation that will impact on the procedures within both their department and the rest of their organisation. Discuss this statement. Particular attention should be given to:

- Methods of enforcing and controlling the protection of data within the organisation.

- Methods of enforcing and controlling the use of software within the organisation.
- The role of the IT department in developing and implementing suitable strategies to assist in these tasks. *(2)*

AQA June 2000 Paper 4

11. An organisation uses a computer network for managing its finance and personnel systems. The network manager is concerned that some members of staff may install unauthorised software onto the network. State six reasons why a piece of software should be designated as unauthorised. *(6)*

AQA June 2001 Paper 4

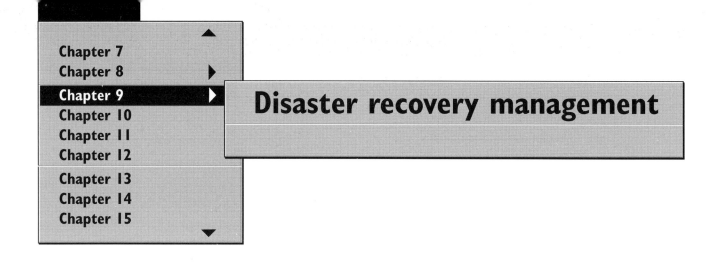

Disaster recovery management

It is important that commercial IT users recognise the potential threats to their information systems, plan to avoid disasters leading to loss of data and have contingency plans to enable recovery of any lost data.

The corporate consequences of system failure

If contingency plans and management are inadequate then commercial enterprises face serious financial losses. They will be unable to process transactions which are at the heart of their business and when the system is restored extra staff time will be required to catch up on the backlog of data. There will also be a financial cost for staff time used in restoring the system. Much day-to-day functioning would cease. This would lead to loss of trade as customers are forced to go elsewhere.

Serious, extensive or repeated failure would lead to loss of confidence in the business and adversely affect its image. The disruption to customers can lead to the loss of goodwill, resulting in the loss of both existing trade on a permanent basis and potential new business. At the worst, a company can be forced to cease trading. A high proportion of businesses never recover from serious failure of their information systems.

Day-to-day data processing functions could be badly affected. Many supermarkets have to close their doors and cease trading if their point of sales terminals fail to function.

Case Study 1

The scale of the problem

Taken from an article in Computing Magazine.

Almost a fifth of European organisations have no disaster recover plan and many of those that do would find them ineffective in an emergency. Research shows that 45 per cent of organisations have not tested their disaster recovery plan in the last twelve months. Figures show that some organisations put out of action by a disaster can lose more than $1 million an hour – a bank could lose $250,000 a minute if systems are lost. An estimated 40 per cent of companies that suffer a disaster will cease to be around within five years.

- Why do so many disaster recovery plans prove to be ineffective?

- Why do so many organisations fail to test their disaster recovery plans?

- Why do so many companies that suffer a disaster collapse?

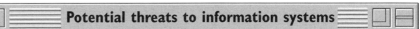

Potential threats to information systems

The threats to an information system are far ranging. Some of the major threats are described below.

Figure 9.1 Threats to an information system

Physical failure

Physical disasters caused by events such as fire, floods or earthquakes may be relatively rare, but when they do occur they can be devastating. The threat of terrorist attack has increased over the last few years and has to be taken seriously by all organisations. Less dramatic damage can be caused to cables whilst building works are being carried out, or even by spilling a cup of coffee on a stand-alone computer.

As well as equipment, files containing vital data could be destroyed by such disasters. Without far-sighted disaster planning, many businesses would be unable to recover from the data loss. Companies and many organisations employ specialist disaster recovery companies to manage their plans.

Hardware failure

Hardware failure is a major cause of system breakdown. Failure can arise from processor failure or disk head crash. Computers are dependent upon a constant supply of electricity. The failure of one hardware component can cause the whole system to crash. The growth in networks and distributed systems has in some ways made disaster recovery easier as it is possible for alternative sites to take over the functions of a site which has a hardware failure. On the other hand, as sites become more dependent upon each other, a failure at one location could cause a universal shut down.

Software failure

Software can contain bugs which only occur when a particular combination of unusual events occur. Such bugs may not be detected in testing and lead to systems breakdowns at any time. They can be hard to locate and put right and cause considerable damage to data as well as delay in processing. Software can fail because it is unsuitable for the task or over time the volume of data used in a system may grow too large for the system to cope with.

Telecommunication failure

The growth of data communications as wide area networks become more commonly used increases the potential for breakdown. Causes of such failure include faulty cables, a gateway that is non-functioning, thus denying access from a LAN to the WAN, or the corruption of data as it is transmitted.

Computer crime and abuse

Data is very vulnerable to illegal access such as hacking. The company's IT security policy should state exactly how to prevent problems occurring and what to do if they do occur. Viruses can alter the way that programs function and lead to breakdown.

Invalid data

Data can be invalid either due to user error on entry or through corruption that has gone uncorrected. Such errors can be copied from one backup version to the next without the corrupt data being detected.

System design failure

Many failures arise as a result of poor system design which failed to build in appropriate measures to deal with all situations. Very often exceptional situations, or combinations of data, are missed by the designer.

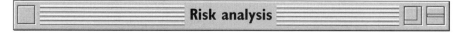

Risk analysis

Risk analysis for any particular system involves determining what the risks are and designing appropriate countermeasures to the appropriate level. The risks will be different for different systems and will change over time. For each risk identified, it is necessary to establish the likelihood (or probability) of such an event occurring and the gravity of the consequences of the event.

For example, a single stand-alone PC on the reception desk of a veterinary practice storing details of appointments and pet treatments is at greater risk than an aerospace company's mainframe system storing its latest designs. However, the latter is more likely to be a target for illegal access.

Computer security involves reducing the risk to electronic data. A risk is made up of three factors: the potential threats to the data; its vulnerability; and value to the organisation. Risk will increase if any of these factors increases. Thus risk analysis is the process of assessing vulnerability to threats, the potential losses, the current security controls and identifying possible countermeasures to reduce risk. It compares the cost of the potential loss with the cost of countering it.

In order to determine risk a review of threats must be undertaken. The review may be on a quantitative basis to work out likelihood, as well as subjective where information is gathered through consulting with staff. Very often a checklist of potential problems can be used as a starting point.

Determining the risks, that is, the threats against and vulnerabilities of a particular computer system, is no easy task. The value of the data to the organisation will vary. Each situation is unique and the overall risk will differ. To undertake a risk analysis, a manager would need to know a considerable amount about the organisation, for example, its aims and objectives or its history and future plans. This knowledge is as important as information concerning risks to the hardware and software. Managers may have statistical data on power failures, crime levels, and so on, when making decisions. However, it is necessary to consider whether they reflect the risk to this particular organisation.

A risk can be categorised in two ways: the likelihood of it occurring and the seriousness if it does occur (see Figure 9.2).

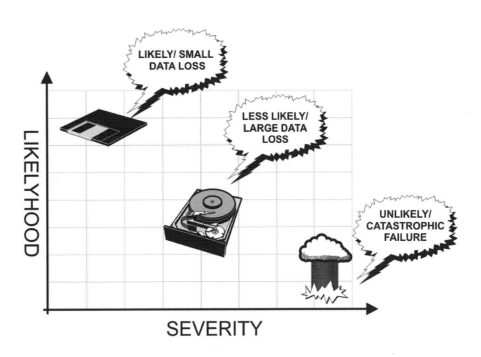

Figure 9.2 Categorising risks

Where a particular risk lies on the graph will influence the type of measures put in place.

The criteria likely to be used in selecting appropriate measures are:

- the cost of measures to protect against and recover from failure
- the potential cost of the loss of data
- the inconvenience to staff – security measures are useless if everyone bypasses them
- the statistical likelihood of the problem occurring.

The risk review may be made either on a quantitative basis (for example, probability of fire over 10 years (0.02), cost of fire (£1,000,000)) or on a subjective basis by consulting with staff and using knowledge of the business.

Software packages are available that provide a checklist of all recognised dangers for a particular type of installation or activity. The package attaches weights to risks and provides an index rating of risks.

A security incident can lead to loss of data confidentiality, integrity or availability which in turn may give rise to impacts of direct or consequential harm. Security management means reducing risks to acceptable levels by implementing procedures to lessen the likelihood or impact of a threat.

Disaster avoidance

There is much that can go wrong when using an IT-based system and it is important that any potential problems are identified before they occur. Some failures in a system can be avoided.

The use of **fault tolerant computer systems** provides protection against hardware failure. A fault tolerant computer has extra hardware such as memory chips, processors and disk storage in parallel. Special software routines or built-in self checking logic detects any hardware failures and automatically switches to the backup device. Some systems automatically call in the maintenance engineers. Faulty parts can be removed and repaired without disruption to the running of the system.

The chances of damage from fire, tempest and flood can be minimised by having detectors in the computer room with CO_2 extinguishers available or by placing the computer room on the upper floor of the building and using fireproof safes for disks and backup tapes. Breakdown of power supplies can be avoided by having an uninterrupted power supply and a standby generator.

Malicious damage to the system can be addressed, in part, by having computer equipment in rooms protected by swipe card or other security methods. Strict codes of conduct need to be enforced to avoid illegal access to systems. For example, rules banning the use of personal floppy disks on the workstations can be established.

Hacking and associated problems could be countered by such measures as checking all accesses to the system and only allowing three attempts before shutting down a terminal. The encryption of all data sent along communication channels should be considered.

Case Study 2

Disaster avoidance

Dawson and Mason Ltd. is a medium-sized manufacturing company which, over the last few years, has become more and more dependent on IT. The company has decided to adopt the following disaster avoidance plan, which consists mainly of common sense practices – reasonable and inexpensive measures to avoid a disaster that could cost the company thousands of pounds in loss of revenue.

- Hardware and software inventory

Each department of the company must keep a detailed inventory of all computer equipment and make sure it is up to date. The inventory should cover all hardware, software, communications equipment, peripherals and backup media, including model and serial numbers.

- IT facilities

Administrative procedures are a vital part of security and disaster avoidance.

- All perimeter doors must be kept locked if the room is unattended.
- Windows and other access points should be kept locked if unattended.
- Access should be restricted to authorised personnel.
- Strangers seen entering office areas should be challenged and asked for identification.

- Local Area Networks

- Backup of server files is automated on a nightly basis.
- A rotation schedule for backup tapes should be used and several generations of backup kept.
- Two copies of the server backup tapes are generated. One backup copy is available on-site in case recovery is necessary. The other copy is stored off-site.
- Disk mirroring is used to duplicate data from one hard disk to another hard disk. (Mirrored drives operate in tandem, constantly storing and updating the same files on each hard disk in case one disk fails.)
- In the case of vital and sensitive data hot backup is used. (Two file servers operate in tandem and data is duplicated on the hard disks of both servers. If one server fails, the other server automatically takes over.)
- A UPS (Uninterruptable Power Supply) has been installed for every LAN server. The batteries should be checked regularly to ensure that they are not drained and that they are charging properly.

- Storage media

- Magnetic media should be kept away from sources of heat, radiation and magnetism.
- Backup media should be stored in data safes.
- Vaults used for storing critical documents and backup media should meet appropriate security and fire standards.

- Preventing theft
  - If a computer is used to store sensitive data, the data should be encrypted so that the data cannot be accessed even if the equipment is stolen.

continued

Case Study 2 *continued*

- Anchoring pads and security cables are used to prevent equipment from being stolen.

- Employee awareness

Security and safety awareness is critical to any disaster avoidance program. A lot of problems will be avoided if employees have been trained to look out for conditions that can result in a disaster.

1 Disasters can be caused deliberately or accidentally. Give one example of a disaster caused deliberately and one caused by accident.

2 Explain the reasons for keeping an inventory of hardware and software.

3 Dawson and Mason's plan does not mention computer viruses. Describe the actions that should be taken to prevent infection by a virus.

4 Describe the process of encryption.

5 List further measures that could be taken to prevent theft.

Planning for recovery from disaster: a contingency plan

Those failures and catastrophic situations that cannot be avoided can, with an appropriate contingency plan in place, be prevented from having disastrous consequences.

A **contingency plan** is a preparation for recovery from a failure. It is a planned set of actions that can be carried out if things go wrong so that disruption is minimised. It is necessary first to identify what could go wrong and then what should be done if it did. For example, if you are organising an event to take place out of doors, it would be sensible to have a contingency plan in case of rain. Your plan could be to make a provisional booking in a local hall or provide guests with umbrellas!

Any organisation that is in any way dependent on a computerised information system needs a plan which details how operations can be resumed after an occurrence of the disasters described earlier in the chapter. The scope of such a contingency plan needs to be established. It is likely to be broad. It should cover equipment, data, staff and business functions. It should take into account that an organisation is dynamic: staff, procedures and equipment will change over time so reviews of the contingency plan must be built in. Obviously the plan should be appropriate for the size and nature of the organisation.

Staff must be trained to react appropriately if a disaster should occur. The contingency plan needs to be tested regularly to ensure that staff are fully aware of their responsibilities as well as to check that the plan actually works. A document should be produced that clearly defines the roles of staff and the procedures to be carried out if the plan has to be put into action.

Elements of a contingency plan

It is usual for a contingency plan to provide for immediate access to alternative computer hardware. In setting up a successful plan, it is essential to identify the most critical business functions and work out how each is vulnerable, by carrying out a risk analysis as described above. It is then possible to establish the hardware, software, files and human resources required to resume processing of these critical applications if disaster occurs. Personnel must be trained to follow the contingency plan correctly and a step-by-step course of action for implementing the plan must be drawn up.

For successful recovery from disaster, data for critical applications must be backed-up and storage media taken off site. A business will have many backup tapes or disks, including the most recent global backup and several incremental backups. Backup tapes must be date stamped as the order in which data is restored after any data loss is vital. The disaster recovery plan must include the order for restoring.

Disastrous effects from hardware failure might be addressed by having a maintenance contract with a specified call-out clause to a specialist company. Alternatively, a business could make an arrangement with another firm or bureau to run their software in the event of major problems.

Distributed processing facilities can be used for disaster recovery. If a business has distributed processing to local branches then the branches can operate for several days if the main computer centre is lost. Another option available to large organisations is the use of multiple computer centres. Disaster recovery firms are used by businesses that do not wish to build their own backup facilities.

Large organisations, such as supermarkets and banks, have more than one computer site in case of hardware problems. Contingency plans are set up so that the critical tasks of one site can be carried out at another. An example of such a contingency put into action is illustrated in the description of the terrorist attack which caused problems for Royal and Sun Alliance (see Case Study 4). Alternative network routes are also maintained so that, if one cable is severed, for example, an alternative route can automatically be used.

For a large multinational bank, the cost of downtime would be enormous, so disaster planning is taken very seriously. A separate physical location is maintained where hardware, software and data replicate that of the main system. The data is updated in real time and mirrors the main site storage. In case of a disaster, the site will provide all the current functions, at a reduced scale, but at the same level of performance. One person in each system team is likely to be made responsible for the business recovery procedure so that, if a disaster did occur, he or she would be able to initiate a swift change to the backup site and system.

Nearby companies can come to an arrangement to provide emergency facilities for each other in case of disaster so that vital systems can be run. Specialist disaster recovery firms will help in the drawing up of a disaster recovery plan. They will have the expertise and the equipment that will let them act swiftly when necessary.

Case Study 3

System failure

Lloyds cashpoints fail for five hours

A power failure paralysed Lloyds Bank's entire national cash machine system leaving thousands of Christmas shoppers without cash. For more than five hours, Lloyds' customers were unable to obtain money from any automated teller machine.

Almost all the Lloyds' machines flashed up the message 'sorry, cashpoint service closed'. Bank staff in shopping centres reported big queues as shoppers struggled to get money from cashiers inside branches. The timing could not have been worse: nine days before Christmas demand for cash is at its yearly peak.

The system was brought down by a power failure at the computer in Peterborough which authorises cashpoint withdrawals nationwide. Damage to a single power cable may have been to blame.

○ What contingency plan could have avoided the five hour downtime?

Case Study 4

Terrorist attack: Royal & Sun Alliance

On a Saturday in June, one of the biggest bomb blasts in peacetime Britain ripped through the Arndale shopping centre in Manchester, injuring 206 people. Longridge House, home of the Royal & Sun Alliance insurance company bore the full brunt of the blast.

The building was almost destroyed and, as it contained the company's mainframe, it was initially feared that core business operations could be seriously jeopardised. In spite of extensive damage to all seven floors, Royal & Sun Alliance staff in Liverpool detected signs of life in the IT system, but when the fire brigade cut off power to the site later in the evening, all systems effectively died.

Fortunately for Royal & Sun Alliance they had a contract with data recovery partner Comdisco. Key Royal & Sun Alliance staff were rushed to Comdisco's Warrington centre. With the help of recovered backup tapes, Comdisco's mainframe was able to mimic the characteristics and requirements of the insurance company.

Meanwhile, 200 Royal & Sun Alliance staff were switched to the company's Liverpool centre. When the sun came up on Monday morning the company had a makeshift, temporary switchboard which was up and running for 9 a.m. Luck and effective disaster recovery planning meant that not a single day of trade was lost.

○ List the features mentioned that were taken into account in the contingency plan.

○ The final sentence attributes part of the successful outcome being due to luck. Where did luck come in?

Case Study 5

Fire: William Jackson, food manufacturer and retail group

(Business Computer World)

6 July was pay day at food manufacturer and retail group William Jackson, based in Hull. Anticipating her busiest time of the month, payroll administrator Diane Rush was at work by 7 a.m. preparing wages data to be transferred from the company's AS/400 computer to BACS, the system for paying wages directly into banks.

Diane noticed smoke billowing from the food factory next door and phoned Safetynet, the company's disaster recovery partner at 7.45 a.m. All staff had to be evacuated from the offices as fire swept through neighbouring buildings.

Although tapes and a modem had been recovered, the continuing blaze meant that the payroll could not be processed on site. Under protection from the fire brigade, Safetynet successfully rescued the AS/400 from the ashes and installed the charred machine alongside their own mobile unit. Using a parallel recovery process, the payroll was successfully relayed to BACS and all 2500 staff were paid on time.

○ List features from the William Jackson contingency plan.

Summary

IT users must:

○ recognise the potential threats to their information systems. Dangers include:

- ○ physical failure
- ○ hardware failure
- ○ software failure
- ○ telecommunication failure
- ○ computer crime and abuse
- ○ invalid data
- ○ system design failure.

○ plan to avoid disasters leading to loss of data. Examples of disaster avoidance measures include the use of:

- ○ virus scanning software
- ○ fault tolerant components
- ○ smoke detectors in buildings
- ○ uninterrupted power supply or standby generator
- ○ strict password management policies
- ○ extra network links
- ○ regular maintenance.

○ have contingency plans to be able to recover any data lost. Examples of elements of contingency plans to prevent disaster in case of failure include:

- ○ backup strategies
- ○ contract with a company specialising in disaster recovery
- ○ arrangement to use the hardware of another firm or bureau in case of failure
- ○ distributed systems maintaining duplicated data on different sites.

Measures taken to prevent problems will depend on the perceived risk and the cost of potential loss of data. The process of risk analysis is used to determine the need for such measures.

Disaster recovery management questions

I. A fire service relies on computers to direct the driver of the fire engine to the fire by the quickest route. Experience suggests that a second backup computer will be needed at a cost of £30,000, although it may never be used. Councillors making the decision on what to do are reluctant to spend the money. Advise them what to do. (8)

2. 'Only 60 per cent of companies in the UK have adequate disaster recovery plans'. Discuss this statement, including in your answer:
- why such plans are necessary
- the potential threats to information systems
- the contingency plans needed to combat these threats. (12)

3. 'Information stored in a typical computer system is more secure than information stored in a typical manual filing system'. Discuss this statement, including in your answer the threats to security to a manual filing system and those to a computer system and the ways of minimising the threats to a computer system. (12)

4. Define the term risk analysis. Explain the circumstances under which such analysis is important. (8)

5. Suggest some essential elements of a disaster recovery plan for:
a) a major high street bank (10)
b) a small corner shop (8)
c) your school or college administrative system. (10)

6. Define the term fault tolerant computer system. (2)

7. List five distinctly different potential threats to an information system. Give one way of countering each potential threat. (10)

NEAB 1999 Paper 4

8. A medical practice has installed a new information system that links patient records and prescriptions to the financial systems of the practice. The financial records must be secure against fraud as they are used to claim money from the Health Authority.

a) Describe four factors that should be included in an IT security policy for the practice. (8)
b) Describe one measure the practice could take to show that their records were accurate. (2)
c) Describe three criteria that could be used to select a disaster contingency plan to recover from a breakdown of this system. (6)

AQA June 2002 Paper 4

9. An insurance company is reviewing its disaster recovery management policy.
a) At a strategic level, state **six** potential threats to an information system. (6)
b) Explain the concept of risk analysis. (4)

AQA June 2000 Paper 4

10. 'Information systems are critical to the running of any organisation, the consequences of failure could prove disastrous.'
Discuss this statement, including in your discussion:
- the potential threats to the system
- the concept of risk analysis
- the corporate consequences of system failure
- the factors which should be considered when designing a contingency plan to enable recovery from disaster. (20)

AQA June 2001 Paper 4

11. A growing organisation has realised that so far they have been lucky in that their information systems have not failed. Before they expand their business operational reliance on ICT, they have been advised by their insurer to carry out a risk analysis and then plan what to do next.
a) Explain what is meant by risk analysis. (3)
b) State **three** different potential threats to an information system and describe a countermeasure for each one. (9)
c) Describe **three** of the criteria that could be used to select a disaster contingency plan. (6)

AQA Jan 2003 Paper 4

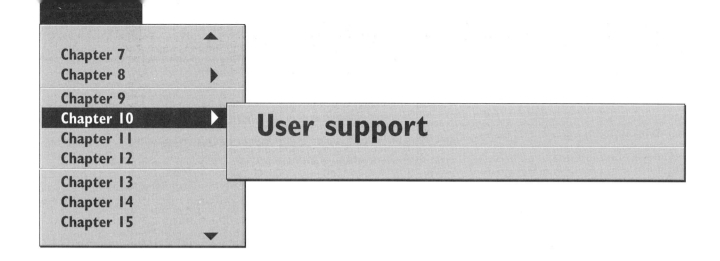

User support

Most software producers provide some form of support for users in case they have difficulty in installing or using their software. Support is sometimes provided free under the product warranty or an entitlement to help can be bought for a fixed period of time. Large organisations will have an IT support team whose members will provide hardware and software support for users in-house.

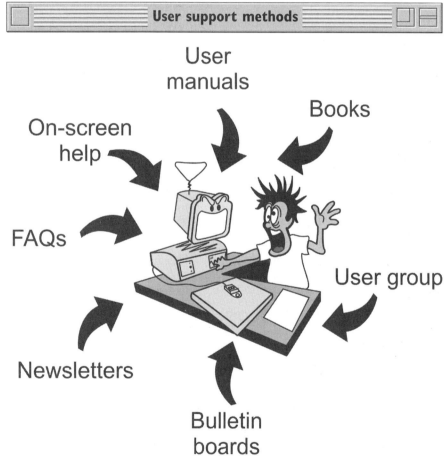

Figure 10.1 User support methods

Many industry standard packages have a very large user base, who between them will need to know all aspects of the software's functionality, although each individual user is likely to use only a part of the range of options a software package offers. Support is provided in a variety of ways.

User manuals providing written instructions in a book form usually come free with the software. They describe how to install and use the software. For complex packages, there can be a number of different books: perhaps one aimed at a first time user, in the form of a tutorial, and another involving a complete description of all functions to serve as a reference document.

On-screen help within packages is just about always provided, at least at a basic level of support usually by pressing the F1 key. Many packages provide very extensive on-screen help facilities.

Books about using popular software are produced independently by publishers and sold in most bookshops or over the Internet. For the most popular packages there are a very large number of titles available. A user needs to ensure that any book purchased is designed for a user of their skill level as books will vary from those suitable for absolute beginners to those designed for the most advanced user.

Publishers of widely-used software may send **newsletters** to all registered users, including articles on tips, solutions to common problems and advanced functions. These newsletters provide a forum for users to share ideas and problems.

Software houses provide a considerable amount of information on packages via **bulletin boards** on the Internet, often in the form of **Frequently Asked Questions** (FAQs). Users can search through questions that other people have asked and are likely to find a solution that resolves their current problem.

Logic Programming Associates Ltd

| Products | Support | Downloads | Information | Latest News |

Frequently Asked Questions (FAQ)

This page contains some frequently asked questions, together with their answers: please check these to see if they solve your problem.

Running WIN-PROLOG

The following questions have been asked about running WIN-PROLOG:

Q: When I try to install WIN-PROLOG 4.100, I get a "String Too Long" error: what's this all about?

A: This error occurs on certain Windows 2000 systems, where one or more of the "Environment Variables" has a value that exceeds 512 characters in length: the most common case is the "PATH" variable. This problem has been completely overcome in WIN-PROLOG 4.200, and we recommend you to upgrade your system if you experience this problem.

Q: When I try to "assert" or "retract" programs in WIN-PROLOG, I get a "Predicate Protected" error. Why does this happen?

A: The "Predicate Protected" error is due to a feature of modern Prologs: if you load a file

Figure 10.2 An example of Frequently Asked Questons (FAQs)

For complex software, **user groups** are set up, where users can get together to share problems and ideas. Such groups can either meet physically, or more often these days, via bulletin boards on the Internet.

Very often the help that a user needs is closer to hand. It is possible that a colleague or friend who is familiar with the software can help with their problem.

Helpdesks

In addition many software publishers offer telephone support 24 hours a day, 7 days a week, for immediate help and advice. The user phones the 'help desk.' Help desk operators are technical troubleshooters who provide technical assistance, support, and advice to customers and end-users. They are experts in the program and have a computer on the desk in front of them, which they will use to try to replicate and solve the users' problems. This support can be provided free of charge to registered users.

What is logged?

When the call is taken, the user will need to give some information to the Help Desk operator. This should include:

- their name and telephone number
- the nature of the problem
- the name and the version number of the software
- the specification of computer it is being run on (the type and speed of processor, and the size of memory will be needed here)
- the operating system in use
- any error messages being displayed
- the licence number of the software so that the help desk can check that the software is being used legally.

The help desk operator will record this information together with the date and time.

Telephone support problems

A number of problems can arise when using a manufacturer's telephone help desk. The waiting time on the phone can be considerable at certain times of day. Many of these services are popular and it is not unusual to spend a lot of time listening to 'music' whilst a call is queued.

Some problems are common and are easy to answer but other, complex, ones will not be able to be answered on the spot, as several experts may need to confer. In these circumstances, it will be necessary for the help desk operator to phone back at a later time.

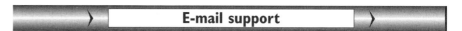
E-mail support

If the problem is not time critical, then e-mail could be used as an alternative to the telephone. This has the advantage of smoothing out the demand, so that the operator can answer queries in order throughout the day. A priority system could be used which would ensure that critical enquiries were answered first. She or he will be able to spend all their time finding solutions to problems without being interrupted by a ringing telephone.

From the user's point of view, the use of e-mail avoids wasted time on the telephone. However, instant answers to simple problems will not be possible. E-mail lacks the opportunity for human interaction offered by a telephone conversation.

Monitoring the help desk

A help desk is likely to use a computerised call logging system giving a unique call reference number for each user query. This allows the performance of the help desk operator to be monitored as well as providing a reference for follow-up calls.

The help desk employees should have access to a file of registered users to enable a check that the caller is entitled to help whenever a phone call is received. A computerised database of known errors and their solutions, together with answers to frequently asked question should be available. This could take the form of an expert system.

The performance of the help desk should be monitored to ensure that it provides a high level of service.

Performance indicators could include:

- the number of calls logged daily or per hour
- the response time to the initial call
- the time taken to resolve the problem
- the number of repeat calls on the same problem for a particular user.

It may also be possible to record the level of the user's satisfaction of the problem resolution using a qualitative code.

The manager responsible for the provision of help desk facilities would review the performance indicators on a regular basis and make necessary changes to staffing levels and procedures. It might prove necessary to provide extra training for help desk operators.

Package credibility

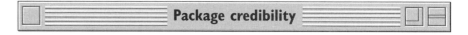

It is not cheap for software companies to provide and staff a customer help desk. Of course the support is not free. Someone has to pay for it and it is likely that the price of the software reflects the provision of user support. Despite its cost, user support is necessary and is a major factor in determining the credibility of the software.

The provision of user support reassures the customer when they buy the product. They are more likely to buy the product if they know that support is available. If user support is not available, business users are unlikely to risk using the software.

User support shows the customer that the software company has confidence in its product. A poor quality product could result in thousands of help desk calls and would be expensive for the company.

If the user suffered a problem and no support was available, they would be unlikely to buy a product from the same company again. A help desk helps retain customers.

Which method of support?

The method of support a user will use will depend on the nature of the problem and the skills and circumstances of the user. Many users rarely look in a manual, preferring to find out the answer for themselves although this is not always the most efficient way of operating. The first point of call is usually the on-screen help as it is always available. In a large company it may be easy for a user to find someone who knows the software well enough to solve a problem.

Checking the Internet for a bulletin board may be more convenient for an office worker than buying a book. The information given also may be more up to date. Using a telephone help desk is often the last resort for a user; it can be time consuming and require great patience.

Documentation

All types of software should be supported with appropriate documentation. In fact, the quality of the documentation will be one of the criteria considered when choosing software.

Different types of user will have differing documentation needs. The technical support team will need documentation that provides installation instructions including disk, peripheral devices and memory requirements. They will need to have documentation of backup routines and recovery procedures. An explanation of all technical error messages, together with the necessary action to correct them, will be required.

A data entry clerk, using the same system, will need clear instructions on how to use the functions needed for tasks. Details of appropriate error messages due to incorrect data entry should be included, together with a list of useful keyboard shortcuts.

Case Study 1

Helpdesk

Computer help desk operator
Salary: £14,500

I went straight from A levels to work when I joined UMIST (University of Manchester Institute of Science and Technology) at 19 as a receptionist in the computer department. Now, two years later, I work as a computer help desk operator. I work from 8:45 a.m until 5 p.m. I don't suffer from stress, I feel valued and everyone in my department treats me as an equal.

In the morning I organise computer training courses. In the afternoon, I staff the walk-in help desk. I deal with staff and students complaining they can't log in, print or set up an account.

We get around 60 calls a day. People turn up saying, 'You're the help desk, it says on this leaflet you'll fix it.' They expect instant results and the high-ranking professors tend to get more hysterical on the phone than the students. I tend to keep calm when people lose their temper.

At the beginning I was amazed that so many students in a place specialising in technology needed help with logging in.

(From The Guardian, 21 March 2001.)

- Describe any help desk facilities available at your school or college.

- Find out the five most frequent problems taken at this help desk.

Case Study 2

Help desk job advertisement from www.hotrecruit.com

IT help desk operator
Salary: £14,000 per annum
Purpose of job
To deliver a high level of customer care to staff who call the IT help desk.

Main activities/responsibilities
- To staff the IT help desk.

- To answer the IT telephone helpline.

- To log calls in the help desk system, set initial priorities and assign calls to IT support engineers.

- To liaise with customers to keep them informed of progress on their calls.

- To monitor outstanding support calls and alert support engineers when calls are overdue.

Person specification
Essential
- A minimum of two years experience using IT in an office environment.

- A good grasp of PC hardware terminology and a knowledge of Windows 95/98/XP and Microsoft Office software.

- Demonstrable commitment to providing a high standard of customer service.

- Excellent interpersonal skills, a good clear telephone manner and the ability to communicate diplomatically and effectively at all times.

continued ...

Case Study 2 *continued*

- Able to work methodically and accurately, and prioritise work, under pressure.

- Able to work on own initiative as well as part of a team.

- Able to prepare reports.

Desirable

- Previous work experience in a customer-facing role.

Use the Internet to find five other help desk jobs. Computer magazines and the site given above could be good starting points. List the requirements that are common to all the advertisements.

Summary

- Knowledge of software is backed-up by user support. Often this is a telephone line providing access to immediate advice for a particular problem. Software providers may also provide help on the Internet.

- A range of support can be available to users. This can take the form of:
  - On-screen help

- Documentation – different forms available for different categories of user
- User manuals
- Books about using popular software
- Newsletters sent to all registered users
- Bulletin boards with Frequently Asked Questions (FAQs)
- User groups
- Colleague or friend
- Help desk.

User support questions

1. Each day a software house logs a large number of calls from its users to its support desk.

   a) In order to resolve a user's problem, list **four** items of information that the support desk would require after getting the identification of the user. *(4)*

   b) The software house is introducing an ISDN-based system so that it can communicate directly with its software at the users' sites.

   i) Describe **two** potential benefits to the software house, other than speed, of such a system. *(4)*

   ii) Describe **one** potential disadvantage for the customer of such a system. *(2)*

   AQA June 2000 Paper 4

2. Each day a software house logs a large number of calls from its users to its support desk.

   a) Describe how the support desk might manage these requests to provide an effective service. *(3)*

   b) Describe three items of information the support desk would require to assist in resolving a user's problem. *(3)*

   c) The software house receives complaints from its users that the support desk is providing a poor service. Describe three reports that the software house could produce in order to examine the validity of this claim. *(6)*

   NEAB 1997 Paper 4

3. Many software companies offer a user support line.

   a) Describe three items of information a user support line would log when taking a call from a user. *(3)*

   b) Many user support lines need to share problems and potential solutions between a number of

operators who are answering calls. Describe one method of achieving this. *(3)*

   c) Some user support lines also offer a mailbox facility to enable users to log their problems using e-mail. What advantages does this have for:

   i) the software user

   ii) the user support staff. *(4)*

   NEAB Specimen Paper 4

4. A software house has a user support department that provides a range of services to customers including telephone advice and the supply of data fixes for corrupt files. The department uses a computer-based logging system to store details of incoming telephone calls from users (a call management system). The system is capable of producing a variety of reports via a report generator.

   a) The software house receives complaints from its users that this department is providing a poor service. Describe three reports that the software house could produce to examine the validity of this claim. *(6)*

   b) The department currently uses traditional mail to receive disks containing corrupt files and to return them with the data fixed. However, the department now wishes to use electronic communications based on ISDN. Describe two potential advantages and one potential disadvantage to the customer of this proposed change. *(6)*

   NEAB 1999 Paper 4

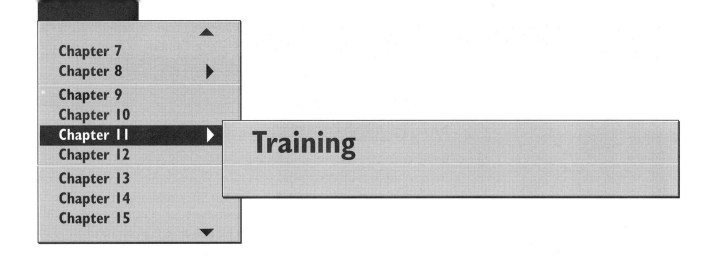

Training

Training is '*the acquisition of a body of knowledge and skills which can be applied to a particular job.*'

Today the job market is very flexible. People do not stay in one single job for the whole of their working life, but are likely to make one or more major career changes. As well as this, the nature of a particular job changes as new technological advances are made. This is particularly true for IT users. New hardware is appearing every few months. New versions of software appear every few years. Employers need to give IT training to their workforce on a regular basis: training should consider both the needs of the company and the needs of the individual.

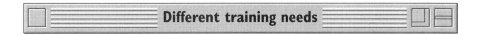

Different training needs

Different users have different training needs, depending on their previous experience, their knowledge and their job and its requirements. Some jobs involve IT tasks that are repetitive and specific; others call for a more open-ended use. It is crucial that the level and pace of the training fits the user and the task.

Someone who has not used a computer before will need initial training. A more experienced user may need training in higher level skills. Users of special equipment (for example, a bar code scanner), or special facilities (for example, e-mail) will need specific training.

A database package such as Microsoft Access can be used at a number of different levels. So training needs to be available which meets these differing needs. For example, an operator of a database whose job is to enter data may only need to be taught how to access an existing database, add and modify records.

The manager who uses the information from the database as a tool in decision-making may need to be taught how to produce standard reports and carry out a range of queries. A database programmer will need to learn much more about the package, such as how to set up a new database and amend an existing one, how to write reports and macros, and much more besides. It would be inappropriate for all the above users to attend the same course.

Skills-based or task-based training

Skills-based training

Some training is based on learning a skill, such as typing on a keyboard, using Windows or using a program like Word or Access. This skill could be used in many circumstances. This type of training is often offered in standard courses that teach participants how to use a range of facilities according to their current skills level. Such training can be fairly open-ended, leaving the trainees to decide exactly how to incorporate the skills learnt into their current jobs.

Task-based training

Other training is based on learning how to do a particular task. Examples of this could be: how to use a hand set for recording electricity meter readings; how to process a sale with a Visa card; and how to load transaction and master file tapes in a batch processing system. In such circumstances, the training is designed specifically for the occasion. It is more likely to take place in-house. Skills acquired will be very specific and will often not be transferable into other situations.

When training to use a software application such as a sales database, different personnel will require different training based on the tasks that they are required by their job to carry out on the database. A telesales person is likely to need training in data entry. They might need to know what data has to be entered and what is optional, what order to work the data entry process, how to deal with errors and unusual data and how to answer enquiries.

A sales manager using the same database might need training in how to produce a range of reports and how to 'drill down' from summarised information to find more detailed information when searching for explanations.

Database administrators will need a more technical and complex training that provides them with an in depth knowledge of the software. They will need the skills to carry out a wide range of tasks including writing new reports, modify the database structure to meet changing needs, as well as troubleshooting when problems occur.

Skill updating and refreshing

For employees in many jobs, keeping IT skills up to date is a nearly constant need as job requirements and facilities change. Employees will need to update their skills on a regular basis, particularly as new or updated versions of software or hardware are installed. Old skills may be superseded when new systems are installed.

Employees may also need to refresh old skills if they have not used some piece of hardware or software for some time. Some activities are only carried out at irregular intervals and it is easy to forget how to use features of software if they are not constantly being practised.

When an employee changes job within an organisation, either because of promotion or as a result of changes in the structure of the organisation, he or she might need to be trained in new IT skills that are needed in the new role.

Case Study I

Training for use of a college electronic attendance system

A college uses an electronic attendance registration system that allows teachers to enter the details of attendance in each class using a hand-held device.

A member of the tutorial staff can access the system, on an office computer, to view the information collected in classes and is able to produce a variety of reports relating to individual or whole class attendance over a selected time period.

The college information department manage the system. They will maintain the interface between the registration system and the college MIS. They have to write new reports from time when requested and they troubleshoot the system. From time to time they need to contact the developers of the registration system.

Different training is needed for each different group of staff.

- Outline the training needs for:
    - Teachers
    - Tutorial staff
    - Information department personnel.
- When would training be required?

There is a wide range of training options available. It is important that the method is carefully chosen to meet the specific needs of an individual.

Face-to-face or instructor-led training

Formal training with an instructor training a group of trainees is a popular but expensive option. However, this method has the advantage that the trainer can answer questions and provide immediate help and feedback. Face-to-face training may take the form of on-the-job training or be delivered through in-house courses or external courses. Instructor-led training remains very popular as students are able to interact with each other and their tutor, sharing ideas and information.

A disadvantage of instructor-led training is that it is usually planned for a specific time in advance which might not coincide exactly with the time the trainee actually requires instruction; in this way it lacks flexibility. If the training is not followed up by immediate practice, much of what has been learned is quite likely to be forgotten.

On-the-job training

This, as the name implies, involves learning while at work. A trainer from inside or outside the company may come and give instructions to a trainee. Although it has the advantage of providing training in a realistic setting, it is often difficult for the employee to learn with the day-to-day stresses of the job present.

> Xylos (www.xylos.com) trains more than 18,000 people each year in using ICT. Depending on needs, a team of 35 trainers use different methods, including on-the-job training, instructor-led training and fully automated e-learning.

In-house courses

In-house courses are courses specially organised for a group of employees. They are normally held on-site using an internal or an external trainer. The trainees may all have the same needs, for example, if the software used by the company has recently been replaced or upgraded. The biggest advantage of providing in-house training, run by employees of the organisation, is the cost. Outside trainers are usually very expensive. In-house trainers will have a very good understanding of the organisation itself, its procedures and structures, and will be able to tailor the training to meet the needs of the employees exactly.

When electronic registration of students, using Bromcom's EARs system, was introduced at a college, the IT department undertook to train all teaching staff. A number of sessions were put on and teachers were invited to join a session at a time suitable to them. During the training session the teachers were each given their own EARs hand-held device and were shown the different functions that the system offered. They were also handed an A4 sheet of hints to remind them what to do. The IT staff were then available at the end of a phone to deal with problems and queries. As the only way to get a device was to attend the training session, everyone attended!

External courses

Many local colleges offer training courses in various aspects of ICT. A company may send employees to the college for a course that is offered regularly there. As the trainees could include employees of different companies, the costs will be shared and so are less.

A college may also put on courses especially for a group of employees of a company, either in the college or at the company.

> **Canterbury College** offers many ICT courses. There is an *Introduction to databases* course looking at Microsoft Access including:
>
> ○ creating a database
>
> ○ running reports
>
> ○ using queries and searching
>
> ○ editing data
>
> Start dates, times and durations can be tailored to suit the trainees.

Commercial companies also put of training courses. These are often very specialised and can be very expensive. However, many such companies offer a wide range of courses.

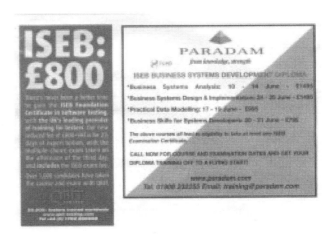

Figure 11.1 Private training courses

E-learning means using electronic methods to teach the trainee. These methods include online tutorials, interactive video and on-screen help. A few years ago some people felt that e-learning would quickly take over all other forms of learning, but change has not been as rapid as these people predicted. However, e-learning is growing in popularity; its big advantage is that staff can learn when and where they want. If someone needs a particular skill for a project, then e-learning allows them to gain it straight away without having to wait for a relevant course to be run. So training can be provided at the convenience of the individual, to meet his or her specific work needs.

A factor that has held back the growth of e-learning is the lack of enthusiasm by many employers for staff to learn in this way. E-learning, which is often very heavily graphics based, is demanding on computer and network resources (such as memory, processor time and bandwidth) so its use will only be feasible in organisations that support a good ICT infrastructure.

Case Study 2

Reuters using e-learning

Reuters, the news agency, is planning a change from classroom-based training to e-learning that could save them up to £1 million.

The move is an attempt to make learning a more built in part of normal working life. The head of training sees classroom-based training as an inefficient way of transferring knowledge. He is aiming for 25 per cent of all training to be delivered online.

● What changes will Reuters have to put in place to ensure that the move to e-learning is successful? Your answer should cover a wide range of issues.

Online tutorials

There are many tutorials available online via the Internet. Some are free, others are available cheaply. For example there are lots of courses available at www.freeskills.com. For an annual membership fee of US$99, the trainee has access to every training course. Trainees can study what they choose, when they choose, at their own pace and within a small budget.

The database courses available include: Access 2002 (XP), Access 2000, Access 97, FoxPro, SQL Server, Visual Basic, Oracle, Lotus Notes, Informix, Paradox and Approach.

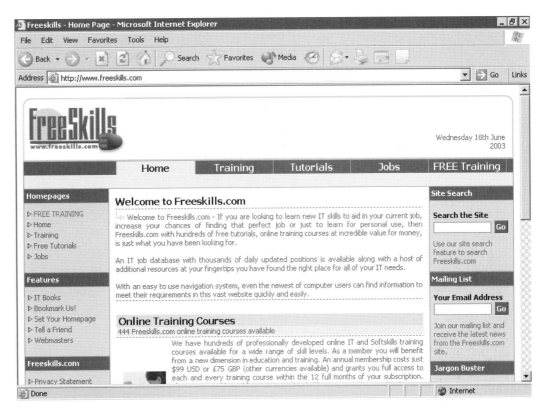

Figure 11.2 freeskills.com

On-screen help

Most software packages offer on-screen help simply by pressing the F1 key. On-screen help is used very often as it is so freely available.

On-screen help allows you to search on keywords or to type in your question in a natural language and be given an explanation as well as examples of use. Sometimes animated demonstrations and cue cards are also available. Cue cards are small help windows that appear over the application screen to help the user. On-screen help has the advantage of being always available while the software is in use, is quick to use, free to use, and user friendly.

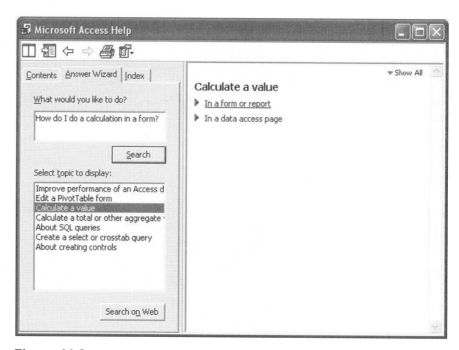

Figure 11.3 Microsoft Access on-screen help

Interactive video

Interactive video can provide professional training at your computer. The video is normally stored on CD-ROM. It is interactive in that users can choose which sections to cover, miss out sections or go back over sections. The video may require the user to make responses which will re-enforce their understanding and determine how quickly the trainee progresses through the video.

Interactive video is a low stress learning environment and the videos can be navigated in a logical way using an easy-to-use interface.

Paper-based materials offer a traditional method of learning. These methods include user manuals, training manuals and books.

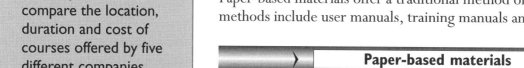

Paper-based materials

The manual

Manuals usually come free with the software. They claim to teach you all you need to know, but they vary in quality and are not always very easy to follow. A manual can prove to be a good reference book in case of a problem. Manuals can be used when and where the user wants and progress can be made at the individual's own pace.

Books

Books are commonly available from bookshops for popular software packages. Many books are available at an introductory level. Titles include *Access for Dummies*, *Field Guide Access* and *Ten Minute Guide to Access*. These books take the reader step-by-step through the basic functions of the program. There are also books available which introduce the more advanced features of such packages. Books tend to be more user-friendly than the user manual and include good screen shots. They, too, can be used when and where the user wants. The book also provides a useful guide to dip into from time to time when a particular problem is met.

Training manuals

Training manuals give the user the opportunity to work at their own pace and refer quickly to the appropriate section.

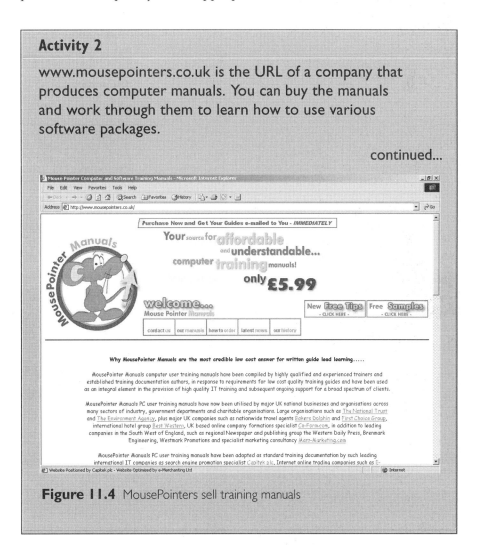

Activity 2

www.mousepointers.co.uk is the URL of a company that produces computer manuals. You can buy the manuals and work through them to learn how to use various software packages.

continued...

Figure 11.4 MousePointers sell training manuals

Activity 2 *continued*

For example in Microsoft Access 2000 there are manuals in:

- understanding databases

- creating tables and controlling input

- basics of Access queries

- going further with queries

- creating reports

- creating forms

- using macros.

Each manual costs £5.99. Figure 11.5 illustrates a page of the manual.

Visit the web site above to explore the range of manuals offered.

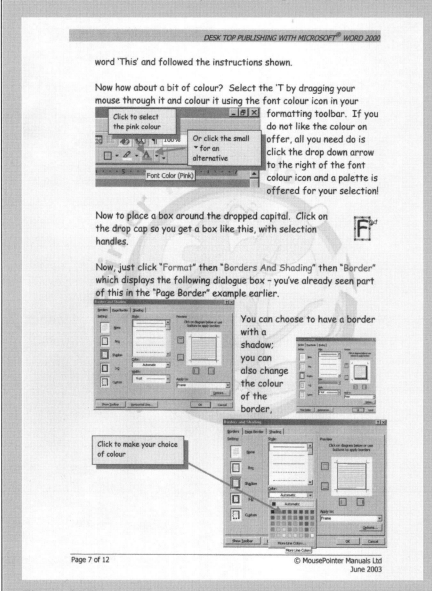

Figure 11.5 An extract from a training manual

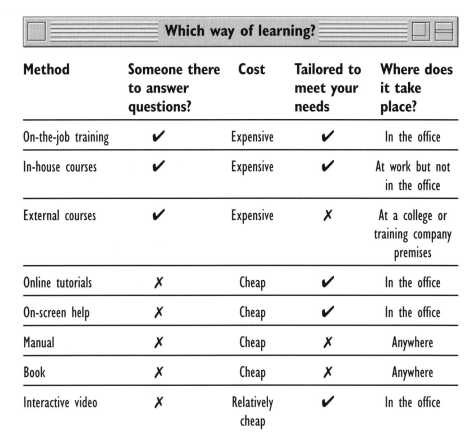

Which way of learning?

Method	Someone there to answer questions?	Cost	Tailored to meet your needs	Where does it take place?
On-the-job training	✔	Expensive	✔	In the office
In-house courses	✔	Expensive	✔	At work but not in the office
External courses	✔	Expensive	✘	At a college or training company premises
Online tutorials	✘	Cheap	✔	In the office
On-screen help	✘	Cheap	✔	In the office
Manual	✘	Cheap	✘	Anywhere
Book	✘	Cheap	✘	Anywhere
Interactive video	✘	Relatively cheap	✔	In the office

Case Study 3

Training in context

Middleton College is a large FE college that offers a wide range of courses. For many students IT forms a large part of their course. There are also a number of students whose course is totally IT based.

Middleton College has over 25 administrative staff and the turnover of staff is quite high. Recently the whole college has been networked. The new principal has made it a priority that all his senior managers make greater use of IT as a tool for decision making – this has caused some anxiety for several managers.

Before the network was installed, a variety of word-processing software was used by different sections of the college. The new system will only be supporting Microsoft Office XP.

Different groups of staff have different word-processing training needs to allow them to use Microsoft Office XP appropriately.

⊙   Identify these different types of need and for each suggest an appropriate training programme.

Developing IT training strategies

IT training in a company needs to be planned and strategies developed based on that company's objectives. Training is often vulnerable to budget cutting as some managements see it as an expensive luxury that has to be dropped when times are hard. This can lead to a reduction in the amount of training altogether or management may look to deliver training in different ways: perhaps a move to e-learning rather than sending employees on expensive courses at distant locations that also bring travel and living costs. However, if a training strategy is to be successful, it is important that decisions involving the ways in which training should be acquired need to fully take into account the needs of both the organisation and the individual employee. It is likely that a range of different methods will be used.

Training must be planned to coincide with the installation of new hardware and software. In some organisations the training of personnel when new software is installed is left to the IT department. This does not always result in the needs of the user being met in an appropriate way.

When a national museum implemented an e-mail system for the first time, the user training was not carefully planned and did not take into account their real needs. The IT department decided when the training sessions should occur and the form that they should take without talking to the users to find out what would be most appropriate. As a result many people were unable to attend any of the sessions due to other commitments. The content of the training sessions was also inappropriate and did not address the protocols and procedures that need to be established if e-mail is to be successfully implemented within an organisation. It took a number of months to overcome the bad feeling and confusion caused by the mishandled training.

New legislation may bring new training needs and these must be planned for in advance. New ventures within an organisation may also generate IT-training needs. These need to be identified early and planned for.

The IT training needs of specific jobs must be established. These are often highlighted through the annual appraisal process, where employees discuss their progress with a line manager and set targets for the forthcoming year. An IT skills audit could be carried out to compare the skills required by each post with the skills of the person holding the post; this process will highlight training needs.

As employees are becoming more computer literate, so their training needs are changing. More people are likely to demand more IT training because they are interested in developing their skills further.

The IT training needs of all new employees and current employees taking on new roles must be carefully assessed. Their current skill level should be compared with the requirements of the role and training put in place to plug the gaps.

A company's IT training strategy will include who needs to be trained, what training they need and how this training will be delivered. Large companies may have their own training suite and in-house trainers, while small companies can probably only use outside agencies.

The training strategy should fit in with other strategies within the organisation.

Case Study 4

IT training at Ellis Paints

Over 800 office staff at Ellis Paints, from senior management to office juniors, have been trained in Microsoft Office as part of the company's switch from MS-DOS to Windows NT.

The company used a training organisation with experience in IT training that did not exist in-house. The training organisation analysed individual needs and found a very wide range of skills. Some staff had hardly ever used a computer, while others had a very high level of IT competence.

A programme was developed to cater for the different individual needs. The programme was based on a series of seminars and one to three days of classroom-based training designed to cater for the different levels of competence. The training included one-to-one tuition for some staff and workshops looking at specific professional requirements. According to the trainers 96 per cent of the company's staff are now trained to the initial level of Microsoft Office proficiency.

The training has not finished. Future plans include the provision of on-going support, lunchtime user clinics and the provision of online training in Microsoft Office via an intranet.

- Ellis Paints chose to bring in outside trainers to train their staff in Microsoft Office. Describe other methods the company could have used for staff training, for each method indicate its appropriateness for Ellis Paints.

- The senior management of Ellis Paints feel that they need to draw up an IT training policy.
  a) Explain why this is necessary.
  b) Describe what such a policy should contain.

Summary

- Training is vital in a highly skilled area of business like IT. The rapid pace of change means that training is not something that happens when you start a new job but is continuous.

- Training can be skill-based or task-based.

- Different levels of training are required for different situations, for example, beginner, intermediate, refresher course.

- Training courses may be:
  - on-the-job
  - in-house
  - external.

- Other methods of training include:
  - reading a user manual
  - buying a book
  - on-line tutorial
  - on-screen help
  - interactive video.

Training questions

1. A small legal firm is about to replace stand-alone computers with a new computer network. Industry standard software will be installed. As new users of both the equipment and the software, the firm is concerned about the levels of support and training that will be needed. There are three levels of system user: the solicitors themselves, the practice management and the administrative staff.
   a) Explain two factors that need to be taken into account when planning the training. *(4)*
   b) Describe two different ways of giving technical support to these users. *(4)*
   c) State two means of providing the training material and give an advantage of each. *(4)*

   AQA June 2002 Paper 4

2. A school is considering the introduction of an IT-based display system to replace the existing daily newsletter read out at registration. The new system will have several display screens at various locations throughout the building. The system will be operated via a PC which is connected to the school network.
   a) The existing daily newsletter is currently typed by a member of staff in the school office who will be responsible for the new system. The introduction of this system will cause considerable change for the member of staff involved. Describe two alternative ways of collecting the data on which the messages will be based. *(6)*
   b) The member of staff will require training in the use of the package in order to create an effective display. List three ways in which training could be provided. *(3)*
   c) The system may also be used to display urgent messages. Give an example of one such use, and describe one safeguard which should be put in place to prevent misuse of this feature. *(3)*

   AQA Specimen Paper 4

3. A building society is introducing a new software package for use across the whole range of its operations.

   a) State **three** different categories of user and for each give one example of his or her potential use of the system. *(6)*
   b) State **three** possible reasons why different users may require different levels of training. *(3)*
   c) The building society is also planning subsequent training for existing users by in-house staff, following the initial training. State **three** reasons why this may be required. *(3)*

   AQA June 2000 Paper 4

4. You are asked to advise an organisation on the introduction of a new software package.
   a) With the aid of three examples, explain why different users may require different levels of training. *(6)*
   b) Following the initial training you advise subsequent training for users. Give two reasons why this may be required, other than financial gain for the training agency. *(4)*

   NEAB 1997 Paper 4

5. The head of a school decides to adopt an IT package to maintain pupils' records of attainment. The package will be used throughout the school.
   a) i) Identify three different potential users of this package. *(3)*
      ii) With the aid of examples, describe the different types of documentation that each user will require. *(6)*
   b) Training in the use of this package may be provided by a variety of methods other than formal training courses. Describe two possible alternative methods. *(4)*

   NEAB 1998 Paper 4

6. Describe, with the aid of examples, **three** different methods of providing training in the use of software and justify their use. *(9)*

   AQA Jan 2003 Paper 4

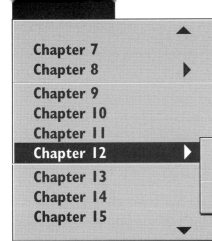
Project management and effective ICT teams

A **project** is an activity with a specific purpose that usually takes months or years to complete. Examples of IT projects could include expanding a school network to include a new building, installing a new booking system for a cinema chain, or upgrading an internal e-mail system within an organisation. Whatever the nature of the project, it is likely to go through the same stages and will need planning and careful management.

It is most important that clear and realistic objectives are set and agreed by all involved in the project. Objectives should include the timescale for completion and the size of budget.

There have been many horror stories of IT projects that have been unsuccessful. Early attempts to computerise the Stock Exchange had to be abandoned. It is important to explore why some projects go wrong while others are successful.

IT projects are usually so large that they cannot be implemented by just one person. They are normally undertaken by a team of people working together. No one person could do all the work on their own, even if they had the time, as a wide range of skills and knowledge will be required. The project team should be selected with care to complement each other so that altogether they possess the drive, skills and knowledge necessary for implementation.

Subdividing a project into subtasks

A large project is likely to be made up a number of **phases**. For example, when developing new software in-house for an organisation the project will be made up of the following phases:

- analysing the user requirements
- designing and prototyping a new system
- writing and testing the code
- acceptance testing
- installing the software and training the users.

Different people are likely to be involved in some different phases of the project as different skills will be required. The tasks will be matched to the skills of the people in the team. For example, a team member who has good interviewing skills could be involved in the investigation stages of the project whilst a member with a flair for and good knowledge of design could be used to produce screen prototypes.

When implementing a project it is usually necessary to divide each phase up into smaller tasks and allocate these tasks to members of the team. Many of the tasks can be carried out concurrently (at the same time). Tasks will be allocated to team members on the bases of their current skills and availability as well as allowing scope for team members to develop their skills and progress. The division into tasks makes the project more manageable as each team member has a clearly defined set of tasks. Very often **milestones** are identified. These are stages that, when reached, will represent completion of significant stages in the project.

Teams can be made up of similar personnel each of who performs a small part of the whole, for example, a team of programmers or a number of different skill holders each providing separate expertise in their own field. Some large projects, such as a new ticketing and passenger tracking system for the London Underground require hundreds of thousands of man hours to complete. Obviously, it would be impossible for the work to be carried out by one person!

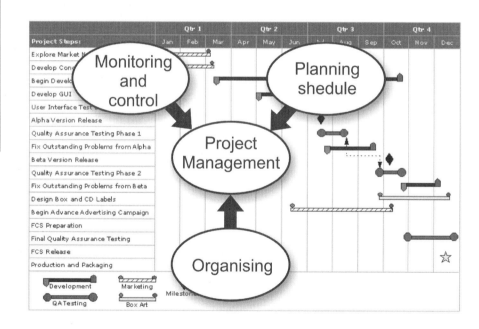

Figure 12.1 Using project-management software

Project management

Leadership

The project will be managed by a **project leader** or **manager** who will need to direct the resources to be used in the best possible way to get the job completed successfully and on time. These resources include people, time, money and hardware.

It is the project manager who will organise the subdivision of the projects into subtasks as described above. He or she will need to possess the skills of leadership and diplomacy if the project is to be successful, the sufficient technical knowledge to assess progress and the inter-personal skills to deal with clients.

Project management has three aspects: planning and scheduling, organising, and monitoring and control.

Advertisements from the IT press

Project Manager Package: £45,000–£75,000

Responsible for the day-to-day management of a client's project. Will interact directly with clients, coordinate work requirements, provide technical leadership, monitor reports on progress, control project scope, and ensure that deliverables, deadlines and budgets are maintained.

Project manager: to £45,000 + car + bonus + benefits

You will be a professional Project Manager with a background in systems design, able to demonstrate strong customer-facing skills. You will possess first class project management experience delivering projects to deadlines and communicating your innovative ideas at a senior level.

Project manager: to £60k

A global leader in e-commerce is seeking a dynamic Project Manager to lead medium to large web projects for clients. You will have a strong customer relation background with the ability to build relationships and understand new business processes coupled with a strong grasp of the technologies involved.

- List the skills and experience needed to be a project manager for an IT project.

Planning and scheduling

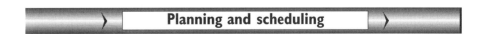

Planning is crucial to the success of any project. It is very important that enough time and thought is given to realistic planning. If they are not then essential tasks can be overlooked which can result in a project overrunning time or going over budget. A careful analysis of risk should be carried out at the start of the project.

Scheduling involves allocating resources and facilities so that they are available when required. Resources can be human or physical. Delay in a resource being available may lead to slippage in deadlines which could incur extra expense. For example, the network cable needs to be in place before the computers can be installed. Under-floor power cables need to be installed early on before the floor is laid. There are a number of project planning techniques and associated software that are used with large projects.

An ICT project should include:

- aims and objectives
- a project leader
- a project team
- a deadline for work to be finished
- a budget for completing the work.

The budget will need to cover staffing, hardware and software costs, outlay for training, expenditure on data entry, as well as other expenses such as travel and subsistence.

At the start, the client and the project manager will agree acceptance criteria for the completion of the project. These are agreed targets that must be met. Examples of such criteria are that all deadlines must be met, work should be completed within budget, the system should be working fully and all agreed security measures should be in place.

Organising

Much of a project manager's time will be spent organising other people! A project manager will need to arrange meetings, ensure that team members have the resources that they need, follow up any problems that arise and ensure that all the necessary things are in place for the next phase of the project.

Monitoring and control

The project manager will need to monitor progress as the project proceeds and report back to clients. Inevitably, unexpected problems will arise and certain tasks will overrun. Sometimes extra tasks arise that were not identified at the start of the project. The project manager will have to adjust the schedule of tasks, perhaps changing around team members, authorising overtime or even contracting extra staff to ensure that deadlines are still met.

The project manager will need to control the budget.

Most projects will include regular **review sessions** where the team get together to compare current progress against the schedule's planned progress. Each team member will report on the progress of the tasks that he or she is currently working on. Any completed since the last review will be noted. The review will enable problems to be highlighted and solutions found.

The client will expect to have a regular report on progress and this will be prepared by the project manager after a review.

Activity 2

Dogged by failures

(Based on an article in The Financial Times)

In theory, IT helps improve productivity, responsiveness and communication. In practice, IT projects are often dogged by management problems that result in delays, cost overruns and failure to meet the original objectives.

IT projects continue to have an extremely high failure rate according to a recent survey by Oasig, a group supported by the Department of Trade and Industry.

It concluded that between 80 and 90 per cent of IT investments do not meet their performance goals, 80 per cent of systems are delivered late and over budget and about 40 per cent of developments fail or are abandoned.

The increasing sophistication of technology can increase the problems. The recognition of these types of problems is focusing attention on how companies should evaluate, plan and implement an IT project. Few companies take these issues seriously. Evaluating the performance and impact of IT developments are not easy tasks, partly because it is not always clear what criteria should be used to judge the value of IT investments. For example, introducing electronic mail in an organisation may transform its internal communications, but it may be hard to justify in terms of specific financial benefits.

The Oasig study says that the main problems with IT projects stem from managers' narrow focus on technological capabilities and efficiency goals. It says that companies often fail to consider how work should be organised and jobs designed following the introduction of new systems. Users rarely have enough influence on systems development.

- Explain, in your own words, why project evaluation is such an important thing.

- What makes project evaluation hard?

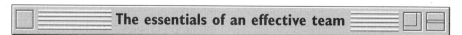

A team is a small group who have come together with the aim of completing a project. Just as in a sports team, they will be allocated different roles, but need to work together rather than as individuals. Tasks are usually allocated according to the strengths of the team members: getting people to do what they are good at is usually appropriate. Complementary skills are required within an IT team (just as having a football team of 11 goalkeepers would not be successful!). Good communication within the team is essential so that progress can be monitored and potential problems avoided. They should develop to the stage where they are able to perform effectively, each member adopting the role necessary to work with others, using complementary skills. Teamwork and cooperation help to produce **consensus** and **avoid conflict**.

A good team needs clear and consistent leadership. A good leader will bring the best out of the individual members and encourage cooperation and exchange of ideas. Tasks should be allocated to the members appropriately, so that every member has work of which they are capable and which, if possible, will help develop their individual skills.

At the start of the project, standards need to be set and agreed by all members. These standards should be adhered to and monitored throughout the project. One widely used example of such standards is SSADM (see box). Standards in program writing could be the use of

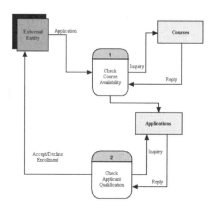

Extension material

SSADM (Structured Systems Analysis and Design Methodology) is a structured methodology (a system of ways of doing things in regular and orderly procedures) that provides a set approach to information systems development. It specifies the stages and tasks which have to be carried out, what needs to be produced and the techniques used in production. SSADM is used in the analysis and design stages of systems development.

SSADM uses three key techniques:

- Logical Data Modelling – identifying, modelling and documenting the data requirements of an information system.

- Data Flow Modelling – identifying, modelling and documenting how data flows around an information system using a set of data flow diagrams with appropriate documentation.

- Event Modelling – identifying, modelling and documenting the events which affect each entity and the order in which these events occur.

particular coding conventions in the choice of variable names, the layout of code and the inclusion of comments.

A good team will keep a careful watch on costs and should complete the project within budget. All aspects of work should be carefully costed. Progress should be monitored and alternative action taken whenever necessary, such as if progress is not being made according to plan. Regular meetings, together with the use of charts and suitable software, can be crucial to monitoring progress and maintaining control.

The leader should have the appropriate seniority for the task, adequate understanding of the project, the ability to see the project through to successful completion, and the skills to adequately and systematically monitor and control progress and costs.

If possible, there should be a balance of skills between team members who could have different backgrounds – in systems, business operations or technical fields.

A team requires good communication skills, both written and verbal. Members need to be able to communicate well with each other, but also with end-users. They need to be able to ask the right questions in such a way that they can establish end-user requirements.

Case Study 1

Camelot

The Camelot Group plc was awarded the licence to run the National Lottery. Within six months, over 10,000 retailers were selling tickets and the first draw was held, yet the first company building (the head office and main data centre) was not finished until three months later.

The National Lottery sells around 100 million tickets every week and receives over 60,000 calls per week to its National Lottery Line, nearly all of them on Saturday nights and Sunday mornings. This requires a complex computer system with high security. With such a daunting task and a tight timescale, good project management was essential.

The project was split up into smaller tasks including:

- installing hardware in the head office and the two data centres
- training staff
- installing hardware in the retailers' shops
- training retailers
- installing the corporate network linking the head office and the two data centres, the warehouse and the eleven regional offices for both voice and data
- testing
- implementing the call centre for the National Lottery Line for customers to claim prizes
- implementing the call centre for the Retailer Hot Line for retailers with technical problems

Geoff Pollock, Telecommunications Manager at Camelot, said, 'In normal circumstances we would have expected a project of this nature to take around eighteen months, but we did everything in only five months'

continued ...

Case Study 1 *continued*

- How could the project be completed in such a short time?

- Suggest reasons why the project was implemented so successfully.

Case Study 2

Sophie – a project manager

Sophie works for a large banking organisation. She manages a team of six full-time members and runs several projects at a time. A major project recently undertaken involved splitting up a current database system into two communicating halves, one dealing with front office (customer-related) operations, the other back office (internal administrative) ones. This was done so that front office services could be provided on a different hardware platform.

The project was split into three main phases:

- initial analysis when data flow and user interface needs were established

- development when the program code was written, tested and the interfaces with all other software also tested

- new system installation.

Sophie worked out that the project would require 20 man months to implement. Four members of her team were allocated to the project. Other contractors with specific skills were also involved. Developers (programmers) who had specific hardware experience and knowledge of both UNIX and NT operating systems were required within the team. Analysts on the team needed both a good technical knowledge and a sound understanding of the banking business. More junior team members were employed in testing.

At the start of the project Sophie drew up a project plan that highlighted what tasks needed to be done to complete the project and who should do them. She made sure to set clear objectives for each task, defining its start and end and giving a set time for its completion. Her plan was produced using Microsoft Project. Sophie also maintained a spreadsheet of all tasks where details of problems that arise were stored.

As the project evolved, she met regularly with team members to discuss progress, giving help and direction as appropriate. If any problem became apparent she would provide extra resources to the task. She was able to monitor and control overall project progress as she could see when individual tasks were complete. She produced a project status report every three weeks which informed all the stakeholders in the project of current progress.

Whenever an unforeseen problem was thrown up by testing, the job of resolving the problem would be delegated by Sophie to a team member. She herself oversaw the progress of the project and carried out many of the tasks herself, such as managing the testing process.

Four months after starting the project it had been successfully implemented.

- Give the reasons that ensured that the project was implemented successfully.

- Describe three reasons why the project was split up into tasks.

- How did Sophie maintain control of the project?

Summary

- IT projects require careful management to ensure successful completion.

- Introduction of IT into a company is too large a task to be performed by one person. As a result IT professionals often need to work in teams.

- The characteristics of a good team include:

- good leadership

- the appropriate allocation of tasks

- adherence to standards

- appropriate monitoring and control of progress

- control of costs.

Project management and effective ICT teams questions

1. Explain why projects are often subdivided into subtasks and performed by teams. (6)

2. Describe the characteristics of a good team. (6)

3. Describe three possible causes of inefficiency in the working of a team. (6)

4. A firm is creating a team to plan, design and implement an IT project. Describe four characteristics of a good IT project team. (8)

   NEAB 1998 Paper 4

5. A company has three departments to handle finance, buildings and equipment maintenance. Each department currently operates a separate IT system. The company wishes to improve the efficiency of the operations by implementing a common corporate system across all three departments. In order to achieve this improvement, the company has decided to select members of staff from each department to form a project team to plan, design and implement the new system.
   a) Describe three corporate level factors the team should consider when planning the new system. (6)
   b) At their first meeting the team decide to subdivide the project into a series of tasks. Describe two advantages of this approach. (1)

   NEAB 1999 Paper 4

6. Large organisations often run their own system development projects, collecting a number of suitably skilled people together to form the development team. Describe **four** characteristics of a good ICT development team. (8)

   AQA Jan 2003 Paper 4

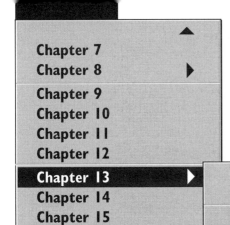

Information and the professional

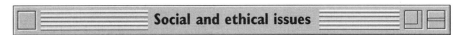

Social and ethical issues

The introduction and use of ICT brings social, moral and ethical issues that affect a professional working within the industry.

Many ICT professionals spend at least part of their week working from home. They are able to use IT equipment and communications to access files and data and to keep in touch with the office. There are advantages in this, mainly savings in travel time and stress and having the flexibility to work around other family commitments, as well as dangers: it is possible to become isolated from fellow professionals and get overlooked by management.

An ICT professional has to be prepared for constant retraining as many specific software application skills are relatively short-lived as new versions of applications and new software are introduced. Currently many jobs in the ICT industry are offered on short-term contracts which can lead to uncertainty and financial difficulty.

Ethics is about making the morally correct decision. An unethical decision is not necessarily illegal. There are many situations when an ICT professional has to make decisions where ethics should play a part.

The following actions could all be considered unethical:

- Knowingly selling out-of-date equipment whilst assuring the buyer that it is 'up to the minute and the best on the market'.

- Putting inadequately tested software, that has bugs that might cause real problems to the purchasers, on the market in order to gain a competitive advantage.

- A developer not telling a client that the system he is developing for them will not meet their needs.

- An employee using company information for their own ends, for example, taking a file of names and addresses to use as a mailing list for a small business that they are setting up at home.

- Disclosing information from the organisation's intranet to someone outside the organisation.

The story of Tom's day at work, given below, highlights a number of unethical practices. Read through the story and then highlight as many examples as you can before reading the suggestions given in the table.

Activity I

Tom's day at work

Tom arrives in his office and immediately switches on his desktop workstation. He has a network user account and when he logs on he is asked for his password. He types it in: 'TOMRULES' and waits for the system to load.

Then he checks his e-mails. He has 20 waiting for him. Eight of these relate to work, six are from friends and six are SPAM (unsolicited messages – the junk mail of e-mail). He opens the messages from his friends. One contains photo images of a friend's holiday that each take a minute or so to download.

After 20 minutes spent dealing with social e-mails, Tom opens one of the SPAM messages that has the headline 'Earn £5000 without working'. The message has an attached document. When Tom opens it he realises that the message is a hoax and immediately deletes the message.

Now Tom gets down to work. He needs to access a database for which he needs another password. He uses the one that was originally assigned to him by the database administrator and, as it is hard to remember, he keeps it on a 'Post-it' note stuck on his computer screen.

During the morning Tom feels ready for a break so he walks out to the water cooler in the corridor where he meets up with some colleagues from a different department. They stay talking for 10 minutes, discussing a new computer game that one of his colleagues has recently bought. Tom borrows the game CD-ROM and returns to his desk. He is keen to see the new game so he installs it on the local hard disk of his workstation and plays the game for half an hour. He is not very good at first but quickly improves.

When it is lunchtime, Tom logs off his workstation and goes to the sandwich bar with a friend. A colleague comes in and asks Tom if he could go back to work as he has forgotten to print out a report that is urgently needed. Tom has not finished his lunch so he tells his colleague where to find the file so that she can print it out for herself. 'You'll need to log on as me. My password is TOMRULES', he says.

After an afternoon of working Tom has another play of his new game, but he doesn't seem to be getting any better so he surfs the Internet for a while instead, visiting a couple of his favourite 'Porno' sites and downloading a couple of images that he stores on the hard drive of his workstation.

continued ...

Activity 1 continued

Some possible unethical practices that can be found in the account of Tom's day

Choice of password – easy to guess	Password should be made up of letters and digits and not be meaningful.
Reading personal e-mail (20 minutes)	Using work time, for which he is being paid, on personal matters.
Downloading photos	Putting unnecessary load on network resources.
Opening SPAM e-mail from unknown source	Likely to be in breach of security policy: virus danger.
Password stuck on screen	Passwords should be kept secret.
Fails to log off	Leaves computer vulnerable to use by others who may obtain access to data to which they are not authorised.
Installing game on hard drive	Likely to be in breach of security policy: unauthorised software installed without licence.
Tells colleague password	Passwords should be kept secret.
Downloading and storing pornographic images	Inappropriate behaviour.

Case Study 1

Misuse of the Internet in the workplace

In a recent survey, Internet and e-mail abuse were found to be the main instances of office work misconduct.

From the information given by the companies taking part in the survey, 'cyber-abuse' accounted for more counts of professional disciplinary action than the occasions of dishonesty, violence, and health and safety breaches combined.

Twenty per cent of companies in the survey said that they monitored staff usage of online facilities, although only half of them had informed the staff of the monitoring.

- Describe the ways in which an employee could use e-mail and access the Internet inappropriately in an office environment.

Activity 2

- Write your own story about an employee's bad day, in which he or she carries out a number of IT-related acts that could be considered unethical.

- Swap your story with that of a colleague in your class.

- Go through your colleague's story, highlighting all the acts that you consider to be unethical. Explain the reasons.

Codes of practice and conduct

Some issues highlighted in 'Tom's day at work' are against the law. More details of the laws relating to IT, together with their effects on business practice, are covered in Chapter 8 as well as ICT for AS level Chapters 7–10.

However, the law does not cover all the modes of behaviour and practice that an organisation could expect for its employees. Other methods have to be used to ensure that employees are working in an ethical and appropriate manner.

Professional bodies

Many professions have bodies which lay down codes of practice for the profession. These include the General Medical Council (doctors), the Bar Society (barristers), the Law Society (solicitors) or the Royal Institute of British Architects.

A doctor's code of practice includes the Hippocratic oath, which states that they must not divulge information about a patient's health to anyone else. Professional bodies have the power to expel members for a breach of their rules. A doctor, for example, may then be 'struck off' for misconduct and not be able to practise.

British Computer Society

The British Computer Society (BCS) is the chartered body for Information Technology professionals. Formed in 1957, the society was incorporated by Royal Charter in 1984. It has over 38,000 members.

The BCS sets standards of professional, moral and ethical practice for the IT industry in the UK. Mr R. J. McQuaker, the vice-President of the BCS said, 'The public expect the same standards of competence and conduct from the members of the BCS as they expect from doctors, lawyers or architects'.

The BCS codes of practice and conduct do not have legal status, but are merely the rules of the society. Breaking the codes is not illegal, but anyone doing so may face punishment from the society, for example, expulsion. This may affect their professional position or their chances of getting promotion or another job.

Extracts from the BCS code of conduct

- Members shall endeavour to complete work undertaken on time and to budget and shall advise their employer or client as soon as practicable if any overrun is foreseen (Clause 6).

- Members shall not disclose or authorise to be disclosed, or use for personal gain or to benefit a third party, confidential information acquired in the course of professional practice, except with prior written permission of the employer or client, or at the direction of a court of law (Clause 8).

- Members shall not misrepresent or withhold information on the capabilities of products, systems or services with which they are concerned or take advantage of the lack of knowledge or inexperience of others (Clause 10).

- Members shall not purport to exercise independent judgement on behalf of a client on any product or service in which they knowingly have any interest, financial or otherwise (Clause 12).

Visit the BCS site www1.bcs.org.uk to find out more about the BCS code of conduct.

Employee code of conduct

All employers have codes of conduct for their employees. A code of conduct lays down the way in which an employee should behave. They may be communicated verbally or formalised in a written document. For example, they may specify the type of clothing an employee should wear, where smoking is allowed and forbid the drinking of alcohol on the premises.

Breaches of the code of conduct may lead to sanctions, such as, verbal warnings, written warnings, loss of pay or dismissal, depending on the frequency and the severity of the breach.

Many jobs will involve secret or sensitive information which must not be divulged, for example, because the information could be personal or be of benefit to a competitor.

For ICT personnel the legal requirements, such as those imposed by copyright law and the Data Protection Act will be included in a code of conduct.

An employee code of conduct will lay down the responsibilities of ICT users, authorisation, security and penalties for misuse.

Responsibilities

The ICT user will be expected to have certain responsibilities relating to the use of hardware, software and data. These should be listed in the code of conduct. Such responsibilities might include sensible use of hard disk space and not over burdening the network system with unnecessary data transfer (particularly at peak times).

The user will have the responsibility to comply with all the ICT-related legislation such as the Data Protection Act, Computer Misuse Act and copyright laws.

Authorisation

An individual within an organisation will be authorised to access certain data that is needed as part of their role. Attempts to access any data or software for which they are not authorised will be a breach of the code of conduct.

To use another user's identification code and password would be in breach of the code.

Security

All aspects of ICT security should be covered. These would include:

● Passwords: these should not be written down or disclosed to anyone. They should be chosen to comply with given guidelines (e.g., not meaningful words, a minimum of six characters, a mixture of numbers and letters and upper and lower case), and changed regularly.

● Prevention of unauthorised access to information: the use of a screen saver with a password to prevent use of a workstation by others, storing of printed information in a secure place (not leaving printouts lying on the desk for anyone to see), taking care to keep a laptop safe when away from the organisation's premises.

● Using appropriate encryption procedures when data is transmitted across public networks.

Penalties for misuse

The code will describe the penalties that could result if a user breaks any part of the code of conduct. Such penalties could include:

● a verbal warning

● a written warning

● reduced access rights

● demotion

● dismissal

● prosecution, if a law has been broken.

However, many minor breaches of the code could occur through lack of knowledge or unintentional acts by the user. An inexperienced user might break the requirement that stipulates that a user changes his password every six weeks. Such breaches would best be dealt with by providing the user with training that demonstrated the importance of the measures in the code.

Case Study 2

The ten commandments for computer ethics

1 Thou shalt not use a computer to harm other people.

2 Thou shalt not interfere with other people's computer work.

3 Thou shalt not snoop around in other people's files.

4 Thou shalt not use a computer to steal.

5 Thou shalt not use a computer to bear false witness.

6 Thou shalt not use or copy proprietory software for which you have not paid.

Case Study 2

7 Thou shalt not use other people's computer resources without authorisation.

8 Thou shalt not appropriate other people's intellectual output.

9 Thou shalt think about the social consequences of the program you write.

10 Thou shalt use a computer in ways that show consideration and respect.

(from the Computer Ethics Institute at www.brook.edu/its/cei)

- Which commandments are legal requirements and which ones are purely ethical suggestions?
- If you think the commandment is a legal requirement, explain which is involved.

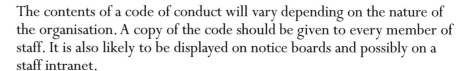

Contents of a code of conduct

The contents of a code of conduct will vary depending on the nature of the organisation. A copy of the code should be given to every member of staff. It is also likely to be displayed on notice boards and possibly on a staff intranet.

A number of ICT-related items might appear in an employees code of conduct, for example:

- No unauthorised disks may be used. (It is possible to install software that means that only the company's specially formatted disks can be read.)
- No unauthorised software can be used on the company's computers.
- Employees may not copy software for personal use.
- How the organisation fulfils requirements of the Data Protection Act.
- How often passwords should be changed.
- What possible passwords are acceptable, for example, only combinations of letters and numbers – not dictionary words or names.
- Passwords should not be written down.
- No action should be taken against the interests of the company.

Case Study 3

Southampton University code of conduct for use of computers

Southampton University issues regulations for use of computer systems and networks by staff and students. The following are excerpts from these regulations:

1 The use of computers is regulated by three Acts of Parliament: the Data Protection Act 1984, the Copyright, Designs and Patents Act 1988 and the Computer Misuse Act 1990. Similarly, the use of the public data telephone networks is regulated by the Telecommunications Act 1984.

2 The following regulations are framed to remind all members of the University of their legal obligations. In addition, the use of computer software may also be subject to the terms of licence enforceable in the civil courts.

3 These regulations have the status of Regulations for Discipline which apply to all members of the University. Any breach of these regulations will automatically be considered a breach of discipline.

continued ....

Case Study 3

4   Data Protection. Members of the University are only allowed to hold, obtain, disclose or transfer personal data (as defined by the Data Protection Act 1984) as permitted by the University's current registration with the Data Protection Registrar and in accordance with Data Protection Principles as set out in that Act. If in doubt, the University's Data Protection Officer should be consulted before any personal data is stored in a computer system.

5   Copyright. Members of the University will comply with the provisions of the Copyright Designs and Patents Act 1988 in relation to any computer program or data set and shall not act in any way contrary to the terms of any licence agreement applying thereto. (This is a formal way of saying 'thou shalt not use pirated software.')

6   Computer misuse. Members of the University are only allowed to use those computing resources, data or voice communications facilities, which have been allocated to them. Computing resources may only be used for properly authorised purposes. (Students do not have authority to grant anyone else access to the facilities that they have been given.)

7   Members of the University may not access, alter, erase or add to computer material which has not been generated by them unless they are explicitly authorised to do so by the originator of the material.

8   Authorised users of computer systems must take reasonable care to prevent unauthorised use of the computing resources allocated to them.

9   Members of the University may not use computer systems or networks in such a way as to compromise the integrity or performance of the systems or networks. (These regulations cover the activity commonly known as 'hacking'. Breach of any of these regulations is prima facie evidence of an offence under the Computer Misuse Act.)

10 Networks. Members of the University must abide by any 'conditions of use' of networks which are published by the responsible computing management for the protection of the integrity and efficiency of the network.

11 Members of the University must not cause obscene, pornographic, discriminatory, defamatory or other offensive material to be transmitted over the University, national or public networks, or cause such to be stored in University computer systems. (It is a criminal offence to publish pornographic material, for example by including such material in a web page.)

12 Withdrawal of service. The responsible computing management may withdraw access to facilities from any user found to be guilty of a breach of these regulations.

13 The University will hold the individual user personally liable for any costs or claims which may arise from any use of University computing and/or communications facilities, whether authorised or not by the responsible computing management.

14 Passwords. All staff and students are given an account with a unique log in name and password. The account is only to be used by its owner. A password is assigned by the System Manager when the account is created. The user must change this immediately. The password must not be divulged to anyone.

15 A password may be changed by its owner but the new password must conform to security measures in force at the time. (The password must be at least six characters, it must not be a dictionary word, name, telephone number, car registration number or anything likely to be associated with its owner.)

16 Account access. Users must take reasonable steps to protect their own accounts from access by others: the owner will be held responsible for any improper use. In particular you must not allow any other person to log in to your account. (If you need to share access to files and data with another user you should use e-mail.)

17 The Head of Department may authorise the system support staff to examine any file if there is reason to believe that these regulations are being contravened in anyway.

continued ....

Case Study 3

18 Use of the Internet and the World Wide Web. Any reasonable use of the Internet is permitted, although users should bear in mind that the load placed on the network by excessive use (for example, downloading large graphics files) will degrade its performance for other users, not only in the Department but also for the University and even on a national scale.

19 Staff and students are allowed to maintain personal home pages on the Web, hosted on Departmental systems.

○ Categorise the statements above as relating to the responsibilities, authorisation, security or penalties for misuse.

○ List those statements that relate to ICT legislation.

Activity 3

Draw up an ICT code of practice for students at your school or college. You will need to include statements that relate to:

○ behaviour
○ use of ICT equipment
○ use of school network
○ access to, and use of, the Internet
○ legal requirements
○ plagiarism (copying the work of others and passing it off as your own)
○ Include any further statements that you feel should be included.

○ Draw up a further code of conduct for teachers at your school or college.

○ For each statement, describe the appropriate sanction if the requirement is not met.

Summary

○ The introduction and use of ICT brings social, moral and ethical issues that affect a professional working within the industry.

○ 'Codes of Practice' exist which are separate from any legal requirements with which any professional organisation is expected to comply. They are based on ethical activity.

○ An organisation will need to establish a code of practice for its users.

○ An employee code of conduct will lay down the responsibilities of ICT users.

○ The code will describe the penalties that could result if a user breaks any part of the code of conduct. Such penalties could include:
  ○ a verbal warning
  ○ a written warning
  ○ reduced access rights
  ○ demotion
  ○ dismissal
  ○ prosecution, if a law has been broken.

Information and the professional questions

1. Bill is an IT consultant advising people on computerising their work. Bill recommends to clients that they should buy their computers from the computer manufacturers Cheapo, run by Bill's friend Clive. These computers are usually out-of-date models. 'These are the bee's knees. They'll never let you down. I swear by them. You don't want that modern stuff – too unreliable,' says Bill. State which laws or codes of conduct have been breached (if any) and why. *(4)*

2. A company uses a computer network for storing details of its staff and for managing its finances. The network manager is concerned that some members of staff may install unauthorised software onto the network.
   a) Give reasons why it is necessary for some software to be designated as unauthorised. *(2)*
   b) What guidelines should the network manager issue to prevent the installation of unauthorised software onto the network? *(2)*
   c) What procedures might be available to the company to enforce the guidelines? *(2)*

   NEAB 1997 Paper 3

3. As the IT manager for a large company, you have been asked to develop an employee code of conduct. Describe four issues which might be included in such a code. *(8)*

   NEAB 1998 Paper 5

4. 'Codes of practice' exist for professionals within the IT industry separate from any legal requirements. Explain, with the aid of an example, the distinction between a legal requirement and a code of practice. *(3)*

   NEAB Specimen Paper 1

5. State three issues that should be included in an Employee Code of Conduct. *(3)*

   AQA June 2001 Paper 5

6. Discuss the social, moral and ethical issues for a professional working within the industry that might arise when introducing and using information and communication systems. *(6)*

   AQA Jan 2003 Paper 4

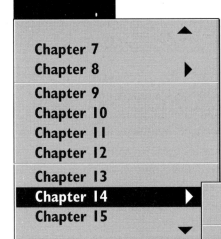
Policy and strategy issues

Information management policy

All organisations store information, even if they don't use information technology. Traditionally, offices need to store information. In the past this information was kept in filing cabinets, stored in a particular order, usually alphabetical or chronological, so that information could be retrieved easily. Decisions concerning what information should be kept and for how long needed to be made.

The senior management of an organisation needs to take a long-term view of information management. Without careful planning, systems can grow in an unstructured way, leading to inefficiency, redundancy and incompatibility. There is the danger of the growth of many similar systems, each created for their own use by an individual. Thus a policy is needed.

Compatible systems are those that are able to share data. Incompatible ones cannot as the data is not in the same format in the two systems and cannot be converted from one format to the other.

There has been a huge explosion in the amount of data that can be stored and information produced. Today a large proportion of an organisation's information is likely to be stored electronically. Data can enter a system from a range of different sources: the Internet; from another company through EDI; from customers. Without careful planning, much of the data can remain unused, stored for no purpose.

Decisions about the archiving of information forms part of an information management policy. Similarly the organisation may have a policy on which information should be stored on computer; whether it is stored on the network hard disk, a local hard disk or on a floppy disk. The policy may include how long is it kept for and who has access to it.

A well thought out policy is even more important if the data is of a personal nature because the organisation is bound by the Data Protection Act. This means that unnecessary, out-of-date information must be deleted and access must be restricted only to authorised personnel.

The organisation may need a policy on how to communicate information internally. In the past, memos, notices on notice boards, passing a note round, weekly information bulletins and internal company newsletters all may have been appropriate. Today, internal e-mail provides a very easy way of informing staff. Mailing lists of, say, directors, personnel, or sales staff can be set up. It is then easy to send a copy to everyone on the mailing list. The use of work group software, such as Lotus Notes, allows users to work on the same documents and provides access to each others' diary.

Strategic implications of software, hardware and configuration choices

The choices that are made concerning the purchase of hardware and software, and also the kind of network infrastructure and operating system that are installed are likely to have major implications within the company. Such purchases are very costly and represent a major investment. New systems are unlikely to be totally replaced very frequently, so major purchase choices will dictate the ICT structure and direction of the organisation for some time.

It is advisable that all ICT purchases are made through a central point so that standardisation can be controlled.

The skills required, both from current employees and future recruits, will be established. A major training may be required. For many employees this training may just show them how to do their current jobs in a different way.

An organisation may become reliant upon the support given by the supplier or manufacturer. If a change in supplier or manufacturer is made then new relationships will need to be made with personnel in that organisation.

When making a configuration choice of the network infrastructure and operating system, it is important to choose a set up that is both flexible to use and able to be expanded as requirements change and grow. Organisations do not stay the same. They can diversify into new areas that will make new, extra demands on the ICT systems.

Software choices

Aspects of software choice are considered in Chapter 16. Decisions have to be made as to whether appropriate software already exists that can be bought and modified if necessary or whether it must be developed from scratch.

The use of an Office-type suite and other commonly used software should be standardised throughout a company. This will allow easy maintenance and support from the IT technical team within the organisation. Documents and other data can be shared easily between users.

The use of a standard operating system across a whole organisation will provide a standard look and feel.

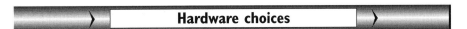

Hardware choices

Ideally, an organisation's ICT technical department would like to have identical workstations for all users. This would simplify maintenance and would allow the best discount deal to be worked out with the manufacturer. However, in reality, such a situation is unlikely to occur, except in very small organisations. To replace all workstations in one go is likely to prove too costly. Most organisations carry out a rolling program of replacement to spread replacement costs more evenly.

Future expansion needs must always be considered, although these are unlikely to be exactly known.

Range of user needs

When drawing up an information management policy, the needs of all users must be considered. These needs are likely to be very diverse. The jobs carried out by different personnel will have very different ICT skills requirements. The skill required by users will vary from basic data entry or occasional word processing to a wide and varied technical knowledge of hardware and software. Some users will use a workstation or other ICT equipment for nearly all their work whilst others will be occasional users. The skills that users already have, together with their confidence in the use of ICT will also be a factor.

Methods of enhancing existing capabilities

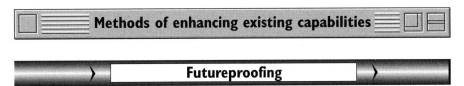

Futureproofing

Futureproofing concerns finding ways of making sure that a system has a reasonable life and does not need to be totally replaced too soon.

Computers have developed so rapidly that machines that are four or five years old seem slow and cannot cope with recent software. It is not possible to predict the future other than to say it is unpredictable.

However, it is sensible to take steps to prevent problems. It is often true that the data stored on computer is more valuable than the hardware itself. If a fire occurred it is possible to buy replacement hardware but the data can only be replaced if backup copies have been stored safely.

When buying a new computer system, it is important to buy one that won't be out of date too soon.

Old data must be able to be used. Programs must have backwards compatibility (the ability to read files from previous versions). High density disk drives must be able to read and write to the old double density floppy disks. Faster CD-ROM drives must be able to cope with older CD-ROMs.

Hardware performance is constantly being improved by manufacturers in terms of both processing speed and memory capacity. New versions of software include extra features and usually require extra main and backing storage memory. It is important that any computer purchased has sufficient RAM and hard disk capacity to cope with likely future requirements, both from software and expanding files. The possibility to expand memory at a later date should be built in as well as the capacity to add extra cards and peripherals if needs change.

Considering future needs is even more important when setting up a network. When establishing the cabling in and between buildings, care must be taken that future growth in network traffic is catered for. The network infrastructure of cables, switches, servers and so on, are costly to purchase and install. Frequent changes to these basic, underlying services can be disruptive to work and need to be avoided through careful forward planning. There must be flexibility in the number and positioning of workstations so that changing future requirements can be catered for.

Upgrading hardware and software

Hardware and software development

After some years of use, a company may wish to upgrade their computers. This may be a result of an increased volume of data or a desire to decrease processing time. Required changes in software might make the hardware upgrade necessary as new versions of software often have greater resource requirements.

If computers are kept for a long time, they can become obsolete and spare parts become unavailable so that they cannot be repaired when they break down.

As technology advances, tasks can be carried out in a way that could not once have been achieved. This could result from such developments as increased processor speed, increased memory capacity or enhanced transfer speed over a network.

Alongside the increase in hardware performance, software development has also made rapid progress. There has been a move towards software that has a greater range of functionality as well as graphical user interfaces which provided an interface that is easier and less frustrating to use.

Organisation ethos

The organisation may have a policy to upgrade hardware after a certain time in order to provide an up-to-date image for the company or to maintain good staff morale.

Having up-to-date ICT resources can inspire confidence in customers and other business contacts. It should also provide the best service to customers.

This is a particularly important reason for regular upgrading in a company whose business is in ICT, for example, in hardware manufacture, software development or support. Such an organisation needs to portray an image that it is 'ahead of the game' and at the forefront of ICT development.

Task-driven change

Changes in the way that tasks within the organisation are carried out might force an upgrade of hardware or software.

A decision that salespersons should collect all information regarding clients directly would require them to be issued with laptop computers. The currently-used software would have to be upgraded to allow for the transfer of necessary data to and from the laptops on a daily or weekly basis.

A decision by senior management to provide the facility of Internet sales for customers would have networking and software upgrade implications.

Case Study 1

Howse, Hulme and Byer (HHB), Estate Agent

HHB is the name of a small estate agent that has eight offices within a 50-mile radius.

Information on customers and the details of houses for sale are stored locally at each of the eight offices. Customer details and data regarding the houses, such as the number of rooms and their dimensions, locality etc., are stored on the local computer. Photographs of properties are stored in filing cabinets.

HHB wishes to upgrade its methods to enable the photos to be stored on the computer together with short video clips. Details of all houses that they are currently trying to sell should be available online in all their offices.

● Discuss the implications of the desired changes in terms of hardware, software and configuration.

Case Study 2

Paying for the Tube after you travel

London Underground Ltd. (LUL) are planning a new billing project that will be based on a smart card system. It will be the world's first post-payment system for travel. A passenger will be able to charge up their card remotely using the Internet or telephone or pay by direct debit at the end of the month.

The software will work out the best deal on the trips that have been made by the passenger. Customers will not have to decide in advance whether they need a weekly or a monthly ticket.

● Why do you think that the LUL wish to install this new system?

Software change

Many commercial software packages are regularly updated and new versions brought on to the market. An organisation will have to decide if and when it is appropriate to move to the new version.

Consideration will have to be given to whether the extra features offered by the new version will be of real benefit to the organisation's users. It is advisable to wait until the new version is tried and tested so that it will prove to be robust in use.

If the new version has a different look and feel from the old version, as well as having extra features, it might be necessary to undertake a programme of staff retraining to ensure that everyone is able to make efficient use of the software.

A new version of a software application frequently has a greater systems resource requirement than an older version. It is likely to take up more hard disk space than the old version, require more RAM and may need a faster processor to run it. Problems can arise when not all the workstations in an organisation are able to run the new version. This can lead to some file incompatibility as it is likely that files produced by the new version cannot be read by the old.

Users may require training in the use of the new version of the software if it includes new features. Although new features could be ignored until the user feels ready to find out about them, upgrades can also include changes to existing features which could cause confusion and irritation. Unless training is provided, users will initially take longer to perform familiar tasks. Extra support will be needed for users when software upgrades have been made.

In a large organisation, an upgrade can be trialled in one department before use throughout the whole organisation. In this way expertise can be built up and problems highlighted on a small scale. However, if this is done there are likely to be complications in file transfer between departments.

Very often, it is not necessary to purchase a full copy of a new version of software, just an 'upgrade' copy that will convert the current version to the new one. This is usually a cheaper option, but does have some disadvantages.

A graphic designer who runs his own business uses the Quark software package on Apple's Macs. Over a number of years he has bought upgrades to the original version that he purchased. Although the original version provided all the features he required, he needed to install the upgrades as his clients and publishers used the more advanced versions and would send files to him which could not be read by the older software.

Recently the system was struck by a virus that resulted in all the software having to be reinstalled. This took a considerable time as every upgrade had to be installed separately, in order.

When an organisation undertakes a major system upgrading a decision has to be made on the new hardware platform. Ideally it should be compatible with the old platform.

Compatible hardware

When different hardware manufacturers produce machines that all support the same software and data files the machines are said to be compatible. Some applications are dependent upon a particular hardware configuration (e.g., processor type, memory configuration, VDU configuration). For example, Microsoft Office 2000 will not run on a PC with a 486 chip. The term compatible hardware is often used to refer to those hardware systems that conform to a particular minimum hardware specification, having similar architecture and supporting the same peripheral devices.

Case Study 3

Pump up the program

(Based on an article by Brian Clegg in PC Week)

Software upgrades are a mixed blessing. Upgrading is plagued with hidden costs and difficulties such as incompatibilities with previous versions or other installed software and insufficient system resources. Even the users who beg for the latest version will need extra training and support.

An important consideration of upgrading is the cost of new software licences. The amount paid can be subject to negotiation: vendors have a variety of approaches. Oracle's support agreement for server products includes free upgrading. This removes any concern about the cost of new licences, but limits the IT manager's choice. IBM effectively insures against upgrades, offering a protection scheme to provide low cost upgrades provided you pay 15 per cent extra on the original licence.

The biggest upgrade expense can be training users. If benefits are to be gained, there is a training need, and companies that aren't prepared to provide that training will have hidden costs in the time taken to perform once familiar tasks.

However, training is the most disputed area. At one large company, a manager comments, 'we do not put much resource into user training. It does not work for most people and they can't afford the time out from fee-earning work. We find most people who want to use software pick it up and use it to a level they are happy with themselves. If they get really desperate they can call my department for help'.

Sometimes an upgrade will generate hidden training requirements. A senior network analyst with the same company recalls problems with a new version of Microsoft Project. 'There were differences in the way Project handled changes, for example, tasks that had slipped. We treated the upgrade as if it was a matter of pure extra benefits, but ignored the differences in the way the product worked, resulting in problems.'

The message from the IT managers is that you should take charge of upgrading – don't leave it to the vendors to tell you when to do it.

- List the costs of upgrades identified in this article.

- Describe the training needs that can arise from upgrading software.

- Explain the reasons why software vendors make such frequent changes to their software.

Case Study 4

Upgrading systems

Camelot upgrade network

Camelot, the National Lottery operator, is upgrading its network infrastructure. They will be replacing the nationwide backbone for its lottery terminals. The new network will be based on ISDN.

This change is part of a major investment in the Lottery technology, terminals and infrastructure by Camelot. By taking advantage of new technology, they will be able to launch new games.

Direct Line

The insurance company Direct Line is upgrading its call centre technology to improve the service to its customers, currently over 5 million. They are replacing 5000 dumb terminals with PCs and installing new software. The call centres can deal with 170,000 a day (about 35 million a year). The computers process 9.5 million transactions daily, so reliability is essential. The old system had reached the limits of its capacity.

The system will provide more customer information so that the operators can answer calls more effectively.

The company have been waiting to upgrade for some time, but did not want to do so until reliable technology that would last was available.

- What do we mean by the term 'network infrastructure'?
- What is a 'call centre'?
- What is a 'dumb terminal'?
- Compare the reasons of the two companies for upgrading their systems.

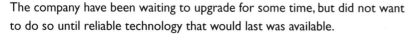

Emulation

When a decision is made to upgrade hardware it is likely that much of the software used will be upgraded too. Indeed the need for new software could well have been the driving force for hardware change. However, it is possible that some of the old software would still need to be run on the new hardware. If a change to incompatible hardware is made, it may be possible to run old software using an emulator.

A software emulator is a program which, when it runs, makes the physical computer appear to run as the old one did. The old software can therefore be used. Chips are available to provide hardware emulation.

Emulation provides a way of ensuring that old software, incompatible with new hardware, can still be used. It is a solution which is an attractive choice when a few, small systems need to be continued using old software. Emulation can also prove useful when a minority of computer users need to work on different hardware platforms from the majority of the organisation's users. For example, the design department in a large organisation might need to use Apple computers rather than PCs for their design work. The use of emulation software will allow them to use certain PC software that is used by the rest of the organisation.

Using software emulation allows access to a greater range of applications than that which is available on the user's hardware platform and allows data to be transferred between platforms.

Using emulation software can provide a cheap short-term solution to a problem without the need to invest in costly hardware until the user is sure that the more expensive change is justified.

Limitations of emulation

Because an extra layer of program is required, the original software will run more slowly and will not exploit the features of the new hardware. The emulator can make heavy demands on system resources such as memory, hard disk space and processor time. Software emulation may not provide full functionality of the application software so that the user can only access some of its features.

Summary

- Organisations should have policies for information management.

- Software, hardware and configuration choices have strategic implications for an organisation. Hardware and software purchased within a company should be standardised to ensure:
  - compatibility with existing data
  - compatibility with existing hardware
  - that colleagues can share data where necessary
  - that colleagues can communicate where necessary (e.g., by e-mail)
  - that technical support is available
  - that legal software licencing requirements are met
  - that training is available
  - that the hardware can cope with possible future demands.

- ICT users within an organisation have a wide range of needs that need to be considered.

- Organisations decide to upgrade their hardware and/or software provision for a number of reasons including:
  - Hardware/software development
  - Organisational ethos
  - Task-driven change
  - Software change.

- When upgrading, compatibility needs to be considered.

- Emulation software and hardware provides a way of running software on a different hardware platform.

Policy and strategy issues questions

1. Explain what is meant by the term 'futureproofing'. *(3)*

2. A computer user has bought a large number of packages for a NEAB PC. Due to increasing workload it is necessary to replace this model with a more powerful computer. The user has a choice of either: buying an NEAB SUPERPC machine which is compatible with the NEAB PC, or buying a MEGAMACHINE which is a completely different piece of hardware but provides the software emulation for the NEAB PC.
   a) Why does the user need to relate the new machine to the NEAB PC? *(2)*
   b) Explain the terms **compatible** and **software emulation**. *(4)*
   c) Discuss the relative merits of adopting one choice of computer as compared to the other. *(4)*

   NEAB Specimen Paper 5

3. 'If I need an IT system I buy whatever hardware and software I want without any regard to anyone.' This statement was made by a manager of a department in a company.
   Why is this an inappropriate approach in a large organisation? *(6)*

   NEAB Specimen Paper 5

4. 'I don't care which version of a word-processing package the rest of the company uses. As a senior company manager I intend to upgrade my department to the latest version.' Give four potential problems this attitude may cause for other IT users in the company. *(4)*

   NEAB 1998 Paper 5

5. A company has been running a large number of application packages on a personal computer. Although the computer works and has no hardware faults, the manager of the company now wishes to upgrade to a more powerful computer to run the same type of application packages.
   a) Give four distinct reasons why the company may wish to upgrade their computer. *(4)*
   b) The company could buy a computer which is compatible with the current machine in use. An alternative is to purchase a different type of computer, with software emulation of the current

hardware. Explain the terms compatible and software emulation. *(6)*
   c) Describe the advantages and limitations of adopting a software emulation approach. *(4)*

   NEAB 1998 Paper 5

6. A graphic designer makes use of a particular hardware platform and particular software packages. Her clients often send her files produced on computer systems that are incompatible with hers. One solution for the designer is to use emulation software.
   Describe one advantage and one limitation the designer will have if she pursues this solution. *(4)*

7. A company has been using a particular accounting package for several years and they are considering whether to upgrade or replace the software with an alternative.
   State **four** reasons why the company may wish to upgrade the software. *(4)*

   AQA June 2000 Paper 5

8. As an IT consultant you have been asked by a particular company to draft a number of policy and strategy documents relating to the use of IT systems at work.
   a) State **four** issues that should be included in these documents and, for each one, give an example of its effect on employees. *(8)*
   b) State **four** reasons why the company would need an information policy. *(4)*

   AQA June 2000 Paper 5

9. A school IT coordinator wants to upgrade the school computer network, which consists of a large number of workstations and two servers, all of which are at least three years old. The operating system (OS) is over five years old.
   a) State five reasons she could give to her senior management that would reinforce her case for upgrading. *(5)*
   She has the choice of either using an established network OS, or take part in the first phase of trialling a new one. She chooses the established OS.
   b) State two reasons why she might do this. *(2)*
   c) Describe two benefits that a software manufacturer gets from customers trialling a new OS before it is made generally available. *(4)*

   AQA June 2001 Paper 5

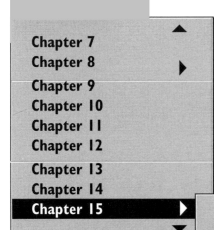
Backup strategies

The aim of a producing file backups is to make sure that a computer system where data has been lost or corrupted can be restored to its original state. This might occur if a hard disk crashes or a file is accidentally deleted for example.

An information management strategy must include a strategy for backing up files. Computer files are very valuable to the organisation. Lost files will result in wasted time and money. It is essential that a company has a backup strategy to cover all eventualities, including accidental damage, deliberate damage and damage due to equipment failure.

After carrying out a risk analyis, a formal strategy should be established that ensures that regular backups of critical data are taken in a consistent and appropriate manner. They need to be done in such a way that, if necessary, the system could be restored in a reasonable amount of time. What is considered reasonable will depend on the nature of the data being backed up. It is important that the backup procedures should not affect the provision of service. Ideally they should be invisible to the user.

Short- and long-term plans should also be made for the archiving of data that is no longer needed online. Archiving removes data that is no longer needed from an online storage medium such as a hard disk, thus freeing up space. Such data may prove useful in restoring data after a failure if problems arise with backed up data.

Activity 1

Backing-up laptops

Many organisations have excellent strategies in place to backup their networked systems and databases but neglect to consider the backup needs of the growing number of laptop computers that are used by employees. Laptops are particularly at risk as they are more vulnerable to theft and potential damage.

An employee's laptop could contain a range of data and programs whose loss could range from annoying to critical, such as software applications, highly configured Windows systems, communication setups to connect to the Internet and the organisation's network, documents and other data, and Internet bookmarks.

Activity I continued

Prepare a backup strategy for an insurance salesman who uses his laptop to:

- download client information from the company database

- update client records using special purpose software when visiting the clients

- produce reports and letters using Microsoft Office

- keep in touch with work colleagues through e-mail.

The responsibility of backing up a system should be allocated to a specific person within the organisation. It is that person's responsibility to ensure that backup and recovery procedures are practised from time to time and that careful checks are made to ensure that whatever backup measures are being taken actually work so that backed up data can be read at any time. It is important that all writing and reading equipment is compatible.

The strategy will need to specify which files need to be backed up and at what frequency. A good management plan will ensure the backups are performed at the appropriate intervals. Most organisations backup at least daily but backups may need to be performed more or less frequently.

> **How long to keep data**

The longer an organisation keeps its data, the more portable media, such as magnetic tapes, are needed. Older backups will be needed in case later backups fail. Consideration of any legal obligations for the business, as well as other business needs, should be made when determining how long backed up data should be retained. If the data needs to be stored for a long time, the media should be periodically inspected for signs of damage.

It is important to establish when a backup should take place and who does it. Backups are often taken at night as many systems only run during working hours. A backup log should be kept. This should record the details of all backups taken with details of time, date, the medium used (identified by a volume number), together with the name of the person who carried out the backup.

With an online system, suitable backup facilities must be in place to ensure that all lost transactions can be restored. Consideration of the volume of data involved in the system and the importance of the speed in which restoring from backed up files must be taken into account. Arranging backup for systems which are online for 24 hours a day can be complicated.

When a network is used the process of backing up can be centralised and all servers can be backed up from one place. In most cases the user is responsible for any data that is stored on the hard drive of their own workstation.

The place where backup copies are to be stored must be specified, as well as the length of time and number of back copies that are kept.

Case Study 1

A college backup strategy

A sixth-form college runs a network used by teachers and students as well all administrative services such as MIS and examinations. The network supports over 20 file servers. Backup is an important part of the work of the IT Department.

The department uses a software utility called Backupexec developed by Veritas to carry out its backup.

As little use is made of the college system outside working hours, the department carries out a full backup every night. The backup is initiated by the software and DLT 7000 tapes are used to store the backed up files. The tapes are slotted in to a 16 slot autoloader.

The rotation system described on page 148 is used. The last and previous weeks' tapes are held off-site while those for this week are held in the autoloader. The monthly backup is kept for a year.

The backup process starts at 1630 in the afternoon and is completed around 0630 the following morning. Jeremy, senior IT Technician at the college, is in charge of checking that the backup has successfully completed when he arrives at work in the morning. The backup software produces a log file which will inform him whether the backup:

- completed with no errors
- completed with errors
- aborted.

Most mornings the backup will have completed with no errors; a complete failure causing the backup to abort is a rare occurrence. If the backup completes with some files failing to be backed up, Jeremy has to follow up each error. If the backup does fail completely he will have to decide whether to risk running without a backup for a day or to slow the network down while the backup is repeated.

If a user of the network deletes or overwrites a file by mistake, Jeremy can restore a previous version for them. The backup software keeps a catalogue of the path of all the files it backs up. It will then read through the tape until it finds the required file.

Files on the servers are not the only things that need backing up, for example, configuration settings for the firewall are stored as a text file. Over time the settings will have received many modifications and if the file were lost it would take many man-hours to recreate.

- What is the advantage of using an autoloader?
- Comment on the effectiveness of the college's backup strategy.
- Why is it important for one person to have the responsibility for backup?
- Explore the Veritas website to find out the functions offered by BackupExec software.

> **Options available for backup systems** >

A number of factors will influence the decision of backup method and storage medium. These include:

- the seriousness of the consequences of lost data
- the volume of the data
- the speed in which the data is changing

○ how quickly recovery needs to take place if a situation occurs when data has to be restored from backed up version(s)

○ the cost of various methods.

> **Selection of an appropriate medium for backup storage** >

When choosing the appropriate medium for backup the capacity (the amount of data that can be stored on the medium), the speed of transfer of data and the cost will all need to be considered. The hardware device chosen can be dedicated solely for backup use or used for other purposes as well.

Many backup strategies rely on the use of removable storage media that can be stored away from the computer system. Some examples of backup media of this type are given in the table below.

8 mm tape	Offers moderate speed (60–80 MB per minute) and good capacities (2.5–40 GB) for medium-sized environments.
ADR (Advanced Digital Recording)	Offers high speed (30–120 MB per minute) and good capacity (50 GB) for desktop computers and servers.
AIT (Advanced Intelligent Tape)	Capacity up to 50 GB and transfer speeds of up to 360 MB per minute make AIT suitable for environments with large amounts of data.
DAT (Digital Audio Tape)	Holds 12–20 GB with transfer speeds from 6–150 MB per minute.
QIC (Quarter Inch Cartridge)	QIC drives suitable for home or small business use are relatively inexpensive. Cartridges can be bought with capacities from 4–50 GB and speeds can range from 30–300 MB per minute.

A tape library is a device that makes unattended large-scale backups possible. They are frequently used when backing up data stored over a network. A tape library consists of tape drive and a robotic device that can move tapes in and out of the drive. By using a tape library, the volume of data that can be backed up without the need for human intervention is increased hugely and limited only by the number of tapes that it can hold.

> **Frequency of backup** >

The frequency of backup must be determined. Obviously, the more frequent the backup, the less out of date will be the data when it is restored. However, whenever a backup is undertaken, processor time is tied up and files can be unavailable for other use. An appropriate balance needs to be found and factors such as the acceptable length of delay in restoring files in the case of failure as well as the importance and nature of the data need to be taken into account. Sales data for a supermarket, which affects orders and deliveries, will be backed up hourly, if not more frequently. User data, such as passwords and user names, need only be backed up every week.

To use removable storage media it must be possible to allocate time when a backup can take place without interfering with the normal running of the system. In many organisations, systems are not in use at night and so full backups can be taken then.

Recording of transactions in a log

Unless a file is backed up after every transaction, which is unlikely to be feasible, a record will need to be kept of all the transactions that have taken place since the last backup occurred. In the case of file failure, the latest backup copy would be used to restore the file. It could then be brought up to date by rerunning all the transactions, stored on the log, that had occurred since the backup was made. Of course, the transaction log itself must be backed up otherwise failure could cause a loss of transaction. Such a transaction could record the bookings for a flight.

In some systems it is necessary to perform transaction log backups every 15 minutes during the day to keep the data entry loss to less than 15 minutes.

Systems that are live for 24 hours a day may need to look at alternative methods of ensuring that data is adequately backed up.

Program files do not change very frequently except during development; backups only need to be created when new versions are installed. However, many software applications need to be configured to meet the requirements of the hardware that is installed. They can also be customised to meet the user's specific needs for macros and templates, for example. It is advisable to keep backups of all such modifications: it is easy for a user to delete the files that store the configuration details and without a backup file the configuration and customisation would have to be undertaken again. All backup copies should be regularly checked.

Data files are regularly changing and will therefore need regular backing up.

Scheduling backups and tape rotation methods

Tape backup systems have been in use for years on computer systems. It would be very unwise to use the same physical tape for every backup session. The backup process might fail part way through execution without producing a complete tape: the old version would have been overwritten. So a number of tapes will need to be kept and, if the tapes are not going to get muddled up they need to be carefully labelled and stored. This will allow the correct tape to be accessed when needed to restore the system.

A **tape rotation system** is used to ensure that the correct versions are kept.

Full backup

Perhaps the easiest way to backup is where a full image of the system is copied to tape every single day. A different tape is used each day. This ensures that the system can be restored from only one tape. It may take many tapes, and, if the volume of data is large, a considerable time to carry out each day. This type of backup is common for small servers that are not in operational use 24 hours a day. The limitation of taking a full backup is that it can take a considerable time to carry out; if a system is running at the same time it is likely to slow down processing.

Differential backup

This is a variation of full backup where one tape is created that contains a full image of the system and subsequent tapes receive copies of the files which are different or were updated after the image backup. This allows the full system to be restored with a maximum of just two tapes. The limitation of using differential backup is that when some time has elapsed since the last full backup, the backup of all changed files will be time consuming.

Incremental backup

This is a further variation in which only the files that have changed since the last backup to the tape are copied. Using an incremental backup would take less time to backup as each file change is only being backed up once; incremental backups could be done several times during the day. Its limitation is that, if a failure did occur it would take more time to restore files to the current position since several tapes may have to be used one after the other to totally restore the system.

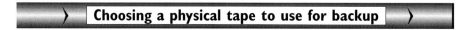

> **Choosing a physical tape to use for backup** 〉

A **rotation method** determines how tapes are fed through the system.

Grandfather, father, son

The Grandfather, Father, Son system is a simple method that has been used for many years. Tapes are labelled by the day of the week with a different tape for each Friday in the month and a different tape for each month of the year. (Using a tape for Saturday and Sunday is optional depending on whether files are updated over the weekend). The rotation would be made as follows:

MONDAY TUESDAY WEDNESDAY THURSDAY FRIDAY1

MONDAY TUESDAY WEDNESDAY THURSDAY FRIDAY2

MONDAY TUESDAY WEDNESDAY THURSDAY FRIDAY3

MONDAY TUESDAY WEDNESDAY THURSDAY MONTH1

MONDAY TUESDAY WEDNESDAY THURSDAY FRIDAY1

MONDAY TUESDAY WEDNESDAY THURSDAY FRIDAY2

MONDAY TUESDAY WEDNESDAY THURSDAY FRIDAY3

MONDAY TUESDAY WEDNESDAY THURSDAY MONTH2

MONDAY TUESDAY WEDNESDAY THURSDAY FRIDAY1

MONDAY TUESDAY WEDNESDAY THURSDAY FRIDAY2

MONDAY TUESDAY WEDNESDAY THURSDAY FRIDAY3

MONDAY TUESDAY WEDNESDAY THURSDAY FRIDAY5

MONDAY TUESDAY WEDNESDAY THURSDAY MONTH3

and so on.

Since, some months have more than four weeks, it will take over 20 tapes for regular backups over one year.

Physical security of backup medium

As data can be lost due to disasters such as fire, it is necessary that backup files should be kept in a separate place from the original storage medium.

In some large cities there exist firms that run a backup service. They come to client organisations at a fixed time, usually daily, collect the day's backup tapes which they take away to store safely at their own premises. At the same time they provide the client with the tapes, correctly labelled, that need to be used for the next day's backups. If the backups are needed to restore the system, the firm will rush the appropriate tapes to the client organisation.

Often a fireproof safe is used for storage. A locality should be chosen that is climate-controlled, secure and easily accessible.

Data files can also be backed up by transmitting them across a network to save a copy of the data in a remote location. (See Case Study: A remote backup service on page 150).

Recovery method

It is important that when files have been backed up that the backup copy is verified, in other words checked against the original to ensure that it has been copied exactly. If this is not done, the backup files could prove to be useless and the original file could not be re-created.

If the original data files are lost or corrupted, the data can be recovered by using programs that restore the data from the backup files. It is necessary to restore the files in the correct order by following agreed recovery procedures. The file will first be re-created using the most recent full backup and then each subsequent incremental backup file should be accessed, in time order, to update the file. Any transaction log should then be used to restore the most recent transactions.

If the files are used in the wrong order, the restored file will not be correct. Care must be taken in the careful labelling and organisation of backup tapes and disks to ensure that no mistakes are made.

Remote backup

An organisation can use a remote backup service, similar to the one described in the case study, by transferring files to a remote site using a wide area network. The limitations of using remote backup are that data is vulnerable as it is being transmitted over a network and will need to be encrypted.

Case Study 2

A remote backup service

Mercer DataSafe is a company that offers businesses an automated off-site backup service. Data from the company's computer is automatically backed up after business hours to Mercer DataSafe's computer in Lawrenceville, New Jersey, USA.

Using Mercer DataSafe's backups, businesses can quickly recover any lost data, usually within 24 hours of a catastrophic loss (such as a flood, fire, theft or operator error), or within hours of a minor loss (such as a deleted file).

To use Mercer DataSafe's system, you only need a modem. At the preset time, the data to be backed up is compressed in a securely encrypted format. Mercer DataSafe's computer is contacted using the modem and after identification checks, the data is transmitted.

When finished, the data is verified. If everything is correct, a confirmation message is sent back to the company's computer and the computer shut down. The backup company won't have access to the user company's records as all files are securely encrypted and only the user has the key.

Users who already have a tape backup system may still find it better to use a remote service. Many users forget to perform a backup even though they have a tape drive. Other users think they may be doing a backup correctly, but when they need to restore a file they find out that their tapes are useless. Few users take their tapes off site so, if they have a fire or other disaster, they lose all their data.

- What is meant by data verification?
- Why is the data compressed?
- Why is the data encrypted?
- List the advantages to an organisation of using the services of a company such as DataSafe.

Online backup

The methods described above are used by many organisations and are appropriate for small- and medium-sized systems. However, organisations with very large systems that hold vast data warehouses of information, need to look at alternative methods for providing backup. As well as having very high volumes of data, the organisations running such systems can neither afford to lose even a small amount of data nor lose operational time while data is being restored from a backup. An alternative way has to be found to provide against the hazards of data loss.

One way is to use disk mirroring: storing identical data on two different disks. Whenever data is stored to disk, it is stored on both disks. If the main disk fails, the exact data is available on the second disk.

The mirror disk does not have to be located in the same place as the first disk. If it is in a different building then the data is still protected from disaster such as from fire or terrorist attack.

Case Study 3

Porsche cars move to online backup

Porsche store vehicle and warranty information as well as customer information. They have recently moved from traditional tape storage to online backup. Tapes used to be stored off-site, so that in the event of a problem, most historical information was safe. But more recent data, that had not yet been transferred, was vulnerable. If a fire, or similar disaster were to have happened on a Friday, then Monday's, Tuesday's, Wednesday's and Thursday's tapes would still be on site.

The new storage technology will reduce manual error as staff have had to swap tapes over.

- How could the manual swapping of tapes have led to error?

- What is meant by online backup?

Batch processing systems

Batch mode is a common method of computer processing used when there are large numbers of similar transactions. It is used when processing such systems as a payroll or utility billing which are run at regular intervals, perhaps once a day, once a week, once a month or once a quarter. All the data to be input is collected together before being processed in a single operation.

In a typical batch processing system all the transactions are batched together and entered off-line into a transaction file which is then sorted into the same order as the records in the master file. The records from the transaction file are merged with the corresponding records of the master file and the updated records are stored in a new master file.

The old master file is called the **father file** and the new version the **son**. This method of processing produces automatic backup since, if the son file were to become corrupted, it could be recreated by running the update program once again using the same transaction file with the father file to restore it.

When the son is in turn used to create a new version it becomes the father and the old father becomes the grandfather. The number of generations that are kept should be decided upon. Obviously it will be necessary to keep the transaction files as well as they will be needed in the process to restore the up-to-date master file.

Activity I

Produce a leaflet on appropriate methods of backup for a new student of ICT A level who has just bought a home PC. Explain in your leaflet:

○ the need for a backup strategy

○ appropriate methods of backing up

○ the hardware choices available for backup and the merits and costs of each (research on the Internet).

Summary

○ A **full backup** occurs when all the data stored on a medium, such as hard disk, is copied to another medium such as magnetic tape.

○ A **periodic backup** occurs at set time periods.

○ A **differential backup** is a variation of full backup where one tape is created that contains a full image of the system and subsequent tapes receive copies of the files which are different or were updated after the image backup.

○ An **incremental (or modified) backup** only stores changes that have been made since the last backup.

○ The following factors need to be considered when establishing a backup strategy:

○ the appropriate medium for backup storage

○ the frequency of backup

○ the use of a log to record transactions (a transaction log is a record of all the transactions that have taken place since the last backup occurred)

○ the use of full or/and incremental backups

○ the number of generations of backup that should be kept

○ the method of recovery

○ how the physical security of backup medium is to be assured within the organisation.

○ The responsibility of backing up a system should be allocated to a specific person.

○ Different strategies are needed for backing up program and data files.

Backup strategies questions

1. A hospital information system holds program files which are rarely changed and large database files which are constantly changing.

Describe a suitable backup strategy for this system, explaining what is backed up and when, together with the media and hardware involved. *(8)*

NEAB 1997 Paper 5

2. A hospital information system holds program files which are rarely changed and large database files which are changing constantly. At present the backup strategy uses a tape storage device and has the following characteristics:

- Each evening the information system is taken off-line and a full backup is made of the entire system. Three sets of tapes are in use and are referred to as sets A, B and C.
- Set A is used one evening.
- Set B is used the next evening.
- Set C is used the following evening.
- This sequence is then repeated, starting the next evening with set A again.

An advisor has suggested a change is required to improve this strategy. Give, with reasons, four changes that could be made. *(8)*

NEAB 1999 Paper 5

3. A large car dealer has a small computer network within its showroom, with a link to the main supplier's network. The server for the dealer's Local Area Network is located in one of the sales offices. Backups are taken daily and a sequence of tapes is used to store the information. The tapes are stored in full view of anyone in the office. Some of the information is sensitive, for example, customer personal details. Several people use the office but no one person is responsible for the backup.

Describe two possible problems with managing the backup process in this way. *(4)*

Suggest three factors that the car dealer should consider in order to improve its backup process. Give reasons for each of your suggestions. *(6)*

Give two additional factors that would have to be considered by an organisation whose information system has to provide a continuous service. *(2)*

AQA June 2001 Paper 5

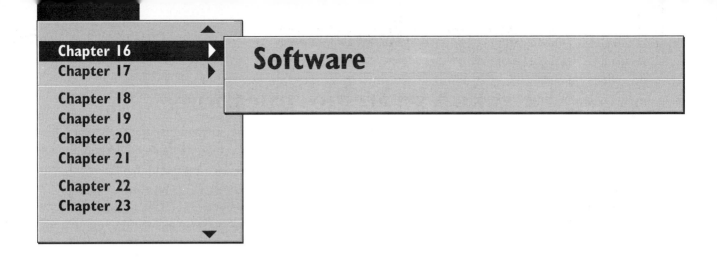
Software

Choosing software

Choosing a software package to use on a home computer is usually relatively simple. There are many magazines and websites that review different software packages, describe features, comment on ease of use and make recommendations.

They will often provide further details such as minimum processor speed, hard disk and memory requirements and the results of benchmark tests.

Figure 16.1 www.pcadvisor.co.uk offers comprehensive software reviews

Software publishers sometimes provide a free demonstration copy, given away with magazines such as *Personal Computer World* or downloadable from the Internet.

Choosing the appropriate software to use within an organisation is a much more complex task. There might be hundreds of workstations throughout the organisation being used for a wide range of tasks by hundreds of different users.

The first step that needs to be taken is to establish the end-user requirements. The capabilities of the software will need be evaluated and then the needs matched with the capabilities.

To establish end-user requirements a detailed investigation will be needed; it should involve interviewing the end-users. The process of investigation should highlight whether or not the organisation has realistic aims that can be met, as well as find out what is important to the user. The investigation should establish the nature of the systems that are already in place. This will allow the current starting position that is to be developed to be clearly seen.

A range of alternative software solutions should be investigated and objectively compared.

The budget restrictions should be made clear at the start of the process; if this is not done, much time can be wasted exploring solutions that are not financially viable.

In such situations, wrong software choices could be very costly. It is important firstly to determine the needs of the user and which aspects of the software type are most important to them. This could be a time-consuming and costly process involving a number of people. It is a process that should not be skimped.

The capabilities of the available software packages should be looked into and compared with the user's needs so that the best match can be found. It may be appropriate to talk to some existing users of the software application being considered. Seeing the software in action can help to highlight problems that might occur and give insight into its suitability for the prospective organisation.

Of course, no suitable software may exist, in which case alternative solutions need to be sought (see Chapter 21).

Establish User Needs

Software Capabilities

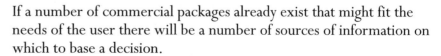

Evaluating software

If a number of commercial packages already exist that might fit the needs of the user there will be a number of sources of information on which to base a decision.

For many packages there will be reports available, either in the IT press or in trade magazines. Very often such publications will carry out extensive evaluations of new software, carrying out benchmark testing and even comparing a range of similar packages. These should prove a useful starting point in making a software choice.

Many software producers will provide a CD-ROM with a version of the software that a prospective user can use for a limited time period for evaluation purposes. An alternative method used for distributing software for evaluation purposes is via the Internet.

Manufacturers will usually provide demonstrations of the system in use. This may be provided at an organisation which is already using the software.

Many colleges are currently considering purchasing VLEs (virtual learning environments) to allow teachers to manage students' learning through IT in an organised way. One of the first things that an IT manager in such an institution would do would be to visit colleges that had already installed one of the VLEs on the market. By questioning the users and observing the software in use, the IT manager would gain useful information on which to base a purchase decision.

When major applications are being considered, personnel from the software producers may provide a prototype implementation that is configured to the specific needs of the prospective user. This would provide the opportunity to see the system in action in the user's environment.

It is necessary to draw up software evaluation criteria that will be used to help decide which product to use. The criteria used in any particular situation will be wide ranging and will enable an objective choice to be made.

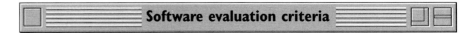

Software evaluation criteria

The requirement specification will be agreed by the user and the developer. The evaluation criteria will need to be based on this specification. The following evaluation criteria are likely to be used

Functionality

The functionality of software is what it actually does. The more features it offers the greater its functionality. Functions of a word processor might include mail merge, thesaurus and grammar check. However, it is important that the functions the software supports are the ones that the organisation needs. There is no advantage in using software that has a number of irrelevant functions and their presence could confuse the user.

A **benchmark** is a standard set of computer tasks designed to allow measurements to be made of computer performance. These tasks can be used to compare the performance of different software or hardware. Examples of tasks are, how long it takes to reformat a 40 page word-processed document, how many pages can be printed in one minute and how long it takes to save 1000 database records to disk. (Taken from the BCS Glossary)

Performance

The performance of a particular software application is determined by how well it performs the required features. Benchmark tests are often used to measure performance. Examples of such tests could include the speed of locating a record or the file storage requirements. It is important to establish whether or not the software can cope with the demands of the user.

Usability and human–machine interface

It is important that the software interface is suitable for the intended user. An interface should be intuitive to use, consistent with clear and appropriate help facilities. An application might have all the functionality required but might prove to be very difficult to use and learn. For a beginner it would need to be very user-friendly with clear screens and instructions. If it is to be used by more experienced ICT users shortcuts would need to be available.

Compatibility

Ideally new software should be compatible with the software currently in use. If it is not, ways will need to be found to transfer data. Many everyday packages, such as spreadsheet, graphics or DTP, are produced as compatible units. Very often the operating system that is used will influence the choice of software as some packages are only produced to run under particular operating systems. If it is similar to the existing software little training will be needed, otherwise extensive retraining might be needed.

Transferability of data

The ease with which data from current files could be transferred into those for the new system is an important factor. This could be achieved easily or there might be a need for major data conversion which could prove unwieldy or expensive. In the worst case, all the data could have to be re-entered.

Robustness

Robustness refers to the extent to which the software will run using realistic volumes of data, supporting the required number of users day after day without crashing or causing errors. It is important to establish how well the software has been tested. If it already has a wide user base it is likely that errors will have been already highlighted and corrected. If it has been used in circumstances similar to those required by the new system its robustness can be easily assessed. It is crucial that the software can be shown to function effectively using the volume of data that is likely to be used.

User support

The kind of support that is provided will need to meet the likely requirements from users. Many software publishers provide a telephone helpline for registered users. If adequate support is not automatically provided, the cost of acquiring it must be considered. This might involve extra training for the IT technicians within the organisation.

The quality of documentation may vary considerably between different software packages. The full range of user needs to be considered: from the beginner to the personnel providing technical backup within the organisation.

There are likely to be books, videos or training courses available for widely-used software.

Resource requirements

It is important to consider whether the software will run on the existing hardware platform or whether new equipment will be required. The processor speed, main memory and disk space requirements will need careful consideration. Whether or not it will run under the current operating system is a crucial factor to be considered.

The choice of particular software might result in the need for changes to other currently used software as well as any software that is intended to be replaced. Some choices might result in further staff being required to run the new software. The costs of retraining current staff to use new packages must be considered.

Upgradibility

Whether or not upgraded versions of the software are likely to become available in the future could be an important factor. The credibility of the company that produces the software will be crucial.

Portability

It is important to ensure that adequate filters are provided to allow data to be transferred to other systems in the way that the system demands. It may be necessary for data to be able to be exported to other software.

Financial issues

Cost will always be a very important factor when deciding upon software purchase. The wider implications of a particular choice need to be explored. For instance, will additional hardware need to be purchased and will other associated software need to be bought?

Considerations such as training needs and file conversion costs must also be included. The development cost of installing the new software will also need to be considered.

Different licensing arrangements will need to be explored as well as the software manufacturer's attitude to upgrades. Some companies provide these free while the cost of others can be a major expenditure.

Other considerations

The supplier of the software must be chosen with care. A well-established company with a good range of products on the market that are well used and well supported has greater credibility than a new, untried company. If a company does not appear to have a stable future any software currently produced may cease to be supported or developed if the company were to cease to trade. Even if it were bought out by a larger company, a particular software application may not be supported under the new management.

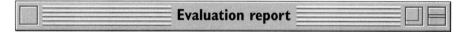

Evaluation report

When an evaluation has been completed, a report is written for senior management who would then make a decision based on the information provided. The function of the report is to document how the different software packages available performed against the criteria set and how they would measure up to the expectations of the organisation. The findings of the report should enable a decision to be made.

After explaining the purpose of the particular report by defining the user requirements, the report should include:

- A summary of the **methodology used** to produce the report detailing how the information was gathered and how the evaluation had been carried out. This would include a description of all benchmark tests undertaken.

- The **actual evaluation**, where the appropriate evaluation criteria are discussed. This would show how well each system compared to the agreed criteria.

- **Recommendations** for purchase would then be made based on the evaluation. The recommendations would be backed up with **justifications**, explaining how the recommendations were arrived at, based on the evidence given in the report.

Activity I

Software choice

This comparison of two well-known Internet browsers was taken from the www.cnet.com website.

Browser	Netscape 6.1	Microsoft Internet Explorer 6
Platform:	Windows 95/98/Me/NT 4.0/2000	Windows 98/98 SE/Me/NT 4.0 SP6/2000
Minimum Processor	Pentium 233	486 DX/66
Minimum RAM:	64 MB	16 MB (Windows 98/98 SE); 32 MB (Windows Me/NT/2000); 64 MB (Windows XP)
Minimum disk space:	26 MB	45 MB (minimal installation, browser only); 70 MB (typical installation); 111 MB (full installation)
CD-ROM required:	No	No
Downloadable full version:	Yes	Yes
The good:	Much more stable than Netscape 6; finally launches nearly as quickly as Internet Explorer.	Cool new user interface elements make it easier to borrow images from Web pages; support for blocking third-party cookies protects Web surfers' privacy.
The bad:	No significant new features.	Won't run on Windows 95 machines.
The bottom line:	Netscape 6.1 is the browser that Netscape 6 should have been, but nine months later. If you're running Netscape 6, upgrade pronto.	This browser promises to stay a bit ahead of Netscape 6.1.

What does the above table tell us about:

- functionality?
- performance?
- the human–computer interface?
- resource requirements?
- robustness?

Summary

- Software evaluation should address the following criteria:
  - functionality
  - performance
  - usability and the human–computer interface
  - compatibility
  - data transferability
  - robustness
  - user support
  - resource requirements
  - upgradability
  - portability
  - financial issues
  - supplier.

- In choosing which software to buy, companies must establish their needs and find software that satisfies these needs.

Software questions

1. A large market research company is considering several different software packages in order to assist with the analysis of data collected on behalf of clients. Give three criteria that should be considered when evaluating these software packages. For each criterion explain why it may be important to this company. *(9)*

   AQA June 2002 Paper 5

2. You are asked to evaluate a software package and produce an evaluation report.
   a) Describe four criteria you would use to evaluate the package. *(8)*
   b) What is the function and content of an evaluation report? *(4)*

   NEAB Specimen Paper 5

3. A company has been using a particular accounting package for several years and they are considering whether to upgrade or replace the software with an alternative.
   a) State **four** reasons why the company may wish to upgrade the software. *(4)*
   b) Describe **four** criteria that the company might use to evaluate alternative accounting packages. *(8)*

   AQA June 2000 Paper 5

4. A company is about to change its accounting software. In order to evaluate the different packages available to them, they have drawn up a number of evaluation criteria.
   a) Why are such evaluation criteria needed? *(2)*
   b) Explain the issues involved with each of the three evaluation criteria given below:
      • functionality
      • user support
      • hardware resource requirements. *(6)*
   c) Identify and describe three additional evaluation criteria that you might also expect the company to include. *(6)*

   NEAB 1998 Paper 5

5. A university has decided to buy a new payroll package. They are considering several options and have drawn up a range of evaluation criteria to help them select the most appropriate one.
   The criteria used by the university include:
   • performance
   • robustness
   • user support.
   a) For each of these criteria, describe two issues that you would expect the university to consider. *(6)*

   b) Describe three other criteria you would expect the university to apply when comparing systems. *(6)*

   NEAB 1999 paper 5

6. A company that specialises in selling bicycles, spares and related items is considering having a website that will allow customers to order online. It already uses a relational database to keep records of customers, stock and orders.
   As an IT consultant, you have been approached to assess the viability of several alternative software solutions. Discuss how you would help the company decide on a suitable software solution. Your discussion should include:
   • what you need to find out in order to carry out this assessment
   • the evaluation criteria that you would consider using
   • the content of the report that you would produce to show the results of your evaluation. *(20)*
   Quality of language will be assessed in this answer

   AQA June 2001 Paper 5

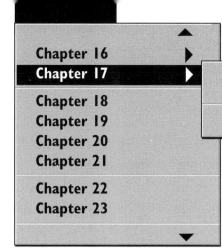
Database management concepts

The British Computer Society gives the following definition for a database: *A database is a collection of data items and links between them, structured in a way that allows it to be accessed by a number of different applications programs.* In other words, a database consists of data. The database is accessed using a database management system. This is a software package that works with the data for the user. A database administrator is employed to manage large database systems with many users.

The Database Management System (DBMS)

A DBMS is software that accesses data in a database. It can find data, change existing data and add new data. The DBMS works directly with the data on behalf of the user who does not himself access the data. The DBMS acts as an extra layer between the user program and the database. It deals with all search and update requests from users and carries out other tasks such as maintaining indexes.

The DBMS may provide its own, user-friendly interface or may deal directly with user programs that request and use the data available in the database. The DBMS will support a number of different user applications. User queries are made via the DBMS using either SQL (structured query language) or QBE (query by example) to communicate with the DBMS.

A DBMS stores the data separately from programs that use the data, thus the programs and the data are independent of one another.

There has been a huge growth in the use of database management systems over recent years. A number of DBMS packages can be bought for use on a stand-alone PC such as Microsoft Access. Multi-user systems, where a number of users, linked to a network, can access the same data are widely used in business. In such a system the data can all be stored centrally attached to a powerful computer. Alternatively the data can be spread over several databases held on different computers (a distributed database).

The functions of a DBMS are summarised as follows:

- **Database definition**. As most commercial databases are relational, the structure of the database will be made up of tables and the links between the tables. A specific language, data definition language (DDL) is used to specify the database structure.

- **Data storage, retrieval and update**. The DBMS allows users to store, retrieve and update information as easily as possible. These users are not necessarily computer experts and do not need to be aware of the internal structure of the database or how to set it up. Data from the database can be retrieved by using queries.

- **Creation and maintenance of the data dictionary**.

- **Managing the facilities for sharing the database**. Many databases need a multi-access facility. Two or more people must be able to access the database simultaneously and to update records without a causing problem.

- **Backup and recovery**. Information in the database must not be lost in the event of system failure.

- **Security**. The DBMS must check user passwords and allow appropriate privileges.

Database Administrator (DBA)

The database administrator is the person in an organisation who is responsible for the structure and control of the data in the organisation's database. The DBA is usually involved in the design of the database and will carry out any changes requested by users. This will be followed up by informing other users of changes affecting them. An example of such a change could be the addition of a new field or the change in size or type of an existing field.

Monitoring the performance of the database is an important task. If the number of accesses increases, the end-user response time might become unacceptably slow. If such problems arise, the DBA will need to make appropriate changes to the database structure.

Many early databases became overcomplicated and failed to fulfil their function – no one knew the whole picture of the data stored. It is crucial that the DBA maintains a data dictionary, a file containing descriptions of, and other information about, the structure of the data held on the database. It is important that all users of the database follow the same naming conventions for elements of the database, such as field and table names, to avoid confusion.

The DBA will deal with queries for the user and provide help and training appropriate to their own use. Training will be required for new staff, as well as for existing staff who may need to be shown ways of using the database more efficiently.

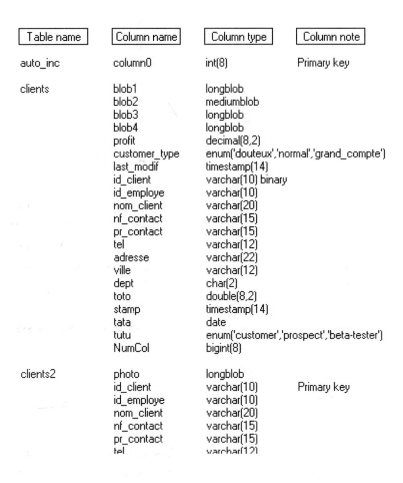

Table name	Column name	Column type	Column note
auto_inc	column0	int(8)	Primary key
clients	blob1	longblob	
	blob2	mediumblob	
	blob3	longblob	
	blob4	longblob	
	profit	decimal(8,2)	
	customer_type	enum('douteux','normal','grand_compte')	
	last_modif	timestamp(14)	
	id_client	varchar(10) binary	
	id_employe	varchar(10)	
	nom_client	varchar(20)	
	nf_contact	varchar(15)	
	pr_contact	varchar(15)	
	tel	varchar(12)	
	adresse	varchar(22)	
	ville	varchar(12)	
	dept	char(2)	
	toto	double(8,2)	
	stamp	timestamp(14)	
	tata	date	
	tutu	enum('customer','prospect','beta-tester')	
	NumCol	bigint(8)	
clients2	photo	longblob	
	id_client	varchar(10)	Primary key
	id_employe	varchar(10)	
	nom_client	varchar(20)	
	nf_contact	varchar(15)	
	pr_contact	varchar(15)	
	tel	varchar(12)	

Figure 17.1 Data dictionary

The DBA will allocate passwords to users and protect confidential information by implementing and maintaining appropriate access privileges that restrict what data an individual user can access and/or change. These are necessary to prevent inexperienced users from mistakenly changing or deleting data as well as for purposes of data security.

The DBA is likely to be required to set up reports for users: the administrator will have a detailed knowledge of the DBMS package and so will be able to create reports that provide the user with the information required in a clear format.

Backup procedures for the database will be managed by the DBA on a regular basis with the responsibility that data is retored if corruption does occur. The DBA will also archive data and carry out any other special housekeeping tasks.

Case Study 1

Interview with Kim, database administrator

Kim is the DBA for a college administrative database. The database includes data on admissions, exam entries and attendance and is used by teachers, tutors, senior management and a range of administrative personnel. Data is used to produce exam entry information, statistical returns for the local skills council for funding purposes, as well as for many internal purposes.

An interview was carried out with Kim to find out what her job involves. This is a summary.

How much time do you spend working on the database?
90–95 per cent of my week is spent working on a database, either our main database, DITA, or one of our in-house databases. The other part of my week is spent liaising with college staff and taking part in meetings.

Can you list tasks in a typical week?
I don't really have a typical week except in very general terms, for example, writing reports, analysing or amending procedures, maintaining existing databases. I have a weekly tasking meeting with the vice-principals and the bursar.

How many users of the system are there?
There are over 80 users who have some access to DITA at the moment.

What different access rights do different categories of users have?
We can assign 'select', 'insert', 'update' and 'delete' rights to individual objects or tables. We assign rights to groups: users have the rights of the group we put them in. We have a read-only group that most college staff are a member of; other groups have additional rights on particular objects.

Do you have a training role?
Each new user needs some training as DITA is not a very user-friendly application. Users need to know how course and class codes are structured and require a basic knowledge of how to search a database before they can really benefit from the system.

Others, who use the system as a main part of their job, will need more detailed training that ensures that data is recorded in a consistent manner. Specific processes that users may have to carry out frequently are documented in training documents so that individuals can refer to them as necessary.

Do you write ad hoc reports for users?
Yes, usually for management. For example, I have just produced a report on the destinations of students on leaving college broken down by the school they came to us from. A requirement will be discussed and its potential assessed for making it available to everyone. If it will serve as a useful tool for the majority of users it will be made generally available via the DITA reporting application.

- What other tasks are often carried out by a database administrator?

- List ten reports that are likely to be produced by the application.

- What is meant by the term ad hoc report?

- Why is it necessary for Kim to meet with the college bursar and vice-principals every week?

The college also employs a data entry clerk, Mary, whose task is to enter details of new students, course changes and other changes to the database.

- What access rights to student data would you expect Mary to have?

- What training would Mary have required when she joined the college?

Organising data in a well-structured relational database brings a number of advantages over older, traditional individual file-based systems.

Data independence

The data and the programs using the data are stored separately. Any changes to the structure of a database, for example, adding a field or a table, will not affect any of the programs that access the data. In a file-based system, a minor change in a file structure may require a considerable amount of reprogramming to all the programs that access this file.

Data consistency

When the database is well structured each data item is stored only once however many applications it is used for. There is no danger of an item, such as an employee's address, being updated in one place and not in another. If this happened the data would not be consistent.

No data redundancy

Redundancy occurs when data is duplicated unnecessarily. In a file-based system, the same information may be held on several different files, wasting space and making updating more difficult.

More information available to users

In a database system, all information is stored together centrally. Authorised users have access to all this information. In a file-based system data is held in separate files in different departments, sometimes on incompatible systems.

Ease of use

The DBMS provides easy-to-use queries that enable users to obtain instant answers. In a file-based system a query would have to be specially written by a programmer.

Greater data integrity

It is important that the data stored in a database is maintained so that is as correct as possible. A range of measures can be taken to ensure the integrity of the data stored in a database. Validation checks can be built in to check that only sensible data can be entered into the database. For example, a range check could be set up for the date of birth of a new student to make sure that the student's age is within appropriate limits. Checks, such as parity and checksums, should be used to make sure that stored data has not become corrupted. All these checks were studied in the AS modules.

Greater data security

The DBMS will ensure that only authorised users are allowed access to the data. Different users can have different access privileges, depending on their needs. In a file-based system using a number of files it is difficult to control access. Relational databases provide different methods of database security.

The simplest method is to set a password for opening the database. The password will be encrypted so that it can't be accessed simply by reading the database file. Once a database is open, all the features are available to the user. For a database on a stand-alone computer, setting a password is normally sufficient protection.

A more flexible method of database security is called user-level security, which is similar to the sort of security found on networks. Users must type a username and password when they load the DBMS. The database administrator will allocate users to a group. For example, in Microsoft Access there are two default groups: Admin (administrators) and Users. Additional groups can be defined. Which group a user is in will determine what level of access they have. For example, some users may be able to see some fields, such as name and address, but not others, such as financial details.

User-level security is essential where users can legitimately access some parts of a database but not those parts which contain sensitive data.

Data consistency: a data item will have the same value whatever application program is being used. In a well-structured relational database, this is achieved by storing every data item only once.

Data integrity: the data that is stored in the database is correct.

Data redundancy: data that is duplicated unnecessarily.

Data independence: data and programs are stored separately. Changes to the structure of the data (for example, by the addition of an extra field in a table) do not result in all programs having to be rewritten.

Case Study 2

A company sells many of it goods through door-to-door salespersons. Each seller has customer details stored in a database table. Some of the fields stored in the table are shown in Figure 17.2.

Forename	Surname	Address 1	Address 2	Post Code	Phone	Last visit	Value last sale
Stephen	Hopkins	22 The Copse	Hightown	PL3 4FR	879654	22/05/03	223.45
Susan	Carville	15 High Street	Kenton	PL4 2FF	445565	25/03/03	176.34
Philip	Higgins	253 London Rd	Hightown	PL3 4FT	809745	12/05/03	87.50
Paul	Fryett	1 Maple Lane	Hightown	PL3 6TG	864351	12/05/03	104.00
Mohammed	Hadawi	57 Greenhill Lane	Kenton	PL4 5RT	476765	09/06/03	338.79
Hamish	MacGregor	12 Wickham Way	Kenton	PL4 6TY	879804	17/04/02	2.50

Figure 17.2 Table showing details of customers (held by salespersons)

The central accounts department deals with the billing of customers. They make use of another database, some of the fields of which are shown in Figure 17.3.

Invoice Number	Forename	Surname	Address 1	Address 2	County	Post Code	Value	Amount Outstanding
2003/34	Phillip	Higgins	253 London Rd	Hightown	Berks	PL3 4FT	87.50	87.50
2003/35	Mohammed	Hadawi	57 Greenhill Lane	Kenton	Berks	PL4 5RT	67.00	0.0
2003/189	Mohammed	Hadawi	57 Greenhill Lane	Kenton	Berks	PL4 5RT	338.79	338.79

Figure 17.3 Table of customer accounts (held by accounts department)

Storing data in this way, in two separate databases involves data redundancy as the customer name and address are stored in two different places, leading to wasted space. This can also lead to data inconsistency, for example, if the salesperson is informed of a change of address for Philip Higgins, he or she can make a change to the address field. It is quite possible that he or she forgets to inform the accounts department, so that Philip Higgins' address is not updated on their records. When such an event occurs, and the same data item is stored differently in two different places, data inconsistency occurs.

- The accounts department of an organisation maintains a file that is used every month to produce payments for all employees. The human resources department maintains a personnel file that stores details of all employees. It is updated when new staff join the organisation or when current employees are regraded. What possible data inconsistencies could arise because of how these two files are maintained?

- Consider inconsistencies that could arise when separate files are used by different departments within a hospital.

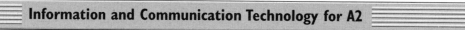
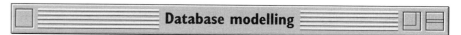

Database modelling

In a complex system it is not a simple task to decide on the structure of the database. The system designer will use a database modeling technique to produce a logical overview, or model, of how the data should be organised. This model is independent of the particular DBMS that is to be used to implement the database. It is vital that the designer takes into account the data needs of all the users of the system and that a clear understanding is formed of how the data is to be used.

It is vital that a formal database modeling system is undertaken in all but the most simple databases. Such modeling ensures that a robust database is produced, that can be extended and altered, and which will not produce data redundancy or inconsistency.

Entity relationship model

One common modeling technique is to produce an entity relationship model.

Entities, relationships and attributes

An entity is an object, person or thing represented in a database. The link between two entities is called a relationship. The information that is held about an entity is called its attributes.

A CUSTOMER is an example of an entity, so is a PRODUCT and an ORDER. Attributes for a CUSTOMER could be Name, Address, Phone Number.

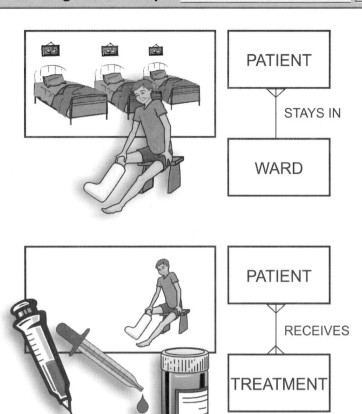

1:1

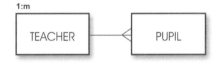

MAN

IS MARRIED TO

WOMAN

Figure 17.4 Examples of relationships

Entity relationships

An **entity relationship (E-R) diagram** is used to show how data (entities) are related to each other. It is made up of entities drawn in rectangles and lines joining the entities that represent their relationships. Each entity is given a unique (singular) name and is written in upper case. The nature of the relationship is written on the line.

1:m

TEACHER ──< PUPIL

Degree of relationship

As well as giving a description of the relationship between two entities, a degree is given which indicated the number of occurrences of the relationship. The degree can be:

One-to-one (1:1)

One occurrence of the first entity is only ever associated with one occurrence of the second.

m:m

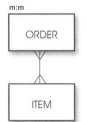

ORDER

ITEM

One-to-many (1:m, 1:∞)

One occurrence of the first entity can be associated with more than one occurrence of the second entity.

Many-to-many (m:m; ∞:∞)

More than one occurrence of the first entity can be associated with many occurrences of the second entity.

Activity 1

Entity relationship diagrams

Draw E-R diagrams for the following pairs of relationships. Make sure that you write you entities in capital letters. Describe each relationship and add the degree.

- ○ pet and vet in a veterinary clinic

- ○ consultant and patient in a hospital

- ○ car and customer in a service garage

- ○ student and hall of residence at a university

- ○ film and customer at a cinema.

The process of entity relationship modeling is carried out by the systems analyst to ensure that all the data needs of the system have been taken into account and the database is correctly set up. It provides a good visual overview of the database structure.

Dealing with many-to-many relationships

As part of your study of relational databases at ICT AS level, you saw how the relationships between tables were made through the use of foreign keys. A foreign key is a field in a table that is the primary key of another table. Thus data can be linked between the two tables.

Figure 17.5 shows how the PET and OWNER tables from a database at a veterinary practice can be linked by the use of a foreign key.

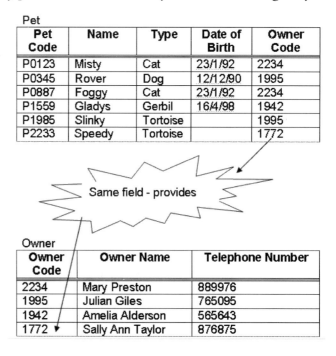

Pet

Pet Code	Name	Type	Date of Birth	Owner Code
P0123	Misty	Cat	23/1/92	2234
P0345	Rover	Dog	12/12/90	1995
P0887	Foggy	Cat	23/1/92	2234
P1559	Gladys	Gerbil	16/4/98	1942
P1985	Slinky	Tortoise		1995
P2233	Speedy	Tortoise		1772

Same field - provides

Owner

Owner Code	Owner Name	Telephone Number
2234	Mary Preston	889976
1995	Julian Giles	765095
1942	Amelia Alderson	565643
1772	Sally Ann Taylor	876875

Figure 17.5 Linking two tables using a foreign key

Unfortunately foreign keys cannot be used directly to make a many-to-many link. In a relational database it is necessary to break up many-to-many relationships by creating an extra entity that will have two one-to-many links.

For example, a company maintains a database of stationery orders made for its employees. Two entities, PRODUCT and SUPPLIER have a many-to-many relationship as each product may be available from more than one supplier and each supplier offers a range of products. To implement this in a relational database, an extra entity must be created, in this case named PRODUCT-SUPPLIER that links the other two entities. The PRODUCT-SUPPLIER table would contain the primary key fields of both the PRODUCT and the SUPPLIER tables as well as extra fields such as Price (see Figure 17.6).

Database normalisation

An alternative way of ensuring that the database is correctly set up to minimise data duplication and without any many-to-many relationships is called database normalisation.

> Normalisation is a process of breaking down complex data structures into simpler forms.

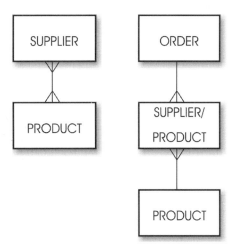

Figure 17.6 Implementing many-to-many relationships using a relational database

The process is made up of a number of defined stages.

Before normalising, write out all the attributes required by the system.

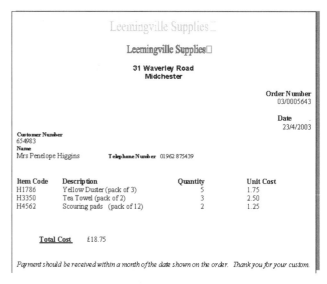

Figure 17.7 Order form showing attributes required to be stored in database

Referring to the order form shown in Figure 17.7, and listing all the attributes:

Order Number
Date
Customer Number
Customer Surname
Customer Forename
Customer Title
Phone Number
Item Code ⎫
Description ⎬ There can be any number (minimum 1) of these fields in any
Quantity ⎪ order. They are called repeated fields. For example, for one
Unit Cost ⎭ order number 12376 there will be many of these values.
Total Cost

This data structure is complex, as it contains a number of repeated fields – one order can contain a number of these fields (Item code, Description, Quantity and Unit Cost). The process of normalisation will transform this data structure into a number of simple tables, linked through the use of foreign keys.

These can be written in **Zero Normal Form** or (**0NF**) in standard notation.

Standard notation for listing fields in a table

- The table name is written in UPPER CASE letters.
- The table name is a singular noun – VIDEO not VIDEOS.
- Fields (attributes) are written in parentheses after the table name.
- Primary key field(s) are underlined.
- Repeated fields have a line over them.

ORDER (<u>Order Number</u>, Date, <u>Customer Number</u>, <u>Surname</u>, <u>Forename</u>, <u>Title</u>, <u>Phone Number</u>, <u>Item Code</u>, <u>Description</u>, <u>Quantity</u>, <u>Unit Cost</u>, Total Cost)

Order Number has been chosen as the primary key as it is a unique number for each order. A line is drawn over the four fields to indicate repeated fields. There can be many entries for these fields in one order.

First Normal Form (**1NF**) is the next stage. 1NF occurs only when there are repeated fields in the 0NF. In the Order example, the fields Item Code, Description, Quantity and Unit Cost are repeated. These fields are removed from ORDER and a new table is created. This will be called ITEMORDER as it consists of the details of the order for one item. The two tables can be listed:

ORDER (<u>Order Number</u>, Date, Customer Number, Surname, Forename, Title, Phone Number, Total Cost)

ITEMORDER (<u>Order Number</u>, <u>Item Code</u>, Description, Quantity, Unit Cost)

Note that the key field Order Number has been copied to ITEMORDER. If this were not done, there would be no link between the items ordered and the main order. However, Order Number by itself is not correct as a primary key for ITEMORDER as there may well be many entries in ITEMORDER for the same order. The **compound key** of the two fields Order Number and Item Code together form the primary key for this table.

Second Normal Form (**2NF**) exists only if 1NF produces a table with a compound key. All attributes in this table should be examined to see if they are dependent upon just one part of the compound or composite key. Examining the table ITEMORDER we find:

- *Order Number* is part of the key.

- *Item Code* is part of the key.

- *Description* is always the same for a given Item Code, regardless of Order Number so it is dependent on Item Code.

- *Unit Cost* is always the same for a given Item Code, regardless of Order Number so it is dependent on Item Code.

- *Quantity* relates to the Item Code but will vary for different orders – thus it is dependent on <u>both</u> Order Number and Item Code.

We can create a table, ITEM, that holds all data about a particular item. The attribute Item Code is also left in the ITEMORDER table to provide a link.

ORDER (<u>Order Number</u>, Date, Customer Number, Surname, Forename, Title, Phone Number, Total Cost)

ITEMORDER (<u>Order Number</u>, <u>Item Code</u>, Quantity)

ITEM (<u>Item Code</u>, Description, Unit Cost)

Third Normal Form (3NF) is a 'tidying up' stage where all tables are examined for dependencies (links between attributes). In other words, in 3NF no non-key field should be a fact about another non-key field. It is exactly the process as that carried out for 2NF except that it is carried out for tables without a compound key.

Such links can be found in the ORDER table where Customer Number, Surname, Forename, Title and Phone Number are all linked. Surname, Forename, Title and Phone Number can be said to be dependent on Customer Number. These attributes can be taken out to form a new table – CUSTOMER. Once again, Customer Number is also left in order to provide a link.

The final design of tables is as follows:

ORDER (<u>Order Number</u>, Date, Customer Number, Total Cost)

CUSTOMER (<u>Customer Number</u>, Surname, Forename, Title, Phone Number)

ITEMORDER (<u>Order Number</u>, <u>Item Code</u>, Quantity)

ITEM (<u>Item Code</u>, Description, Unit Cost)

The database can now be created. The four tables described above should be created with the fields underlined set as key fields. The relationships shown in the E-R diagram should be made between the tables. Note that some data duplication remains, but this is necessary redundancy as the fields are used to create links.

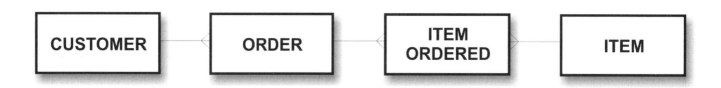

Figure 17.8 Entity relationship diagram for Order database

Activity 2

Data normalisation

For each of the following, write out the attributes in standard notation. Normalise, showing first, second and third normal form. Then draw an entity relationship diagram.

1 A college library system: each record contains data about students and the books they have borrowed.

Student Num	Name	Address	Tutor Group	Tutor	Book#	Title	ISBN	Return Date
3124	Mary Smith	32 Hill Street Bluedale	D22	H Jones	2234	PCs for Fun	1 877556122	13-6-03
3124	Mary Smith	32 Hill Street Bluedale	D22	H Jones	3356	Geography is good for You	1 655536327	21-6-03
5464	John Bloggs	27 Mill Road Grenham	D23	J Pell	5883	Biology for Brilliance	1 223334554	18-6-03
3369	Peter Kelly	119 Leigh Hill Grenham	D22	H Jones	4343	French for Frivolity	2 346798443	16-7-03
3369	Peter Kelly	119 Leigh Hill Grenham	D22	H Jones	2112	History is Hilarious	3 444576661	27-6-03
7765	Gary Tolan	The Heights, Blogdale	D44	M Kelly	3412	Sociology for Slackers	4 558787432	14-6-03

2 Scouting goods suppliers: each record contains data about different scouting goods and the available suppliers, together with the price charged.

Product#	Description	Stock level	Supplier num	Supplier name	Phone	Selling Price
78780098	Large woggle	67	3345	Wogglicity	0131-338675	1.25
78780098	Large woggle	67	5678	Best Woggles	0181-777-8654	1.39
78780098	Large woggle	67	1123	Scouting Bits	01962-874532	1.09
65654333	Cub scarf: green	33	1123	Scouting Bits	01962-874532	4.99
78012544	Cub scarf: red	12	1123	Scouting Bits	01962-874532	4.99
35422123	4 man tent	1	1123	Scouting Bits	01962-874532	123.75
			4659	Tent city	0171-765-0234	101.99

continued...

Activity 2 (continued)

3 Employee training records: each record contains employee details and the courses they have attended.

Employee#	Name	Dept Code	Department	Course	Description	Venue Code	Venue	Date
321-93	Hilary Barr	HR	Human Resources	G1	Getting on with people	IH	In house	23-5-94
566-92	Penny Blyth	F	Finance	EX-A	Advanced Excel	PT	Pembly Tech	15-6-95
566-92	Penny Blyth	F	Finance	M2	Financial Modelling	HH	Highham	02-11-96
566-92	Penny Blyth	F	Finance	AP2	Appraisal level 2	IH	In house	1-2-97
321-92	Neil Flynn	HR	Human Resources	G1	Getting on with people	IH	In house	23-5-94
321-92	Neil Flynn	HR	Human Resources	AP2	Appraisal level 2	IH	In house	1-2-97

4 Fine arts sales: each record contains details of a work of art being sold in auction.

Catalogue#	Title	Painter	Seller Code	Name	Phone	Reserve	Medium Code	Medium
M0134	Hill Sheep	Conrad Dale	AT1	Andy Tomkins	0151-878787	£250	O	Oil
P9009	Abstract	Sally Saeter	CD4	Colin Drake	0121-844444	£1200	I	Bronze
M9843	Abstract	Conrad Dale	PT1	Primrose Tilly	877666	£700	O	Oil
G6677	Tempest	Anonymous	CD4	Colin Drake	0121-844444	£12000	W	Water colour

Activity 3

For the document shown in Figure 17.9 carry out the following tasks:

- List the data fields in 0NF using standard notation.

- Underline the key field and draw a line over all repeating fields.

- Work through the process of normalisation, showing the data in first, second and third normal forms.

continued...

Activity 3 *continued*

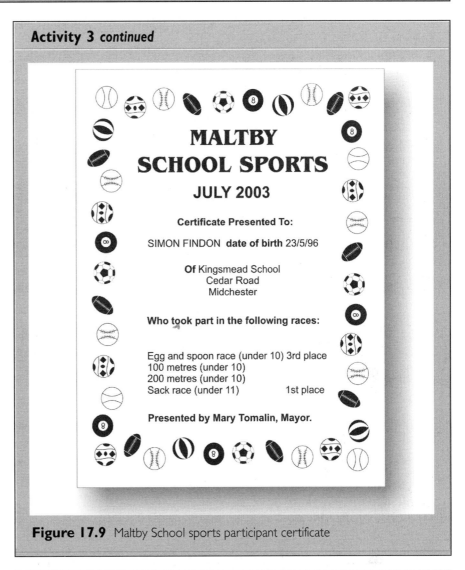

Figure 17.9 Maltby School sports participant certificate

Client/server database

A client/server database is a multi-user database used over a network that has a file server computer that stores all the data for the database. This computer is dedicated to its role as server and would have a fast processor, a large amount of RAM and would access a high capacity storage device.

Users of the database would use less powerful computers (called clients). The querying of the database would be carried out on the client PC and the request for data would be sent to the server. The search of the database would be carried out by the server. Any records selected, that is, those that matched the search criteria sent from the client, would then be sent back to the client for any local processing.

Advantages of a client/server database over non-client/server database

- A large database is an expensive resource. By making it available to a wider user base it will be used more cost effectively.

- As all the main processing is done by the server, the client workstations do not need to be so powerful and are therefore, being of a lesser specification, cheaper to buy.

- Having the data stored only in one place, on the server, rather than keeping copies on different user workstations means that consistency of data is maintained.

- Communication between client and server is minimal as only requests for data and the results of searches are communicated rather than the entire database. Department specific report formats can be held on the appropriate client workstation so that users can produce the required information in the most appropriate format.

- The centralisation of the database allows for a greater control over the data which is less likely to be accessed by the wrong people.

- Backup can be carried out centrally.

Case Study 3

Holmes

Holmes, a national incident management application, is a client/server system. It is used by police officers to organise, process and cross-refer data from big operations.

Any one of 450 terminals can be used to access the data. The system also allows a remote incident room to be set up, from which the Holmes application can be dialed up using a wide area network. Network traffic is kept to a minimum as processing is kept on the central server.

- What are the advantages to the police service of using a client/server system for the Holmes system?

Summary

- A **Database Management System (DBMS)** is software that accesses data in a database.

- The functions of a DBMS are:
  - database definition
  - data storage, retrieval and update
  - creation and maintenance of the data dictionary
  - managing the facilities for sharing the database
  - backup and recovery
  - security.

- A **database administrator (DBA)** is the person in an organisation who is responsible for the structure and control of the data in the organisation's database.

- A DBA's tasks include:
  - designing the database
  - making any changes requested by users
  - monitoring the performance of the database
  - maintaining a data dictionary
  - dealing with queries for the user
  - providing help and training for users
  - allocating passwords and access privileges
  - managing backup procedures for the database.

- **Data consistency**: a data item will have the same value whatever application program is being used. In a well-structured relational database, this is achieved by storing every data item only once.

- **Data integrity**: the data that is stored in the database is correct.

- **Data redundancy**: data that is duplicated unnecessarily.

- **Data independence**: data and programs are stored separately. Changes to the structure of the data (for example, by the addition of an extra field in a table) do not result in all programs having to be rewritten.

- An **entity** is an object, person or thing represented in a database. The information that is held about an entity is called its **attributes**.

- An **entity relationship (E-R) diagram** is used to show how entities are related to each other.

- The **degree** of a relationship can be one-to-one (1:1), one-to-many (1:m, 1:∞) or many-to-many (m:m; ∞:∞).

- **Normalisation** is a process of breaking down complex data structures into simpler forms. It consists of three stages: first, second and third normal form, each of which produces a form that is simpler than the previous one. Third normal form will consist of a number of simple tables, linked through the use of foreign keys.

- A **client/server** database is a multi-user database used over a network that has a file server computer that stores all the data for the database.

Database management concepts questions

1. For each of the following entities, draw an entity relationship diagram to show the relationship(s) between the given entities (choose from one-to-one, many-to-one, one-to-many or many-to-many).
- Context: Doctor's surgery
  GP   Patient   Medical Record
- Context: Family
  Child   Mother
- Context: Car hire company
  Hire Car   Customer
- Context: Library
  Borrower   Library Book
- Context: Football team
  Footballer   Team   League
- Context: School
  Teacher   Pupil   Tutor
- Context: Cruise holidays
  Passenger   Boat   Cruise   Port
- Context: Newspaper delivery round
  Newspaper   Round   Customer   Deliverer

2. A college library uses a relational database management system to operate a membership and loans system. Staff and students can borrow as many books as they wish at any given time.

a) Name three database tables that you would expect to find in this system. In each case, identify the columns and keys required to enable this system to be maintained with minimum redundancy. *(6)*

b) Draw an entity relationship diagram to show the links between the database tables named in part (a). *(3)*

c) Describe the capabilities of the relational database management system that might be used to identify and output details of overdue loans. *(6)*

NEAB 1997 Paper 2

3. A company sports centre use a database management system to operate a membership and fixture system. Normally members register for at least three sports, although they can play any of the sports offered by the centre. Fixtures against many other organisations are arranged in a wide range of sports involving a large number of teams.

a) Name three database files you would expect to find in this system. *(3)*

b) For each of the database files you have named, list the fields required to enable this system to be maintained with minimum redundancy. *(6)*

c) Draw a diagram to show the relationship between the database files named in part (a). *(3)*

Customer code	Customer name	Comp name	Town	Car reg	Make	Model	Lease date	Return date
017312	Johnson, M	CDR	Stoke	N877THJ	Peugeot	406	010895	310796
017312	Johnson, M	CDR	Stoke	P981ESD	Peugeot	406	010896	
013442	Brazil, P	CDR	Stoke	P982ESD	Peugeot	406	010896	
009865	Smith, L	Cooks	Derby	N723KLJ	Volvo	440	010895	310796
016613	Brooks, M	AVP	Crewe	N623TYU	Ford	Mondeo	010196	311296
016613	Brooks, M	AVP	Crewe	P109TYT	Rover	214	010197	

4. A company makes use of a computerised flat file information storage and retrieval system. The company is experiencing problems due to the use of this flat file system.

a) Describe three benefits that the company would gain by using a relational database as opposed to a flat file system. *(6)*

b) The company currently has three files in use; customer, stock and orders. During conversion to a relational database system these files would need to be normalised. Explain clearly what you understand by the term normalisation. *(2)*

c) Examples from the three files are shown below. Normalise these files explaining any assumptions or additions you make to the files. *(5)*

5. A car leasing company stores information about cars and who they have been leased to. Part of the CUSTOMER table is given on the previous page:

a) Suggest why this way of storing data is not efficient. *(2)*

b) Suggest three tables which could be used in a relational database to store this data more efficiently. *(3)*

c) Draw diagrams showing an entity relationship and how the tables are related. *(3)*

6. The secretary of a local tennis club is constructing a database to store data on members' personal details and records of attendance. He has been told that a relational database management system can assist him. Having found an article on relational database construction, he does not understand some of the terminology it contains. He asks you for advice.

a) Explain the following terms:
   i) normalisation
   ii) data independence
   iii) data consistency
   iv) data integrity. *(8)*

b) The secretary constructs his database structure and asks you to examine his work before he enters any data. You notice that he has not included any validation.
   With the aid of an example, explain why data validation is important. *(3)*

c) Give three reasons why he should consult with other members of the tennis club committee before finalising the design of the database system. *(3)*

7. As an ICT manager in a medium-sized company, you have been asked to create a job specification for a database administrator.

a) Describe three responsibilities you would include in this specification. *(6)*

b) The database that this person will be in charge of is a client/server database. Describe two advantages of using this type of database over a non-client/server database. *(4)*

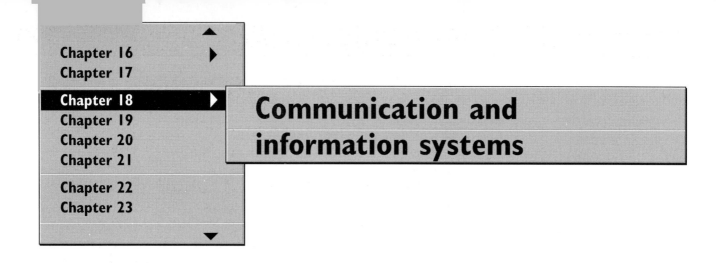
Communication and information systems

Computer networks play an ever-increasing role in modern communications. It is common to find networks used in schools and colleges, doctors' and dentists' surgeries, and shops and offices of all kinds.

There are two types of network: wide area networks (WAN) and local area networks (LAN) although a network may be a mixture of both.

Public WANs such as the Internet can be accessed legally by anyone, either free or on payment of a fee. Private networks have restricted access, for example only to employees of a company.

Local Area Networks (LAN)

A LAN is a collection of computers and peripherals that is usually connected together by cables. It is normally located in one building or site. At its simplest, a LAN consists of a few computers sharing some resources. The computers connected to the network in this way are called workstations or terminals. Wireless workstations connected to the network by radio waves are becoming increasingly more common.

A LAN will usually have one or more **file servers** – powerful, high performance computers with large disk capacity. Data is stored on the server and can be accessed from any terminal. If a printer is to be shared by all workstations, then a printer server is required: a high performance computer that manages the allocation of the printer to different jobs and maintains a queue of waiting jobs. A LAN may have several different printers for different purposes, for example an A4 laser printer for documents, a dot matrix for draft documents and an A3 laser for diagrams.

On larger sites it is common to have more than one LAN linked together with bridges.

Wide Area Networks (WAN)

A WAN is a collection of computers spread over a large geographical area, which can be as small as a few miles or as large as the whole world. Communication between computers is made in a variety of ways including microwave link, satellite link, dedicated cables or the telephone network. The telephone link can either be made through the public dial-up lines where the message is routed alongside others, or through a leased line which provides a permanent connection. Leased lines are practical when the volume of data being sent is large and communication is frequent.

Data sent between two computers on a global network might travel through a number of different communications media. The route is created via switching computers that create the necessary path from source to destination computers.

The Internet

The Internet, a shortening of 'international networks', is more than a WAN. It is a network of networks. The Internet backbone is a high-speed network provided by telecommunications companies. The Internet uses a wide range of different telecommunication media and provides the facility to exchange information on a global scale. Each network that is connected into the Internet can be located anywhere in the world, can be of any size and can be based on any hardware platform. All of this is hidden from a user of the Internet.

The World Wide Web (WWW)

The Internet is the network structure that supports the transfer of information in the World Wide Web (WWW or Web). The World Wide Web is a collection of information held on the Internet in multimedia form. This information is stored in the form of web pages on computer locations called websites. These pages can contain text, graphics, sound or video clips. Organisations and individuals can create websites each of which can contain many pages. These need to be organised into a structure that makes them easy to access by a visitor to the site. Web clients and web servers communicate with each other using Hypertext Transfer Protocol (HTTP). Web pages are usually prepared using Hypertext Markup Language (HTML). There are a range of software tools available, such as Dreamweaver, that enable the relatively easy creation of web pages and sites.

Browser software and search engines, studied in the ICT AS level course, allow a user to locate websites and pages.

Ways in which a network can improve communication and productivity within an organisation

- **E-mail** can increase the speed of communication by replacing paper messages whilst avoiding the constant interruption that can result from the use of the telephone.

- **Video conferencing** can reduce the time and cost of travel for meetings, bringing together participants from different locations.

- An **intranet** allows information to be shared throughout an organisation without the need for circulating, filing and retrieving physical documents.

- **Work groups** allow employees to share documents, diaries and other computer files.

- **Telecommuting** allows personnel to work at home thus reducing office overheads and absence due to family circumstances.

- The **Internet** provides all the facilities of the World Wide Web and opens up the opportunities of e-commerce.

- **Electronic data interchange (EDI)** allows one organisation to transfer electronic data from their computer system to that of another organisation thus removing the need for paper transactions.

- A retail organisation can use **point of sale (POS)** terminals with **electronic funds transfer (EFT)**.

- A **network** allows stock control to be managed in real time. When goods are sold, via a POS terminal, the level of stock can automatically be decreased. Other computers on the network can be provided with up-to-date stock levels.

Internet infrastructure

If an individual user is part of a network, for instance, at school or in the workplace, access to the Internet is likely to be made through a permanent connection between the network and the Internet. If a user is accessing the Internet from a stand-alone computer, a link will be made through an Internet Service Provider (ISP) such as Freeserve or AOL, which in turn is connected to the Internet.

The user links to their ISP's computer using a standard telephone line and a modem, ISDN line or broadband fibre optic cable.

For a network to connect successfully to the Internet it must be able to communicate with it. This requires a set of protocols that are conformed to by all, such as standards for technical details, identification of computers and naming of data files (see Chapter 23 for details of standards and protocols used to support the World Wide Web).

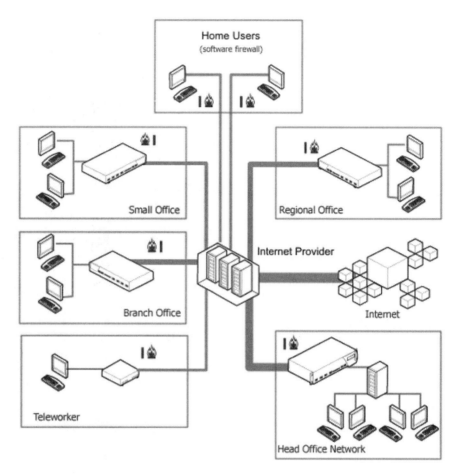

Figure18.1 Ways of connecting to the Internet

When data is to be sent over the Internet it is broken down into small packets of data. Each packet or message is sent individually and can take a different route from source computer to destination computer. When all the packets have reached their destination they need to be reassembled into their original order, as some packets might have 'overtaken' others and so arrived out of order at the destination.

The job of ensuring that data is sent from source to its correct destination via the Internet is carried out by **routers**, dedicated devices that are located around the world. When a router receives a message it checks the destination address and sends it either to the appropriate computer if it is directly linked or to another router on route to the destination. The same process is carried out by every router until the message reaches the destination computer. The best route at any point will be chosen, so if certain links are down or congested, the message can be sent via a different route. Before sending a packet on, the router will check that the packet it has received has been transmitted correctly from the previous point. Integrity checks such as parity, studied at AS, may have detected that data has been corrupted. If this is so, the router will need to request that the packet is sent again.

Each computer connected to the Internet has a unique address, a number known as an **Internet Protocol (IP) address**. This can be

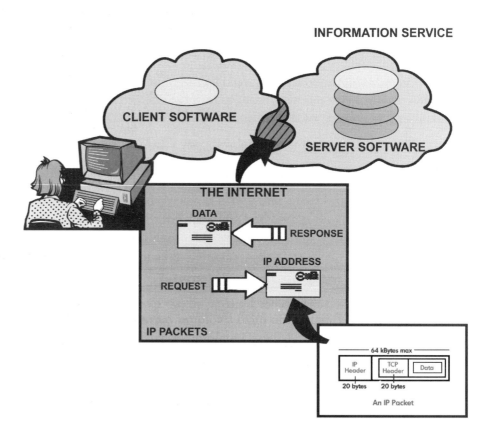

INFORMATION SERVICE

CLIENT SOFTWARE

SERVER SOFTWARE

THE INTERNET

DATA

RESPONSE

IP ADDRESS

REQUEST

IP PACKETS

64 kBytes max

IP Header 20 bytes | TCP Header 20 bytes | Data

An IP Packet

Figure 18.2 Packets of data transferred via the Internet

converted into a **domain name** which is easier to remember and use than an IP address. www.hodder.co.uk is an example of a domain name. Domain names have to be applied for and once allocated they are stored using the Domain Name System (DNS). The DNS is the way that Internet domain names are located and translated. Maintaining a central list of domain names and the corresponding IP addresses would not be practical. The domain name system is a global network of servers that translate host names, such as www.hodder.co.uk, into the IP addresses. The DNS server that is located close to a user's access provider will map the domain name to an IP address for forwarding them to other servers in the Internet.

Applications of communication and information systems

Hundreds of thousands of organisations throughout the world use networks as part of their every day business. The use of the network for most has become an essential tool and they are almost totally dependent on the network and the information it provides.

Computers in all branches of Sainsbury's supermarket chain are linked to computers in the company's distribution warehouses and its head office. Sales information is used in the warehouse to establish order levels for each store. The performance of each store can be monitored centrally. Each store has its own LAN, linking POS terminals to central servers. Each LAN is linked to a nationwide WAN.

Trafficmaster is an organisation that provides traffic information to road users and motoring organisations. They have a WAN linking 7500 sensors located in sites on motorways and trunk roads in Britain. The sensors detect traffic speeds and so the information service can warn motorists of problems ahead. Information can be sent to motorists via radio, telephone or an in-car receiver.

Case Study 1

A college LAN

A sixth-form college uses a computer network throughout its site for curriculum and administrative use.

Since the college purchased its first ten IBM PCs in 1990, the network has grown in size and complexity. It now reaches all the teaching and administration areas; 18 buildings in all. Buildings are linked with fibre optic cables. There are over 20 file servers for curriculum, administrative, intranet, e-mail, backup and other uses.

About 500 Pentium PCs running Windows 2000 are now connected to the network and this, along with the increasing size of applications and data files, means that the IT team is always trying to increase the performance. Configuring the whole college network as one segment where every packet transmitted by a computer is repeated to every other computer would lead to a very high rate of collisions and unacceptably poor performance.

Switches are used to segment the network so that each department has its own server and so reduce traffic. All the computers on the network have access to the Internet via a firewall, router and leased line to the local university and from there to JANET (the Joint Academic Network).

○ List the similarities and differences between the network described and that in place in your school or college.

Case Study 2

The Daily Mirror

Computers are involved in every stage of the production of The Daily Mirror. The main editorial work is carried out at head office which is located at Canary Wharf. Printing takes place in four locations around the country: at Watford, Oldham, Glasgow and Belfast. Editors work at Anderton Quay in Glasgow on a sister paper, The Daily Record. These six locations are linked by a WAN.

Watford also holds The Mirror's picture library. Currently, between 500,000 and 600,000 photographs have been scanned in and held in digital form on disk. These images are available to editors for the inclusion in articles as appropriate and are catalogued according to subject.

At Canary Wharf, a LAN links the Apple Macintosh computers used by journalists and editors. All articles are written using Microsoft Word, pages are built using the publishing package Quark Express and art work is done using Adobe Photoshop. Internal e-mail is implemented using Lotus Notes.

The networks are supported by 21 servers at Canary Wharf and six at Glasgow. Backups are done at night by copying across vital files to a different location.

○ Explain, in your own words, why a combination of LANs linked via a WAN are vital for the successful running of a newspaper publisher.

The London Stock Exchange is over 200 years old but started screen-based trading in 1986 replacing face-to-face trading between dealers on the stock market floor. In 1997 a fully electronic, automated trading system was introduced. Today, a fast, secure, reliable network is essential for trading stocks and shares.

Distributed systems

A distributed system is a system where processing is carried out by sharing tasks between physically separated computers on a network. A distributed system will consist of a network of connected computers which can share resources. One computer may store customer data while another stores product data. Alternatively, data could be distributed between different geographical regions within an organisation. The system allows the data on one computer to be accessed from any other computer and combined in appropriate ways. Distribution should not be obvious to the user and the system should appear to be operating at the local machine.

In the early days of computing, data processing took place in a central mainframe computer. Network stations were purely dumb terminals with no processing power linked to the mainframe. As computers have increased in power but decreased in price, it has become more common for the processing to be performed at a local network station rather than by the central mainframe. This is **distributed processing**.

Distributed processing means data can be processed locally, faster and without continually sending data to and from the central computer. Furthermore processing capacity is spread around the organisation, which allows the work of one branch to be covered by another in case of breakdown.

Most large international organisations will use distributed systems. A company based in the USA selling products online might store the product data in the USA while keeping all client-based data in the local country. It would not be possible to store client data from the European Union in the USA as this would contravene data protection legislation.

A large chain of public houses would use a distributed system. Details of all transactions would be held locally and links made with the head office via a WAN at the end of the day or week to transfer sales details and download any new pricing or product information.

Distributed control

When data was processed centrally, control was firmly in the hands of the data processing department. They could decide in which order work was done and set their own priorities.

With distributed systems, local branches or departments can access the data that they need for themselves given that they have the appropriate access rights. A distributed system can allow the management of a local division of an organisation to set their own priorities and have greater autonomy. The computer at the head office of an organisation would not need to have access to day-to-day information as all operational, and much tactical, decision making would be made locally.

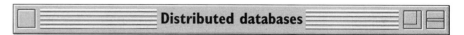

Distributed databases

A distributed database is a collection of different interrelated databases distributed over a network. Some computers on the network each hold part of the data and cooperate in making it available to the user. If the data required is not available on a particular computer, it is able to communicate with other computers in the network so that the data can be obtained. Each computer will usually keep a separate copy of frequently used data to reduce unnecessary network traffic. Distributed database management software manages the distributed database and makes it appear to the user to be a single database.

An example of a distributed database is the Internet Domain Name System (DNS). Details of hostnames and their Internet address are stored in several databases on several computers.

A hotel chain might use distributed databases to store details of reservations. Each hotel stores its own reservations on a local computer. However because all the hotel computers are networked and a distributed database is used, it is possible for hotel staff to see reservations at other hotels and for company managers to monitor reservations throughout the company.

Because the database is distributed, different users can access it without interfering with one another. However, the DBMS must periodically synchronise the scattered databases to make sure that they all have consistent data.

A distributed database can either be online at the host computer in a central location but also available to remote locations, have part of the database at the host computer duplicated and placed in a remote computer, or have copies of the entire database and DBMS at each remote location.

Advantages of distributed databases

The use of a distributed database brings many advantages to an organisation.

- The use of a distributed database can allow local control of processing local data. For example, in a chain of supermarkets, different pricing structures can be used in different shops to reflect local demand.

- As data that is used locally can be stored locally, network traffic is kept to a minimum, this provides faster response times.

- The effect of a breakdown is reduced as distributed processing provides the opportunity of replicating data in more than one location. If failure causes data to be lost at one site an up-to-date copy will immediately be available at another site.

- The use of a distributed database allows data to be shared by different users or branches of the same organisation or even different organisations. The data from one location can be available at another even though the hardware platform or operating system may be different.

- New locations can be added to the database without requiring a complete rewriting of the entire database.

> **Limitations of distributed databases** >

Of course, there are a number of issues that need to be considered before a decision is made to install a distributed database.

- A distributed system, which hides its distributed nature from the end-user, is more complex than a centralised system. This means that such a system is much more expensive to install and maintain.

- The need to transfer data from one location to another increases the security risks to the data. Techniques such as data encryption will need to be used to ensure that data is kept secure.

- As all the data is not stored in one location, if one station were to fail with inadequate backup, other locations might suffer a loss of data.

- If some data is stored and updated in more than one place, there is an increased chance of data inconsistency (see Chapter 17). Procedures will need to be put in place to ensure that the chances of data inconsistency are minimised.

Case Study 3

Home worker

Paul lives in a beautiful, sleepy village in the heart of the Cotswolds where life seems to have been untouched by the computer age. This does not appear to be the most promising place for an IT professional to live.

However, from the converted stables at the bottom of his garden, Paul runs a business which relies on the latest technology. He designs and hosts websites and builds intranets for clients as well as providing a range of other services.

For this work Paul has a high specification server with two client workstations. He has had a leased line installed to provide fast Internet access for both his own and his clients' use. As well as hosting websites (clients rent space on his server), he designs pages using Microsoft FrontPage. He trialled the beta version of FrontPage 98 on one computer, whilst running FrontPage 97 on the other. This provided security in case of bugs arising on the new software which could lead to failure.

continued...

Case Study 3 *continued*

Paul has developed online forms and credit card purchasing facilities for clients. Online credit card clearance can be provided by banks who then pass confirmation of the transaction to the vendor thus making it unnecessary for the vendor to be sent credit card details. This reduces the risk of fraud for the purchaser.

Paul has been working from home for three years now and he never intends to work in a conventional office again!

○ Explain what is meant by the term leased line.

○ What alternatives would Paul have had to having a leased line installed?

○ Why do you think he chose to have a leased line?

○ Describe a suitable backup strategy for Paul.

Summary

○ Local and wide area networks play an expanding role in today's businesses with many companies dependent on their networks for communication.

○ The Internet is the network structure that supports the transfer of information in the World Wide Web.

○ The World Wide Web is a collection of information held on the Internet in multimedia form.

○ The Internet requires an extensive infrastructure of high specification computers and links to support its use.
  ○ **Routers** ensure that data is sent from source to correct destination.
  ○ Data is transferred in **packets** of predetermined size. Each packet can be sent via a different route.

○ Each computer connected to the Internet has a unique address, its **Internet Protocol (IP) address**. This can be converted into a **domain name** such as www.hodder.co.uk.

○ A **distributed system** is a system where processing is carried out by the sharing of tasks between physically separated computers on a network.
  ○ Distributed systems allow processing to be done on local stations rather than centrally.
  ○ Distributed databases are different databases stored at different locations but linked together to appear to be one database.

Communication and information systems questions

1. Distributed systems are very common today.
   a) Define the term distributed database. *(2)*
   b) Describe the problems that can arise due to data being distributed. *(4)*

2. Describe the role of an Internet Service Provider. *(4)*

3. A new home computer user has just registered with an Internet Service Provider to gain access to the Internet. Explain what hardware the Internet Service Provider has to have to be able to offer this service.

4. Describe one LAN and one WAN that you have used. *(4)*

5. Wireless computing is expanding very quickly. Use the Internet to investigate information on wireless networks. Include details such as the hardware required, its range and speed of access. *(8)*

6. A company is considering using a distributed database. Explain to them four reasons why this might not be a good idea. *(4)*

7. A car-hire company has different offices across Europe. Customers can hire a vehicle from one office and return it to any other office. All the offices have network access to the company's internal distributed information system. The network also gives staff access to public local and wide area information systems.
Discuss this system. Particular attention should be given to:
   • the nature and significance of a distributed information system
   • the types of information systems that you would expect to be available on such a network
   • the data that should be distributed on this system
   • the advantages and disadvantages of distributing the data across the network. *(20)*

   AQA June 2000 Paper 5

8. Describe **one** advantage and **one** limitation of distributed database systems. *(4)*

   AQA June 2001 Paper 5

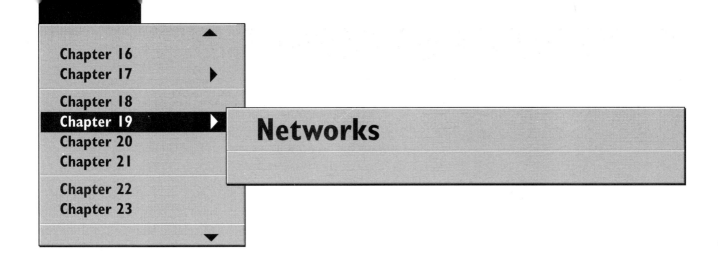

Networks

A network exists when two or more computers are connected to each other by cable, over telephone lines, or by wireless communication. When connected to a network, users can share resources on their computer, such as data files, software, printers and modems.

However networks present a greater security risk than stand-alone machines.

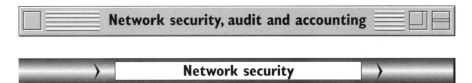

Network security, audit and accounting

Network security

When an individual uses a stand-alone computer, ensuring data is secure is a relatively simple matter. Use of a keyboard and disk lock can prevent other people from using the computer and accessing files. The use of a screen saver with a password can prevent casual prying when the user is away from their desk.

When a computer is part of a network, then security is more complex. The larger the number of workstations and the larger the number of users, the greater the risk of abuse, particularly if the network can be accessed remotely, that is, from a computer off-site.

Since a network is used by most/all the employees of a company then it will contain all the data and information that the company owns. This means that illegal access to the network can be catastrophic for a company.

Security on a network is only as a good as the weakest link, which is normally the staff. A system can only be truly secure if there is a corporate policy on security, which needs to have the appropriate level of support from senior management and an appropriate disciplinary procedure to back it up.

Viruses and illegal software are also easier to spread over a network, especially if all the machines have their floppy disk drives active and the employees all have access to the Internet and e-mail.

Physical controls can be used that limit access to the equipment. Locks on doors and on the equipment as well as keypad access to more sensitive areas, will restrict access to authorised personnel only.

Software can be used to restrict access to specific resources in a system. Such access could be to hardware, for example, only members of the accounts department could be given access rights to print to the printer in their office. Another form of access restriction could be to a specific area of the hard drive. Such access could be granted in different ways: some groups could be allowed to read, others to read and modify, whilst others to read/write/delete and modify.

Network users normally are allocated a unique username protected by a password. This allows a directory to be allocated to each user so that users cannot access each other's files.

Data transferred on a network is vulnerable to misuse. The risk of unauthorised access increases when data is transferred over a WAN using public communication links. Having a password is not enough to prevent unauthorised access.

Staff using networks should follow a number of simple procedures to help avoid breaches of network security, such as:

- Only acceptable passwords should be used. Obvious choices such as SECRET, COMPUTER or the user's name should be avoided. Ideally, the password should consist of a mixture of letters and numbers and should not spell out a meaningful word. The system can be set up so that only certain types of passwords can be used, for example, a minimum length can be specified and that the password contains letters and numbers.

- A password should always be kept secret. It should never be shared with others nor left written down on paper, or even worse, on a Post-it note attached to the computer screen!

- A password should be changed frequently. Many systems are set up to require that a user changes their password on a regular basis, perhaps every month. Usually, the user is given a number (typically three) of log in attempts to access the system by entering the correct password. If all three attempts fail then the network manager is alerted and the user account is disabled for a period of time.

- Logged on computers should not be left unattended without the use of keyboard locks or password protection. The network may also be set up so that a user may be able to log on to only one workstation at a time.

Protecting networks against illegal access through a WAN

Nearly every company will be subject to some illegal attempt to gain access to their computer material. As well as using passwords and sensible procedures, a number of other measures can be taken to reduce the risk.

The danger of break-in can be guarded against by the use of a **firewall**. A firewall is a system placed between an internal network and a public network which ensures that all traffic passing from the inside to the outside, or the outside to the inside, must pass through it. Only traffic which is authorised by the organisation's security policy is allowed to pass. A firewall is designed to protect a safe and trusted system (the internal network) from a risky and untrusted system (the public network). The firewall software will stop access to unauthorised websites or sites containing certain specified key words, stop e-mails and incoming data from certain specified sites and scan incoming data for viruses.

Impostor hackers sometimes use 'packet sniffer' programs to intercept identification numbers and passwords, which they then store for later use. Systems can be designed to prevent the use of such programs.

A widely-used way of countering the effectiveness of sniffer programs is the use of **data encryption**. This is the process of 'scrambling' or coding data so that it can only be recovered by people authorised to see it. It is used when data is transmitted or stored to ensure that the data does not fall into the wrong hands. When the data is to be used, it needs to be 'unscrambled' or decoded using a key that only the appropriate people possess. The use of a callback modem can also increase security.

Activity I

Problems with a virus

The publicity officer of a university was recently caused considerable inconvenience by a virus. Over a period of several weeks, she had put together the proofs of the prospectus for postgraduate courses. This involved considerable effort as entries had to be gathered from a range of contributors in different departments. A number of edits were made and the final versions were recalled from disk and visually checked on the screen with great care. The files were copied to floppy disk and transferred to the printers, who were located on the other side of town, by motorcycle courier. When the files were loaded into the computer at the printers they no longer incorporated the latest edits. The disks were returned. This process was repeated several times as the final deadline got closer and closer. Finally the problem was pinpointed to a virus which affected the copying of files.

- How could the virus have got on to the system?

- Outline precautions that the publicity officer should have taken to prevent this problem from occurring.

- Research some of the effects caused by the latest viruses.

An organisation with a network will need a network manager or network administrator to be responsible for maintaining it. The duties include:

Installing software

Much software will be installed on central file servers. Some frequently used applications, such as Microsoft Office, may be installed on each individual computer. Modern network operating systems allow this installation to be done centrally. The network manager will have the responsibility of ensuring that all the appropriate software licences are held.

Allocating user accounts

When new personnel join an organisation they will need to be allocated accounts with appropriate access rights and levels of resource usage. Each new user will be assigned an initial password.

Making regular backups

A case study that investigates the backing up of network files is to be found in Chapter 15.

Running and updating antivirus software

It is essential that the latest version of antivirus software is in use.

Auditing network use

This involves tracking the use of a network. Software that provides suitable audit information is discussed in detail below.

〉 **Network audit software** 〉

Audit software is used to protect an organisation. It is one of the key tools in hunting down fraud and misuse of the system. It will help to ensure that an organisation conforms to its security policy and help to fulfil duties under certain IT legislation.

Audit software enables the network administrator to keep track of network use. This will help in maintaining security and can also be used to monitor staff. All log ins and attempted log ins are recorded so that illegal attempts at access from a particular workstation can be highlighted. In a similar way attempts to access restricted files can also be recorded.

When a licence has been purchased that allows for a number of concurrent users, audit software can be used to keep a track of the number of users at any time so that steps can be taken to prevent access to more than the allowed number of users.

The increasing use of networks and the Internet by employees within organisations has led many managers to look for ways of keeping track of use. Audit software produces an audit log that can record the following information:

- who is using the system
- the address of the system, normally a unique address held on the network card
- the date and time of access
- what programs have been used
- what files have been opened, modified and deleted
- how many reads and writes have been executed
- how many times a server has been accessed
- failed log on attempts
- websites accessed and time spent there.

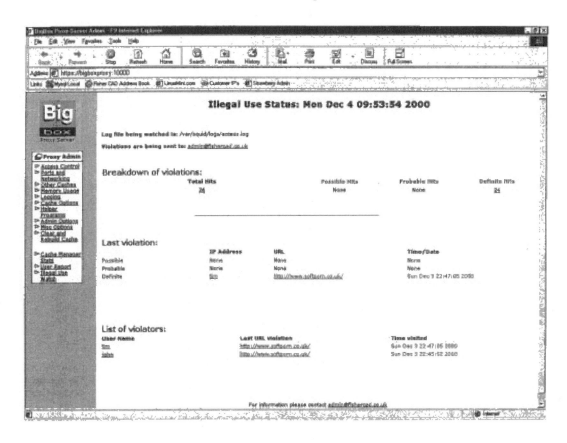

Figure 19.1 BigBOX software

BigBOX see figure 19.1

○ BigBOX™ is Internet access auditing software. As well as filtering unwanted sites, it can provide a list of all network users and sites they have tried to access (including filtered ones).

○ BigBOX™ can also list sites and users who have visited these sites.

○ It is likely that BigBOX™, or similar software, is used in your school or college.

> **Network accounting software** >

Users themselves control the files stored on a stand-alone computer and are able to make best use of the disk space available.

A networked system could have hundreds of gigabytes of disk space to be shared between users. It is important that an individual user is not allowed to use up more than his fair share of this resource. The network manager can allocate each user a maximum allowance. Any requests for more space would need to be justified.

Network services software such as Novell NetWare allows the network manager to set a wide range of parameters for an individual user's account. Log-in can be restricted to certain times of the day with an expiry date and time. If necessary, an account can be disabled.

Restrictions can also be set for password use. A minimum length can be specified and the user can be forced to change the password within a timescale that can be set by the network manager. The number of times that a password can be tried can also be changed.

Access rights can be given for different files and directories. For example, all users might have read access to a common area but only have write and delete access to their own area. Auditors would have read access to the whole system. Users can be assigned to different user groups which can then be assigned access rights. The individual user would have all the rights that have been assigned to the group.

When a printer is shared on a network, it can be important to keep track of the amount it is used by individuals. In some environments, individuals might be charged for the paper used, either individually or to a departmental account. Alternatively, each user might be allocated an allowance. The network operating system could perform this tracking function, but on the whole this currently is an area of weakness of many network operating systems. Utility software is available which can carry out this tracking function. Users or individual printers can be assigned a limit which, when reached, will prevent further printing until some action is taken.

Activity 2

Setting up a college accounting policy

Create an accounting policy for a college of 1500 students and 200 members of staff. You need to specify:

- the hard disk space allowance

- any restrictions on dates for which they are allowed to use the network

- any restrictions on time

- any printing restrictions and/or allowances

- the groups you would create, (e.g., staff, students... but all students do not need to be treated in the same way)

- the minimum allowable password length and period of forced change

- any access rights to shared drives.

The costs to an organisation of running a computer network will usually be significant. Traditionally departments within an organisation have been billed for consumables such as paper and other stationery, secretarial support and the cost of phone calls. Until recently, similar costings were not undertaken for use of a network.

The transfer of graphics uses considerable network time compared with text. As the transfer of voice and video become more and more common the growth of network traffic will be immense. Such potential growth is leading many organisations to begin dividing the costs for network time between its users as the use of video conferencing and other techniques is becoming more widespread.

Network accounting software can be used to monitor network usage (such as connection time, access and storage) by individual departments.

It can provide the network manager with a range of information including the departmental use which can be the basis for billing individual departments. This can also be used to check if the system is providing value for money. Information on usage trends can also be obtained and these can be used to plan future service provision.

Case Study 1

Maxtrack Systems use network accounting software to deliver reports on network usage by users, groups, departments or applications.

The benefits include improved security, assessment of network effectiveness and justification of future network investment. The software also provides information on network usage that enables costs to be allocated between departments or business units.

Activity 3

Network accounting

It is likely that your school or college has a network and that you have a user account. If so, answer the following questions.

- What is your user ID?
- How are these IDs allocated?
- What rules govern your choice of password?
- How frequently do you have to change your password?
- Can you log in to more than one workstation at the same time?
- How many grace log ins are you allowed?
- What happens if you exceed these attempts?
- List the directories/folders/drives that you have full access rights to.
- List the directories/folders/drives that you have no access rights to.
- List the directories/folders/drives that you have read-only rights to.
- What categories of people have different rights from you, and how do they differ?
- Is printing monitored?
- If so, explain how this is done.
- What disk space allocation do students have?

The network environment

Although a business network user may be using the same software as on a stand-alone machine at home, in fact the network environment is very different. Some ways in which it is different are:

- hardware
- user interface
- security
- control of software
- control of files
- access rights.

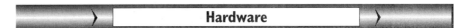

Hardware

You will have learned in Module 2 of the ICT AS course that the following items of hardware are normally required for a network:

- one or more network file server to store and distribute files over the network

- a network adapter card inside the computer that physically connects your computer to the network

- cabling to connect each network computer and printer to the file server.

User interface

The user interface provided on a network will differ from a stand-alone machine in a number of ways. Security will be enforced centrally so the user will always have to log on to the network before they can start to use their machine. When a computer that is attached to a network is switched on, it can boot from the network file server. The user will then be presented with a log on screen and will need to enter their ID number and correct password before being able to access any files or software.

Software is likely to be restricted to what has been authorised and is available on the network.

The GUI might be controlled centrally to stop individuals customising their environment. This will create a consistent corporate image and will also ensure that anyone can use any machine.

The user will have more drives available. Conventionally, on a PC-based system, **A:** to **E:** are reserved for the local floppy, hard disk and CD drives while **F:** to **Z:** are network drives. Typically, the **F:** or **N:** drive might be the user's own private storage area on the file server and other drives such as **P:** could be used to store shared files and software.

Once a user has opened a program, their view will be little different from that of a user of the same package on a stand-alone machine. Certain activities are more complicated for a user on a network than on a stand-alone computer. The use of shared printers is one such example. All documents for printing would be sent to the appropriate job queue and printed when the printer was free. The user would need to ensure that they had selected the correct print queue from their software, otherwise they could find it hard to track down their document!

Security

Password protection gives networks greater security than stand-alone machines. However, there are additional security hazards associated with networks. One such hazard comes from viruses. A virus on one workstation can quickly spread to the rest of the network and destroy the files of a whole business.

Viruses are transferred to systems from floppy disks that have themselves been infected from another computer. Some CD-ROMs have been distributed containing a virus. Access to public networks such as the Internet also pose a threat as downloaded files can contain viruses.

A number of measures can be put in place to help prevent a network becoming infected by a virus. Antivirus software can be bought which will check all new files for viruses. This software is relatively expensive and needs to be upgraded on a regular basis as new viruses are being developed all the time.

Preventing viruses is better than trying to cure them. It is important to follow good practice to avoid infection. Users can be forbidden from using a floppy disk in a networked computer without first checking it for viruses.

Another hazard is hardware failure. The need for backup becomes crucial when a network is in use as the implications of data loss could be enormous. Good practice is important. For example, backing-up should occur regularly and backup copies should be checked as soon as they have been created to ensure that the process has been carried out correctly.

Control of software

The network manager has responsibility for the software used on a network. This software must only be used in adherence to the conditions of the licence. If a licence only allows 20 users, the network can be set up so that no more than 20 stations can access this software at once. The licence documentation and original software discs must be stored safely in case they are needed.

Users' access to certain software must be restricted. Password management software and software to add or delete users would not normally be available to ordinary users. The users' accounts must be set up so that access to these programs is not available.

Control of files

Users can normally only access their own data files and not anyone else's. However, in some applications users must share data. In a hospital, different doctors, nurses and clerks' will need access to parts of the patients' database. In a college, students will need to access shared software and files containing assignments created by their teachers. There needs to be some means of allowing different users different levels of access.

Typically, the **S:** drive on the server will be used for shared data. Users may or may not have read-only or read/write access to folders in this drive, depending on their status and access rights.

Access rights

When a new user account is added to a network, it is necessary to decide on more than the username and password. A networked system does not have unlimited disk space and an individual user cannot be allowed to use up more than their fair share of this resource. The network manager can allocate each user a maximum allowance. Any requests for more space would need to be justified.

The manager can specify exactly which software the user can use. Log in can be restricted to certain times of the day and an expiry date and time for access set. If necessary, an account can be disabled.

Users can be assigned access rights to shared directories by the network manager. These can be full rights (allowing the user to read, alter or delete files), limited to read-only, or access may be completely forbidden.

It is likely that a user will have different access rights for different drives. Access rights to files will be based on business or security necessity. Different people will have different levels of access based on their job, for example, staff in a personnel department will be allowed to look and change everyone's records whereas an individual will be able to only look at their own details, all changes to data going through personnel. A manager might be able to look and edit the details for all of his or her staff but would not be able to delete records or add new employees.

Activity 4

Extranets at Tesco

In January 1998 the Tesco supermarket chain launched the Tesco Information Exchange (TIE). TIE is a pilot project which allows some of Tesco's main suppliers to access Tesco's own intranet via an extranet.

This means the suppliers can get up-to-the-minute sales data for their products, enabling them to adjust production accordingly and avoid over or understocking. Suppliers only have access to their own data and not on other products.

The scheme involves five big suppliers (Britvic, CCSB, Nestlé, Proctor and Gamble and St Ivel) and two small ones (Kingcup mushrooms and St Merryn Meats).

Tesco expect to extend this service to all suppliers in the future. TIE can be accessed via the Internet but is a secure website. A combination of firewalls, passwords and security protocols provide security for the project.

- Tesco have spent a lot of money to set up this system to provide more information to their suppliers. Describe the advantages that the new system would bring for:

    a) the suppliers
    b) Tesco.

- Explain in your own words the terms:

    a) firewall
    b) protocol.

- Explain why security is such an important issue.

Summary

- The use of networks gives rise to increased problems of security. WANs are particularly vulnerable to illegal misuse.

- A major role of a network manager is to maintain security.

- A firewall can be used to reduce the risk of break in.

- Viruses pose a major hazard to network security.

- Use of encryption can keep data secure.

- Network auditing software is used to monitor access to the network and highlight misuse.

- Network accounting software is used to keep track of the use of network resources.

- Users of a network are assigned different access rights to data files.

Networks questions

1. a) Describe two changes that may be evident to end-users when they change over from using a stand-alone computer to a networked environment. *(4)*

   b) A multinational company has recently created an intranet, connecting all of its computer systems. All its sites are now connected using high-speed dedicated links.

   i) Describe **one** facility that could now be made available to the company which would improve productivity. *(2)*

   ii) Describe **two** possible problems that may arise as a result of using this network of computer systems. *(4)*

   iii) Describe **two** possible measures that the company can take to combat problems caused by the use of this type of network. *(4)*

   AQA June 2002 Paper 5

2. An international company wants to set up a new computer network. Although many staff currently use stand-alone desktop systems the company has no experience of networking. As an IT consultant you have been asked to prepare a report for the company directors outlining the issues and the potential benefits to communications and productivity that such a network could bring. Your report should include:

   • a description of the various network components which would be involved

   • a description of the relative merits of different types of network which could be considered

   • a description of the security and accounting issues involved

   • an explanation of networked applications which could improve communications and productivity within the company.

   Quality of language will be assessed in this question. *(20)*

   AQA Specimen Paper 5

3. A manager has upgraded his computer so that it can be connected to the company network. State two additional steps that have to be taken, either by the user or the network manager, to maintain security on a network that would not apply to stand-alone computer systems. *(2)*

   AQA June 2000 Paper 5

4. A manager has upgraded his desktop computer to take advantage of his company's network environment. State two changes that you would expect him to see as a result of such an upgrade. *(2)*

   NEAB June 1999 Paper 5

5. A GPs' practice has a networked system with a database of patient records. Doctors need to access details of a patient's medical history and drugs that have been prescribed. Nurses and receptionists need to access basic personal information. Describe the security problems associate with such a system, together with suggested ways of protecting against them. *(12)*

6. A company has a computer network system.

   a) Activity on the network system is monitored and an accounting log is automatically produced.

   i) State four items of information that this log might include. *(4)*

   ii) Give four reasons why such a log is useful. *(4)*

   b) An IT consultant has suggested that the company changes from a peer-to-peer network to a server-based network. Give six features of these network environments which contrast the two different approaches. *(6)*

   NEAB June 1999 Paper 5

7. A university provides staff and students with access to its computer network.

   a) Activity on the university's networking system is monitored and an accounting log is automatically produced. Suggest what this log might include and explain why it is useful. *(8)*

   (b) Appropriate staff have access to personal and financial data. What steps should be taken to preserve the security of the data in such a system? *(4)*

   NEAB June 1997 Paper 5

8. The IT manager of a large college is about to change the software that is used to record student attendance in classes. Given that this new software must provide different access permissions and types of report, what capabilities and restrictions should the IT manager allocate in order to satisfy the needs of each of the following groups of users: *(8)*

- students?
- teaching staff?
- office staff?
- senior managers?

NEAB June 1999 Paper 5

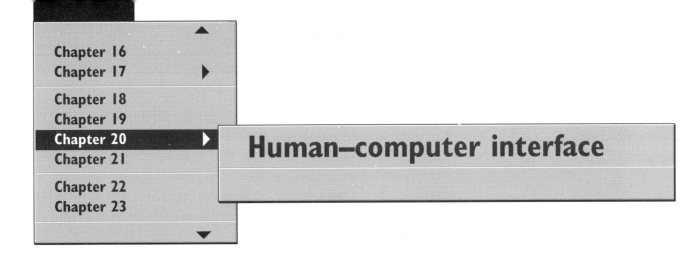

Human–computer interface

It is often said that a system fails because of 'user error'. However, the fault does not always lie with the user, but with the computer professionals who failed to foresee the error during the analysis, design and implementation of the system. It could be possible that greater attention to the human–computer interaction, the way in which communication takes place between user and the computer, would have prevented such an error from taking place.

A recent BCS (British Computer Society) conference on human–computer interface (HCI) research and practice focused on the theme 'Memorable yet invisible'. Making systems memorable is one way to make them easier to operate and thus reduce errors, but users also want systems to make the technology in use invisible to them.

Human–computer interface is a term used to describe the communication between people and communication systems. Considerable attention needs to be given to human–computer interface when a new system is being designed and developed: a poor design will give rise to user frustration and a high error rate. A good design will allow the user to work quickly, making few errors, thus operating more productively. A bad design that does not address the user's needs can reduce job satisfaction and increase unnecessary stress.

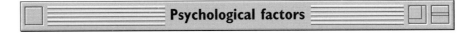

Psychological factors

Computer systems are used most effectively if they take into account the psychological factors which affect human–computer interaction.

User-friendliness and help

The interface should be user-friendly. This means that the software should be easy to use and new features easily learned. It should have a consistent 'look and feel': wherever users are in the software they should be presented with things in the same way. For example, the date might always appear in the top right hand corner or messages pointing out when data has been incorrectly entered should be given in a standard way.

Figure 20.1 Microsoft Office Help Assistant

An interface should be designed to appeal to the widest audience and should be as obvious to use as possible with an easily navigable screen layout so that users do not become frustrated. Of course, not all users are the same and some features may appeal to one user and irritate another. An example of this is the Microsoft Word Help Assistant shown in Figure 20.1. While many users find this to be a helpful facility, others consider it to be an annoying distraction to their work. The software offers the facility to switch off the Assistant so that it does not appear.

Many packages provide a range of options that the user can choose so that his or her own preferences are met as far possible. Figure 20.2, shows a dialogue box from Microsoft Word that allows a user to make some choices about the look and feel of the HCI.

As a general rule, screens should be clear and, whenever possible, self-explanatory, so that a user has all the required information on the screen. It is very important that the screen is not too cluttered as this can lead to confusion. Maintaining a standard 'look and feel' will allow the user to build up confidence. The use of prompts, which guide the user through a dialogue box, reduces the amount of prior learning that is required.

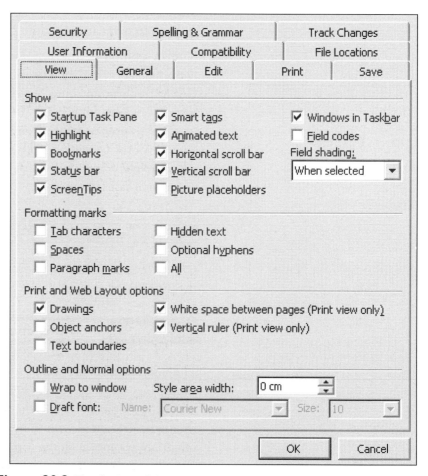

Figure 20.2 The Options dialogue box in Microsoft Word

In many packages the size of the standard font displayed on the screen can be adjusted to meet the needs of the user. An A4 page can be displayed at 75 per cent or 100 per cent of full size for normal work, 200 per cent when details are to be checked or whole page view for checking layout. Sounds can be incorporated to help the user, bringing errors to their attention.

Help facilities

Nearly all recent software includes help facilities for the user to help them to use unfamiliar features. Even an experienced user will need help when wishing to use a feature of the package for the first time. The help screens should be written in clear English, avoiding jargon whenever possible.

Adequate and consistent help should be given to novices. Many software applications include wizards which provide a novice with prompts that take them through a particular task. Some software also offers 'tips' that are displayed when the user is carrying out a particular task. Such tips can provide the user with an alternate way of carrying out the task. Demonstrations or tutorials are also provided with some software to explain the use of complex or unfamiliar tasks.

Help can be context sensitive. This means that when help is requested (via a key press or a menu choice), information is given which relates to the current function being displayed. It is standard for the F1 key to load the help screen and for users to be able to search for help on a key word.

Activity 1

Help facilities should be accessible to novice users. Using a package which you have used before, examine the Help facilities. For each of the following types of help, state whether or not they are available, how they are accessed and how useful you find them.

- context sensitive
- wizards
- tutorials
- tips
- error messages
- other (specify).

Comment on the appropriateness of the language used.

Shortcuts for experts

An expert who uses the same package very frequently can become frustrated if they are taken through a number of menus and prompts when they enter data. It is important that they are provided with shortcuts which allow them to avoid wasting time.

Software can be set up to have hot keys, special key press combinations, which allow pre-set tasks to be carried out without having to make lengthy menu choices. A commonly used hot key combination is CTRL + P used to print out, in place of having to choose Print from a menu option.

Many software packages such as Access, Word and Excel allow the user to customise software. In these packages buttons can be added to run macros, automatically load a customised front end screen interface and set up templates which provide a skeleton for types of documents.

Customisation of task bars or menus allows the user to access frequently-used options quickly and easily so that routine tasks can be done more efficiently.

Make use of long-term memory

Humans remember different things in different ways. Two types of memory have been identified: short- and long-term. We use short-term memory to recall things for temporary use, for example, when you look up the page reference for a word in an index you are able to remember it for the seconds that it takes to turn to that page. Try remembering the page reference a day or even an hour later and you are unlikely to be able to.

When we remember things more permanently we have transferred them to long-term memory. Sometimes we do this consciously by purposely 'learning', at other times repeated use results in our remembering something: a friend's phone number for example. It is easier to commit something to long-term memory if it has a meaning for us, if we understand it. Once we have stored something in our long-term memory we are slow to forget it.

It is good practice to make use of human long-term memory when designing an HCI for a user as it will maximise efficiency. If the on-screen environment is familiar and makes sense to the user then he or she will quickly be able to use the interface intuitively. The development of 'desktop' interfaces that attempt to model an actual desk have been designed to make a user mimic normal actions. Hence the 'trash can' icon is used in some systems for users to dispose of unwanted documents – just as they might throw away paper documents into a waste paper-bin in the real world. In Windows programs the same icon is used to represent a particular action. This reduces the amount of learning needed when a particular Windows program is used for the first time.

However, an icon can be confusing when first encountered. An inexperienced user, when first being introduced to Word wondered why there was an image of a tank. It became clear that she was referring to the print icon!

The use of standard menu items and key strokes reduces the time taken to learn to use new software.

Screen design

It is important to choose a screen design that is appropriate for the likely users. Features such as the size, typeface and amount of text, the use of colour and the incorporation of graphics, need to be chosen carefully. Consistency of headings, menus and layout are very important.

Error messages

The error message is a key feature of an interface. Such messages alert the user whenever a possible mistake is being made, for example, closing a file without saving it. They should be displayed clearly and be consistent in form and positioning. An error message is of little use if the user is not clear how the error can be corrected.

Many modern packages can be configured to modify the number of error messages that appear. Warning sounds can be used to inform the user of an error.

Different types of interface

A range of different types of interface were studied in Module 2 (AS).

A command-based interface (where individual commands are typed in) is most suited to experienced, regular users who can take advantage of keyboard shortcuts. A command-based interface is also more efficient in that one line can give as much information to the system as a number of menu choices. However, command formats need to be memorised.

Menu formats can be full screen, pull down and pop up. They provide an easy way for inexperienced and infrequent users to interface with a system. They provide the user with a range of choices and do not require any prior memorising of key strokes.

A graphical user interface (GUI) uses features such as windows, icons, dialogue boxes and menus to provide an interface that is easy to use. The screen designs are similar across a range of packages and users can set up their own desktop menus. Data can be taken from one application to another very easily.

Resource implications

The use of a user-friendly, sophisticated interface such as a GUI will make heavy demands on the computers resources. They require considerable memory to run, will take time to load and need large amounts disk space. Online help makes considerable demands on system resources including extra hard disk space to store help files which can be very large if a wide range of help facilities, such as wizards and demonstrations, are used.

If a software application is being transmitted over a network, the use of larger files, for graphics and help facilities for example, will increase network traffic and could impair performance.

If complex graphics and large help and other files are required, powerful computers with large amounts of memory (RAM) and fast processing speeds are necessary. Without a fast processor the programs will run too slowly.

A high RAM capacity is needed to store graphics. The use of bitmaps for high resolution screens displaying a large number of colours requires a large amount of memory. A high-speed, high-resolution monitor will be needed to display the graphics clearly.

To run Windows 2000, it is recommended that you have at least a Pentium II 300 MHz processor with 128 MBbyte RAM and a 4 Gbyte hard disk. This would be the absolute minimum however. Recommended would be a Celeron or Pentium III 600 MHz with 256 MBbyte RAM and a 10 Gbyte hard disk.

The following features of a sophisticated HCI make considerable demands on resources:

- On-screen help. Context-sensitive searching on different topics, tutorials and wizards all require considerable storage (hard disk) space and large amounts of RAM when running.

- Use of colour enhances user-friendliness, but results in a high use of Immediate Access Store (RAM). The use of a greater number of colours requires more bits of storage for each pixel.

- The use of graphics and animation add much to the user-friendliness of software. However, complex graphics require a fast processor if the changing images are to be displayed smoothly. Complex graphics, high-resolution screens with many colours require large amounts of memory to store bitmap images. Large amounts of disk space are needed to store graphics files and the complex programs needed to manipulate the graphics.

- The use of GUI features such as icons, scroll bars and dialogue boxes require considerable amounts of disk space and immediate access store. The complex programming needed to run the interface requires a fast processor.

- Many sophisticated interfaces allow for multitasking, where several tasks can be run concurrently. For example, a document can be repaginating whilst other tasks are being carried out. A spreadsheet can be recalculating whilst a user is word processing a letter. Multitasking involves the sharing of the processor between tasks. Such activity requires a fast processor as well as adequate immediate access store otherwise the user will suffer frustration having to wait for task and window swapping to complete.

- Many current developments that attempt to improve HCI for a user make high resource demands. The use of voice recognition to replace keyboard entry uses complex programming that requires a fast processor and large amounts of immediate access store.

Activity 2

Draw up a table like the one below and enter details for eight major application packages used in your school or college. Use manuals, the Internet and magazines to gather the required data.

Package	Minimum processor speed	RAM needed	Disk space required for full implementation	Disk space required for Help files

Customisation of software

Certain software packages can be customised to meet an individual user's specific needs.

Many packages allow the user to choose the toolbars and icons to be used. The contents of menus can be altered to meet specific needs. A personal, supplementary dictionary can be set up so that commonly-used names and words specific to the business can be added. A package such as a spreadsheet can be customised to hide unwanted functions from an inexperienced user and add a user-friendly, task-specific interface.

Features such as macros and templates are common in general-purpose applications packages. Macros allow the keystrokes of frequently used tasks to be automated so that time can be saved. Macros can be set up to allow novice users to carry out more complicated tasks than they would otherwise be capable of. Templates allow users to pre-set and save their own document styles.

Activity 3

Using a package that you are familiar with, explore the ways that the package can be customised. List 15 different features that can be customised, explaining why a user might wish to make each customisation.

Implications of customisation

Customisation of software can allow a user to make the best possible use of it. An inexperienced user can be provided with a simplified set of choices, maximum help and hints and a range of pre-set options, for example, through the use of macros. An experienced user will customise the same package in a completely different way that will allow them to save time and remove unnecessary and intrusive help.

However, the customisation of software can lead to complications. Support staff within an organisation might have greater difficulty troubleshooting when every installation of a particular piece of software is customised in a different way. Identifying a source of error or guiding a user through a new task will be much more complicated when many option settings differ from the norm. If the software has to be reinstalled for any reason, it will need reconfiguring to the user's own requirements.

If users move between workstations, as they do in a school or college environment, finding differently configured workstations will complicate access; users will be unfamiliar with the layout and options.

Summary

- Psychological factors affect human–computer interactions. It is important when designing an interface for new software to take the following factors into consideration:
  - ensure that the software is user-friendly
  - provide a range of help facilities for novices

- provide shortcuts for experts
- use long-term memory to maximise efficiency.

- Sophisticated HCI's are demanding on resources. These resources include:
  - processor speed
  - RAM
  - hard disk space.

Human–computer interaction and interface questions

1. Describe, in your own words the psychological factors that effect human–computer interaction. *(8)*

2. With reference to a spreadsheet package that you have used, describe how software can be customised to meet the needs of an individual user. *(6)*

3. A technical author purchases a new word-processing package which he customises to fit his specific needs. Explain the term customise in this context. Describe what such customisation would involve. *(6)*

4. a) What are the factors you would need to take into account when designing a screen layout for a database application? *(6)*
   b) What are the resource implications for providing a sophisticated human–computer interface? *(4)*

5. Give three factors which should be considered when providing a sophisticated human–computer interface, explaining the impact of each one on the system's resources. *(6)*

   NEAB 1997 Paper 4

6. A university uses a complex CAD (computer aided design) package. The package has a sophisticated human–computer interface which also places considerable demands on the system's resources.
   a) Give two examples of a system's resources that would be affected by such a package and explain the demands placed upon them. *(4)*
   b) Describe three features you would expect to find in the human–computer interface which would merit the description 'sophisticated'. *(6)*

   NEAB 1998 Paper 5

7. A supermarket chain has recently implemented a new stock control system in each of its branches. Many of the staff have described the system as being 'user-friendly'. Give four features of software packages that would merit the description 'user-friendly'. *(4)*

8. a) Describe two resource implications of providing an effective interface. *(4)*
   b) Some users may customise their interface. Describe one consequence this may have for support staff when providing technical assistance. *(2)*

9. The workstations on a particular company network are set up to allow each user to change software, menus, icons and colour schemes to suit his or her own preferences. These variations make support for users difficult to manage.
   The network manager wants to change to a standard user interface, so that all the users will be given the same set of menus, icons and colour schemes.

   a) i) Describe **two** benefits for the users of this standardised approach, other than improved support. *(4)*
      ii) Describe **two** of the disadvantages for the users of this standardised approach. *(4)*
   b) What are the resource implications for planning this standardised interface? *(4)*

   AQA June 2000 Paper 5

10. A composer has decided to invest in a music software package to aid his productivity. He already uses a generic office package and is competent in its use. Both software packages operate with a graphical user interface (GUI). Describe two features of his PC hardware that will be necessary in order for the GUI to operate efficiently. *(4)*

    AQA June 2001 Paper 5

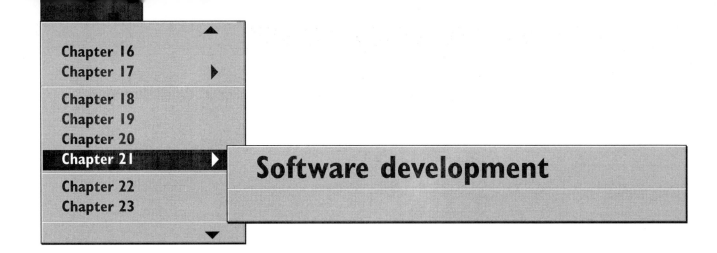
Software development

Activity 1

Specialist Software

Find out a specialist software application that has recently been developed. Prepare a report for your class using presentation software.

You should include details of:

○ the purpose and nature of the application

○ why specialist software is needed

○ any problems that were encountered in its development

You will be able to research the applications from specialist IT magazines and web sites.

If a small business wishes to install a new stock control or payroll system, there are many off-the-shelf products available and it is likely that a suitable package could be found to meet their needs. A description is given in Chapter 16 of the process that should be followed to ensure that an appropriate choice is made.

However, off-the-shelf software does not meet all potential needs. Very often specialist software is required for a system when it is not possible to purchase an off-the-shelf package as the software simply does not exist. For example, if a retail organisation wishes to develop an entirely new form of customer reward scheme there would be no suitable software on the market. Many public sector systems, such as those for the Inland Revenue, the Passport Office or the London Underground need software to be developed specifically for their own needs.

Bespoke software

Software that is developed specifically for a particular system is known as bespoke software. An organisation will choose to develop bespoke software when they wish to implement a new system that performs things that no other system has done. For commercial organisations this might be seen as a way of keeping ahead of the competition.

Bespoke software has the advantage that it can be designed to meet the precise user requirements and that a solution can be produced in such a way that the system will be able to grow and adapt to changing business circumstances. The development of the new system can be phased so that costs can be distributed. In some cases, bespoke software that is developed for a particular organisation may then be sold to other organisations in the same sector.

The main disadvantages of commissioning bespoke software is that it is likely to be costly and will take much longer to implement than if an off-the-shelf package had been used. When something new is being done, perhaps incorporating new technology, there can be a high level of risk: it might turn out that the new system cannot be made to work as intended. Many such systems go substantially over budget and are not implemented on time, indeed some have to be abandoned.

Customising a generic software package

In many systems, there is often a combination of bespoke and off-the-shelf software in use. Very many specialist application systems are built by customising generic software packages. Databases such as Oracle form the basis for many such systems: the functionality of the DBMS in incorporated into the specific application. An alternative generic solution which has become increasingly common is to use a web-based format. This solution would store the data as active server pages – a database format that could be accessed by a browser such as Internet Explorer.

As the volume of programming is much less, both the development time and implementation costs will be less than would be incurred if a fully bespoke system were to be produced.

A large multinational organisation recently needed to replace a 15-year old system. This system had been programmed from scratch as at that time there was no other option: no software in the field was on the market. When considering the replacement options, the analysts rejected the idea of producing bespoke software as it would take too long: the scope of the project was huge and would require many thousands of man hours to develop. Software currently on the market met approximately 90 per cent of the requirements. The team negotiated with the manufacturers to buy the product together with the right to modify it to meet their specific needs. This core product provided the basic functionality; programmers would have the flexibility to build on this so that the extra features could be added and the software made to integrate with other existing software in use within the corporation.

Choosing a suitable way of producing specialist software

When an organisation decides that bespoke software is required or existing software is to be modified, a decision will need to be made as to how the development is to be undertaken.

There are three options:

- The user could write their own software.

- A team within the organisation, perhaps part of a dedicated IT development department could write the software.

- An external software house could be commissioned to write the software.

User-written

If users have the necessary skills, it may be appropriate for them to develop their own program. This is usually only an appropriate option for very small systems or for a small business. Many users have developed their own websites; before packages such as Dreamweaver and Flash were developed this involved a considerable amount of programming.

This is not a commonly-used approach. Most user-produced applications are likely to consist of customised generic packages. For example, within your school or college you are likely to find that members of staff have customised a spreadsheet or database package to meet specific needs within their department. You will have experience of this kind of customising as you produced an application in this way for your AS coursework and are probably working on another project at the moment.

The main advantage of a user developing a software solution is that the requirements of the system will be fully known and understood. No one else will need to be involved, so there would be no chance of misunderstanding. However, it is rare that a user would have the required skills to develop a system, and even if they did have it might not be an appropriate use of their time.

> ## Internal development team

Large organisations may employ a team of IT staff. Very large organisations may have a complete IT department that consists of analysts and programmers who will produce bespoke software solutions. An advantage of maintaining a dedicated team is that that the people developing the software will have a thorough knowledge of the work done by the organisation, its current systems and its procedures. Continuity will be provided as the team that produced the software will be on hand to maintain and modify it.

Case Study 1

International banking

David works in the IT department of a large multinational bank. The department is made up of several hundred people. He works in a section that develops and supports the systems used by the bank traders in the cities that house the main international money markets.

He is working on a project that will produce a back office system to replace the current, rather outdated system that will soon not be able to cope with the demands placed on it. The system involves sending out payments and confirmation of deals done. The requirements of the system are wide ranging but very specific to the organisation. There is no one piece of software on the market that will carry out the required tasks.

An estimated 150 analysts and developers will be needed to work on the project over the next three years.

- David could have chosen to use a software house to develop the software instead of producing it in house. What factors do you think influenced the decision?

- Why might it be appropriate for such a large organisation to develop an in-house solution whilst it would not be appropriate for a small business?

- What are the dangers of choosing to develop an in-house solution?

Getting a software house to produce a bespoke or tailor-made program to the specific user needs is an alternative way of producing specialist software. A software house is a company that employs a number of analysts and programmers with a range of skills, usually in a number of programming languages. Good software houses will employ professionals who are well qualified, reliable and adaptable. Many software houses specialise in different types of work. Some may specialise in Internet-based systems, others may work mainly within a particular business sector such as retail or banking. Many offer a wide range of services. Analysts from the house will work closely with the client organisation to ensure that they have a clear understanding of the system requirements.

As the programs developed by a team from a software house are written especially for the user, they should fit all their needs. However getting a company to develop the solution for a user is likely to be expensive and take time. It is important for a client company to choose a software house that has a good reputation in the given field of work. This can be found out by talking with previous clients of the software house. The range of skills available within the software house should be appropriate. The client will also need to be assured that any system that is produced for them will be adequately supported so that if things go wrong they will be sorted out quickly. There will also be a need for system maintenance so that when minor program modifications are needed to reflect changes in the organisation, the software company will be able carry them out.

Case Study 2

IPL create a system for Teachers Provident Society

Teachers Provident Society (TPS) provides a range of financial services that include advice on mortgages, investment management and unit trusts as well as a large range of other financial investments and products.

TPS called in the software house IPL in the late 1990s when competition was fierce in the financial world. They had identified a need to develop systems that would take advantage of new technological developments as well as cut costs within the organisation. They currently had an assortment of business applications that could not communicate with each other effectively.

TPS required an integrated, customer-focussed set of systems that would make use of common components for a range of functions. The systems should cover all aspects of the business. The new systems should enable them to reduce the costs of launching new products, respond to a percentage of customers' queries immediately and analyse the preferences and profiles of individual customers.

A decision was made for each of the systems currently in use to determine whether to upgrade it, replace it with another off-the-shelf solution or to develop a bespoke replacement.

A development team from IPL worked closely with TPS users and managers. The user interface was prototyped before an appropriate system was designed and developed. Where possible, common components were identified that could be used in future developments of systems to support other types of financial products.

continued...

Case Study 2 *continued*

The development team started in March 1998 and the system was ready to go live in January 1999.

- What ICT developments were taking place in the late 1990s that would affect TPS?

- What is prototyping? Explain why its use would be important in this project.

- Explain why TPS chose a bespoke development of their new systems.

- Why do you think that TPS did not develop the new software in house?

- How do you think TPS went about choosing an appropriate software house? List the criteria that they should have used to make their decision.

Activity 2

Computer services

Specialist software houses are companies that can be commissioned to write software for a user.

In recent years these companies have offered a larger range of services to users and are often called **computer bureaux**, **software consultancies** or **software houses**. The services offered may include:

- selling and installing standard, off-the-shelf software

- tailor-made software

- customising generic software

- computer consultancy and advice

- networking advice

- Internet advice

- website design

- web hosting and maintenance

- selling and installing hardware

- hardware and software rental or leasing

- help in data preparation.

Use the Internet to find an example of a software house that provides the service for each of the services listed. What other services can you add to the list?

Prepare a presentation for your class describing the services provided by one particular software house.

If no suitable software already exists to meet a user's needs, a decision will have to be made to decide upon the method of development.

The following criteria are likely to be among those considered.

Development time

The time that it will take to develop and implement the system will be most important when deciding which approach to use. The timescale within which the system must be completed is likely to be determined by factors within the organisation. New organisational functions that are needed by a certain date may depend upon the new system, for example, the start of another project that has already been planned might require this system to be up and running.

The required timescale for implementation may not allow time to develop the new system from scratch, which is what has to be done when developing a bespoke system. As well as producing all the new program code, the new system will need extensive and time-consuming testing. Customising a generic package will usually take less time compared with other methods. The generic package will already have been coded and tested.

An organisation that does employ its own IT development team may still need to use the services of a software house if all their own staff are committed to other projects and could not complete the project within the required timescale.

Cost

Cost is likely to be a major factor. The cost of producing bespoke software will be high as programmers will have to be paid for all the time that it takes to develop the software. The costs incurred when customising a generic package will consist of the cost of the package together with payment for the time taken to customise it for the specific needs. The amount a client pays for generic software is considerably less than the amount that it costs to create it. The development cost for generic software is spread as such software will be sold to a number, in some cases a very large number, of users.

Costs of developing bespoke software can sometimes be partially recouped by selling the software to other, similar organisations who may be able to adapt it to their needs.

Flexibility to extend

In some situations it is very important that the new software that is created is able to be extended in the future to meet changing needs within the organisation. When developing bespoke software in-house, the developers are likely to have a very clear understanding of what the future requirements of the system could be.

Appropriateness of solution

It is important that the chosen solution will adequately meet the needs of the users. A bespoke system should be able to meet these needs exactly. A generic package might need very extensive customisation which even then would only partially meet the requirements.

Compatibility with existing hardware and software

When a solution is being chosen, considerations of compatibility must be made. It may be that extra memory or an upgrade processor will be required to run the new software. Data files from other systems may need to be read by the new system.

Skills within the organisation

If an organisation does not employ its own IT developers, it will not be able to develop bespoke software in-house. If bespoke software is required, the organisation will have to use the services of a software house. Even if the organisation does employ its own developers, they may not be familiar with the programming language or languages required to implement a particular system and the best option in this case may be to use a software house rather than retrain staff or employ new extra programmers.

Do other, similar systems exist?

Very often, similar systems already exist in other organisations that can be adapted to meet the needs of the new system. Whether this is a feasible option will depend up on degree of competition between the organisations and whether such systems are compatible with current hardware and software.

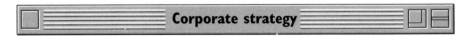

Corporate strategy

An organisation's senior management will produce a corporate strategy that will include plans for future developments within the organisation. These will include the development of new IT solutions and will lay down the scope and timescale for each such project.

Decisions to purchase new software cannot be taken in isolation. Although only one department in a company may use the software, other departments may use the data generated. A sales system might record sales, but the data is needed to reorder stock, to send invoices, to pay staff commission, to plan future services, etc..

The company's IT technicians may be familiar only with one hardware platform. Purchasing software that requires different hardware may mean that the same level of technical support is not available.

In a rapidly changing environment where hardware and software becomes out of date very quickly, it is vital to plan ahead and have a corporate IT strategy. This strategy will cover the whole company and not just individual departments. Any software development must be in line with the corporate IT strategy.

Summary

- Specialist software cannot always be bought off the shelf.

- The main ways a business can provide software solutions to specialist applications are:
  - Getting the user to write the software themselves.
  - A team within the organisation, perhaps part of a dedicated IT development department could write the software.
  - An external software house could be commissioned to write the software.
  - Customising a generic software package.

- When choosing between different software solutions to specialist applications the following criteria need to be used:
  - development time
  - cost
  - flexibility to extend
  - appropriateness of solution
  - compatibility with existing hardware and software
  - skills within the organisation
  - do other, similar systems exist?

- Software purchases must comply with the corporate IT strategy.

Software development questions

1. You are the IT manager of a college. Your principal wishes to implement a computerised student identification card system. One way of providing the software for this system is to use a generic applications package and to customise it to meet the project specification.

a) Describe **two** ways of providing the software other than using a generic applications package. *(4)*

b) The college has a clearly set out IT strategy, however this project has not been included. Identify and describe **four** issues that should be considered when making a final choice from the above three methods. *(8)*

NEAB 1998 Paper 5

2. An examination board is considering developing a system which is to be used for maintaining and processing module test results of candidates.

a) Describe the different ways in which the examination board may be able to provide a software solution.

b) Discuss the issues the examination board should consider before choosing any particular solution. *(20)*

NEAB 1997 Paper 4

3. A company that specialises in selling bicycles, spares and related items is considering having a website that will allow customers to order online. It already uses a relational database to keep records of customers, stock and orders. As an IT consultant, you have been approached to assess the viability of several alternative software solutions. Discuss how you would help the company decide on a suitable software solution. Your discussion should include:

- what you need to find out in order to carry out this assessment
- the evaluation criteria that you would consider using
- the content of the report that you would produce to show the results of your evaluation. *(20)*

Quality of language will be assessed in this answer (see also Chapter 16)

AQA June 2001 Paper 5

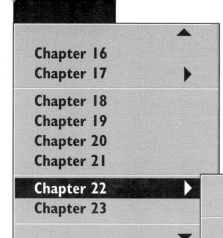

Software reliability

Users expect software to be reliable. It should carry out the function for which it is designed, be robust (i.e., not 'crash') and be free from errors.

To ensure that software is reliable a process of rigorous testing needs to be carried out. Testing is a process of running a program with pre-selected data to make sure that it performs in exactly the way that the specification lays down. The choice of data is not a random thing: every test will have a specific purpose and the output that is produced will be checked against the expected output.

Testing may also highlight other desirable changes to software. For example, the user interface may prove unwieldy or inappropriate or default values for some fields may need to be changed.

When testing highlights an error, a process of debugging will need to be followed. This involves studying the program code to find the source of the problem (the bug). This can prove to be a time-consuming activity.

The process of rigorous testing must take place before the software is released on the market. If new software contains errors, it will, at best, be embarrassing for the software company. At worst, it will lead to a loss of confidence in the company's products and affect sales.

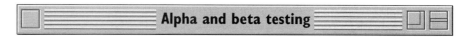

Alpha and beta testing

Software is tested in stages. Alpha testing is carried out in-house by the company who wrote the software. It will test the software with its own test data and will check the software matches the design specification. The people carrying out the testing process are unlikely to be the same people who developed the software as it is very hard for programmers to look objectively at a program that they wrote themselves. Alpha testing will involve testing with different hardware platforms and different operating systems.

When alpha testing is complete and any changes made in the light of the results of the testing, beta testing can be undertaken.

Beta testing is carried out by real users, perhaps companies or individuals who have bought previous versions of the software or who have expressed an interest. The software will be tested using real data in a real situation, using different platforms (different processors, different memory sizes, and so on). This may detect errors not previously found. The beta testers will provide the software manufacturers with constructive comments on the product.

With the growth of the Internet, beta software is often distributed freely over the web to enable a wider audience to test it, for example, Microsoft distribute beta software over the Internet and often release their operating systems in different beta stages.

Prosoft Property Solutions Ltd

| Features | News | Screen Shots | Price list | Demo Disk | Support | Smart Money | Home Page |

News: Last Updated.
Monday, 20th February

RentAccom 2002
Available Now !!

RentAccom 2002 is a Windows based property management system which contains not only a powerful nominal ledger and accounting system with smart error deletion routines, but also extensive automated documentation procedures to enhance document production and improve office efficiency. Please see features for more details.

New Features !!

- Optional documents available under licence from '*The Letting Training Centre*'
- Optional *AFD Post Code* add-on.
- Seasonal charging for holiday lettings.
- Improved upfront commission charging

Figure 22.1 The Windows beta testing site

Why is beta testing used?

There are a number of advantages of getting real users involved in the testing of newly-developed software.

The testers are independent of the producers and therefore impartial. They are interested in finding out whether the software actually does the job they want it to do.

The product is tested in the 'real world' under realistic conditions. There are many modes of use of software that reveal bugs (errors) only when real users use it. Users can sometimes try to do things that have not been thought of by the designers and programmers. Sometimes a particular, unusual, sequence of key presses or option choices can lead to an unexpected error. The volume of data and frequency of access may far exceed that used in alpha testing. More platforms can be used for testing that the software company is likely to possess.

The users can provide valuable feedback to the developers so that problems can be put right before the software is distributed more widely.

Beta testers are able to try out new software before most people. For many people it is rewarding to be involved in an important part of the production of new software.

Beta testers may enter into an agreement with the software house to test the software in certain situations. They must not distribute the software to any other users. The agreement might state that they will be entitled to a discount when the software is eventually marketed.

Some beta testers may even pay for the privilege so they can get early copies of the software. Beta testing is a vital part of software development. A company needs a sufficient number of beta testers to test the product fully but not too many so that the product becomes too public before it is fully released.

Only if both types of testing are successful will the software be released for sale. Windows XP took several years to develop. Firstly, faults had to be ironed out in house. Eventually, six months before the program went on sale, beta copies were sent out to testers. Several bugs still remained which had to be corrected before distribution. Of course, distribution outside the company reduces security. By the time Windows XP was released, the press knew exactly what it would do.

Case Study 1

A beta tester

Julian Voelcker is a computer consultant who volunteers to beta test software. He first got involved with beta testing after being approached to look into an early version of Windows 95. 'I was disappointed about a number of things in the beta version not getting into the final release, so I vented my anger by writing to Mr B Gates at Microsoft,' he said.

Not expecting an answer, he was surprised when a personal reply arrived. The upshot was that he was invited to join a group of beta testers called Club Internet Explorer.

Voelcker gives many reasons for being a beta tester. He gets to know the software. As a computer consultant, customers with a problem expect him to know their package inside out. He gets the chance to use software before it is released on the market. He had Windows 95 up and running a year before it went public.

'You get a lot of free software,' he says. 'There are always goodies from the computer firms.'

Voelcker's real satisfaction comes when his suggestions are incorporated in the final released version of the product.

The group of beta testers are not paid and as the beta software is not finished there is a relatively high risk. 'I've never lost any data through using beta software,' Voelcker says. 'But frankly, if you use beta test software to run your business you are daft.'

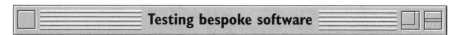

Testing bespoke software

When software has been specially written for an organisation by a software house, a programme of testing will have to be agreed between the two parties. It is likely that the client organisation will provide the software house with realistic test data.

Once the software house has completed testing and put right any errors that have come to light during the testing process the software will be handed over to the organisation to carry out its own testing. This phase is known as **acceptance testing**. Users will run the software with real life data under normal working conditions. Only once they are happy that the software fully meets the original requirements will the software be accepted.

Software errors

However well they are tested, programs can still be sold with faults in them. The commercial demands to get software into the shops, the many different platforms and operating systems that are now available and the huge number of possible paths in a program means that making software bug-free is almost impossible. The errors may only come to light when the program has been marketed.

In September 1999, a NASA spaceship costing around $125 million crash-landed on Mars after a voyage of 122 million miles taking nine months. The craft was destroyed and the crash blamed on software error.

In 1988, St Albans City and District Council bought software from ICL to collect poll tax. However, errors in the code meant that the council collected £484,000 less in poll tax than it should have.

In 1997, Intuit admitted an error in its personal finance software, QuickTax 97. QuickTax, which was designed to help income tax payers fill in a new self-assessment form, was given away free with Quicken. However, the error led taxpayers to fill in their self-assessment forms wrongly. Several errors were reported by users, which the company said were the result of inadequate testing.

Fixing bugs

If software companies discover (or are informed of) a bug in their software they will want to provide a corrected version of the program. They will try to develop a bug fix to edit the program to remove the bug. These fixes, called **maintenance releases**, may be supplied free to all registered users.

There are three reasons why a software company may need to supply a maintenance release:

- **corrective** – to fix bugs in coding which have only come to light after release

- **perfective** – to improve performance: speed, memory usage and so on

- **adaptive** – to make changes to meet changing needs, for example, the introduction of the euro, to fix the millennium bug problem or a new operating system.

The software producer must ensure that all purchasers are given details of maintenance changes. These can be dealt with by carrying out a mailshot to all licensed users including copies on floppy disk or CD-ROM of the changes needed to be made. It is therefore important that users register with the software producer by completing and returning licence agreements.

Increasingly, users can access bulletin boards on the Internet where they are able to find out details of known errors and ways to deal with them, as well as download program fixes.

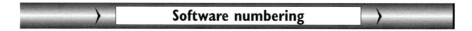

Software numbering

Software is often given a version number or a number representing the year it was introduced, for example, CorelDRAW 10 or Microsoft Office 2000. When an upgrade version of CorelDRAW 9 was produced with more features it was called CorelDRAW 10.

A corrected version of software is not an upgrade. It will usually be given a .1 number, for example, Netscape 6.1.

Maintenance updates of these products may be numbered .11, for example, 6.11.

Why things can still go wrong

Even when rigorous testing has taken place software may fail to operate successfully as part of an information system.

This could be because the software was not designed for the situation in which it is being used. Perhaps the volume of the data and the size of the resulting files are much greater that the software was designed for.

It could be that the software is being used in a different environment (see the Air Traffic Control case study on page 232).

Another reason could be incompatibility. The software might need to interface with parts of an information system and compatibility problems might arise.

The hardware resources provided to run the software may not be sufficient for it to run at its optimum. This could cause systems to run unacceptably slowly or even to crash frequently.

All these problems could result if insufficient time and care is taken in the process of selecting software that meets the needs of the prospective users. If errors occur in bespoke software then it is likely that the system analysis phase of development has not been carried out satisfactorily.

Case Study 2

Air Traffic Control problems at Heathrow

Several years ago a new computerised air traffic control system was installed at Heathrow airport. The software was tried and tested, having been in use for a number of years at several airports in the USA.

The original system took 1600 programmer years to write and a further 500 programmer years for developers to modify it for the more crowded skies of southern England.

When the system was put into action there were a number of serious bugs still remaining. One problem concerned the way in which the program dealt with the Greenwich meridian. The program contained a model of the airspace it was controlling, that is, a map of the air lanes and beacons in the area.

As the program was designed for use in the USA, the designers had not taken into account the possibility of a zero longitude, consequently the need to consider negative values was ignored. The software caused the computer to, in effect, fold the map of Britain in two at the Greenwich meridian, placing Norwich on top of Birmingham.

○   Describe, in your own words, the nature of the error and how it arose.

Summary

○   Testing is a process of running a program with pre-selected data to make sure that it performs in exactly the way that the specification lays down.
  ○   Alpha testing is in-house testing by a software company.
  ○   Beta testing is testing by volunteers from outside the software company, testing the software in realistic situations.

○   Maintenance releases are fixes to problems within software. They are supplied free to registered users. They are not an upgrade.

○   Maintenance releases are issued for three reasons:
  ○   corrective
  ○   perfective
  ○   adaptive.

Software reliability questions

1. Software houses go through a long testing programme before releasing a product. Despite this, problems can still occur with that product. Give **three** reasons why testing may not be completely successful. *(3)*

   AQA June 2002 Paper 5

2. A software company has notified customers of a maintenance release for its accounting package. The notification states that a programme of alpha and beta testing will be carried out to ensure that the maintenance release is reliable.
   a) State **three** reasons why a maintenance release might be necessary. *(3)*
   b) What is meant by the terms:
      i) alpha testing?
      ii) beta testing? *(2)*

   AQA Specimen Paper 5

3. A common saying in the IT world is 'never trust a version 1 release of a software package.'
   a) Describe one example of a problem you may encounter when using a version 1 release. *(2)*
   b) Explain why such a problem might still exist when the package is released. *(2)*

c) Suggest two reasons why many users still purchase a version 1 release. *(2)*

Northern Examination and Assessment Board (A Level Computing) 1995

4. A software company is preparing to release a new application program. Describe the two types of testing carried out before the final release of the software. Explain why both are needed. *(6)*

   NEAB 1997 Paper 5

5. Software houses often produce maintenance releases during the life of a product.
   Describe **three** different types of circumstance for which a maintenance release is required. *(6)*

   AQA June 2001 Paper 5

6. Describe two benefits that a software manufacturer gets from customers trialling a new operating system before it is made generally available. *(4)*

   AQA June 2001 Paper 5

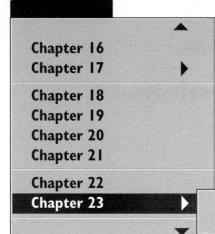
Portability of data

The ability to transfer data to or from another package or hardware platform is a feature that is increasingly becoming an important requirement for users. This means data does not have to be typed in again, which would waste time and could lead to errors.

Data is said to be **portable** if it can be transferred from one application to another in electronic form. Portability has a specialist meaning here – it doesn't mean 'you can put a floppy disk in your pocket and carry it around'!

It is vital that different applications can share data. This might mean two different pieces of software on the same PC, two different PCs sharing the same software, or even two different platforms running different software. For example, web pages can be accessed from different platforms with different browser software. Not only should text be transferable but graphics, sound and video files too. A user may have different applications, or versions of an application, available at home and at work and will need to be able to transfer data between the two computers.

The growth in the use of networks has increased the need for portable data files. Portability ensures that data files produced on one application can be accessed by other applications, or by the same application on different hardware platforms.

For example, a freelance journalist carries out much of his work at home using Microsoft Word on a PC. One of the magazines he works for has a network of Apple Macs on which they run Microsoft Word as their word processor. The second magazine uses WordPerfect on PCs. The journalist needs to be able to transfer documents produced at home to either place of work.

Consider a sales manager who is writing a report on the performance of her sales representatives during the past year. She is producing the report using word-processing software. Details of sales throughout the year are maintained on a spreadsheet that has graphing capabilities. The sales manager would like to include graphics and tables into her report. Ideally this data could be **imported** from the spreadsheet into the word processor.

Users buying new application software will want to be able to import files from their previous software. Portability is an important marketing feature for companies producing new software. Early microcomputers had no common standard for storing data. As a result it was very difficult to transfer data between computers made by different manufacturers. Now manufacturers have standardised the PC format, making it easy to transfer data between different computers, for example, data can be quickly transferred from a pocket organiser to a PC.

The IT industry has helped portability by:

- introducing standards for formatting disks so that different manufacturers' equipment can share disks

- adopting standard methods of storing pictures, for example in bitmap (BMP) format

- adopting standard methods of storing files (for example CSV files – Comma Separated Variable) which can be accessed from many programs, for example Excel

- adopting standard methods of storing text (for example TXT files that just store the text, RTF – Rich Text Format that also stores font sizes as well as text)

- selling utility programs which convert from one version of a program to another.

Standards for the interchange of text, numeric data and graphics

Each type of software is designed to meet particular needs. For example, a relational database management system provides an excellent means of storing, accessing and manipulating data. If complex analysis needs to be carried out on the data, it would be best to transfer it to a spreadsheet. If a complex document were then needed, a word processor would be the most effective software to use. To enable data to be transfered without loss of information from one software application to another, standards are required.

Application Programming Interface (API) is a set of standards that allow organisations to generate software which interfaces with other software.

Object linking and embedding (OLE) enables data to be transferred from one Windows application to another. The data can be transferred as a copy or can still be linked to the original. The technical complexities are hidden from the end-user.

Graphical images can be used on the World Wide Web and accessed freely because a limited range of standard formats is used.

Object Linking and Embedding (OLE)

Very often users wish to transfer numerical, textual and graphical data between software applications. For example, when producing an article using a word processor the user may want to include a graphical image that was developed using a graphics package.

Windows has the facility of Object linking and embedding (OLE) that provides a means of linking or sharing information between different programs. When using a word processor to produce a report on sales, a manager may wish to include extracts from a spreadsheet together with some charts.

This can be done in two ways. The first uses an **embedded object** that is a selected part of the spreadsheet included as part of the document file. The document now actually contains all the data that makes up the object. The original spreadsheet can be modified or even deleted but the embedded object will remain unchanged. Using a number of embedded objects can result in a high storage requirement.

Using a **linked object** does not involve any storing of data in the document. Instead, a link is created to the spreadsheet file. If the data is changed in the spreadsheet the updates will be shown when the document is displayed. If the spreadsheet file were to be deleted then the link would be lost. Using linked objects allows reports to be kept up to date as data in other files is changed. Using linked files will minimise storage requirements as the spreadsheet data is only stored once.

Hardware standards

Hardware standards are needed to allow users to purchase devices from different manufacturers and link them together without problems. In the early days of computing, a user was linked to one manufacturer for the purchase of all hardware as no standards existed.

Common elements for connecting devices are used, such as: RS232 (serial), power cable connectors, mouse and keyboard connectors and Universal Serial Bus (USB). The use of common connecting standards ensures that a wide range of peripherals and internal components can be produced by any company and be guaranteed to work. Such competition means cheaper prices for the buyer. The components themselves conform to standards, which mean that you can buy a hard disk from a variety of different suppliers and be sure that it will work in your PC.

Most internal PC hardware uses either a PCI, AGP, EISA or ISA connector. Modem standards are essential. During the late 1990s there were two competing standards. If your Internet Service Provider (ISP) did not have the same type of modem as you then you could not connect to the Internet.

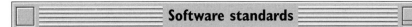

Software standards

The use of standards in software makes applications easier to use as different applications will have a consistent human–computer interface (HCI), the same 'look and feel'. SAA (systems application architecture) was developed to ensure a consistent approach to software development. It stated that F1 should be Help and that the menu names and positions should be consistent.

All software can save its work in a variety of different formats which enable portability and compatibility. To be able to view information on the Web it is necessary to save the data in HTML, most modern packages have this feature.

Common operating systems

With a few, common operating systems in use there is a wider range of software available as the software manufacturers only have to develop their software for a limited range of operating systems, for example, Linux, Apple and Windows.

Windows is the de facto standard for the PC platform. This has ensured that there is an extensive range of user support options available.

Protocols and standards

To be able to transfer data between different computers, it is important to define **standards** and **protocols** first.

Standards

Most programs store data in its own particular format. Data is stored in binary-coded form and a program will need to be able to recognise the coding used appropriately. It is important that programs and computers have access to common standards for coding data, otherwise one program would not be able to intepret the data created by another program. So without such standards, portability would be impossible. A number of standard file formats have developed over the years.

Many ICT standards are laid down by the International Standards Organisation (ISO), for example, JPEG images are compressed images conforming to an ISO standard.

Some common file standards

All text can be transferred in ASCII format. ASCII (American Standard Code for Informantion Interchange) is an internationally agreed standard coding system for representing characters and certain special codes. It is recognised by virtually all small computer systems.

CSV (Comma Separated Variable) format is used for transferring data to and from databases and spreadsheets. Each field or cell is separated from the next by a comma.

Graphics can be stored in a number of formats and most programs can import in a number of formats, for example, **BMP** Bitmap picture, **PCX** Paintbrush picture, **JPG** a compressed image used for storing Internet pictures.

Protocols

Protocols are the formal rules and procedures that need to be followed to allow data to be transmitted, received and correctly interpreted.

TCP/IP (Transmission Control Protocol/Internet Protocol) is a protocol used to define how data is transmitted over the Internet. TCP/IP has become the de facto standard for communication. This has enabled a vast amount of data to be transferred between different computer systems.

Without protocols there would be no agreed way for computers to communicate. Historically many protocols were proprietary, which meant that they were owned and supported by a single company, for example, IBM. This meant that the application, system and communication software would all be optimised to run with the hardware. As a result it was very difficult to link machines from different manufacturers together. Over the last decade this has changed and through the use of gateways and more open communication standards it is possible for machines from different manufacturers to communicate.

Protocols allow the use of **open systems**, computer systems that are independent of the manufacturer and the platform. With open systems several disparate pieces of equipment can be connected together and be expected to communicate effectively.

The main advantage of protocols is that the user is not restricted to one manufacturer's equipment. Even if one company's computers are all the same make, they may wish to communicate with another company whose hardware is different, for example, for EDI. This would not be possible without protocols.

Problems with standards

However as hardware technology develops, standards may become out of date. It is difficult and takes time to get universal agreement on the establishment of new standards. Open systems based on old standards may be unacceptably slow.

Another drawback of standards is that in some cases the full power of the machine might not be available and there might therefore be reduced functionality or performance. Bespoke software, designed specifically for use on a particular platform and ignoring standards, makes better use of the hardware.

Internet protocols and standards

The Internet uses internationally agreed standards so that it can be accessed with a variety of hardware platforms. It is now possible to access the Internet with a mobile phone or a digital TV.

An Internet protocol is a standard set of rules that are used to make sure that information is transferred correctly between computers using the Internet. These protocols define:

- the way in which data is to be structured
- the control signals that are to be used
- the meaning of the control signals.

The protocols used include TCP/IP (Transmission Control Protocol/ Internet Protocol), HTTP (Hypertext Transfer Protocol) used to identify the address of a web page and FTP (File Transfer Protocol) used to transfer files between remote computer systems. Web pages are set up in an agreed language HTML (Hypertext Markup Language).

GIF and **JPG** images are used on the Internet. They use compression techniques to store graphics files. This means that they are a fraction of the size of the same picture in bitmap format. Utility programs like PaintShop Pro can convert between different types of file.

In recent years, the Internet has become more and more commercial and is a very successful marketing tool. Advertisers want their image to be eye-catching – putting new demands on web page design. Animated gifs and Java script allow moving images, which are now common place. Once again commercial needs have driven technological developments.

An Internet protocol is a standard set of rules that are used to make sure that information is transferred correctly between computers. These protocols define:

- The way in which the data is structured
- The control signals that are to be used
- The meaning of the control signals.

File Transfer Protocol (FTP)	Allows a user to send a message that causes a copy of a file to be transferred from one computer to another. The FTP controls the sending of the file copy in blocks and checks for errors in the data when it is received.
Hypertext Transfer Protocol (HTTP)	A standard for requesting and transferring a multi-media web page using HTML (HyperText Markup Language).
Transmission Control Protocol/Internet Protocol (TCP/IP)	Built on a set of agreed standards (part of the OSI model) this protocol allows providers and users to communicate with each other whatever hardware is being used.
Post Office Protocol 3 (POP3)	This protocol defines standards for the transfer of e-mail between computers.
Point to Point Protocol (PPP)	This determines the communication between two directly connected computers. It is very often used between an individual user connected via a telephone line to their Internet Service Provider.

Figure 23.1 Some common Internet protocols

ISO and the OSI Model

The Open Systems Interconnection (OSI) model provides a framework for data to be transferred between two networked computers, regardless of whether they use the same data formats and exchange conventions or are the same type of computer or are even on the same network.

The OSI model was developed by the International Standards Organisation (ISO) as a guideline for developing standards to allow the connection of different types of computers. The OSI model is not itself a communication standard, an agreed method that determines how data is sent and received, but merely a guideline for developing such standards. The OSI model plays a vital role in networked computing.

If a manufacturer's products obey a set of standards based on the OSI model, they can relatively easily be connected to another manufacture's products. Without the communication standards based on the model software development would be very difficult. It would be hard for a manufacturer to sell products that did not adhere to standards.

The OSI model consists of seven layers, as the task of controlling communications across a computer network is too complex to be defined by one standard. Each layer of the OSI model contains a subset of the functions required to control network communications.

The seven layers of the Open System Interconnection model (OSI)

Application Layer (7) This is the level of the OSI model that provides service directly to the end users. Examples of its activities would include dealing with file handling, establishing passwords and determining if sufficient resources were present.

Presentation Layer (6) This layer is usually part of the operating system. It carries out such things as data compression, encryption and formatting to provide a common interface.

Session Layer (5) This layer ensures that a user can exchange information. It deals with synchronisation, grouping data and establishing communication as full or half duplex.

Transport Layer (4) This layer ensures that computers can communicate even if the data transmission systems are different.It provides error recovery between the two end points in the network connection and ensures complete data transfer.

Network Layer (3) This layer routes information around the network. It is responsible for establishing, maintaining and terminating network connections. Standards define how data routing is handled.

Data Link Layer (2) Responsible for the reliability of the physical link established in the physical layer.

Physical Layer (1) This layer is concerned with the transmission of binary data over the transmission medium. It sets standards for electrical and mechanical aspects of interface devices (cables, etc.). The physical layer is concerned with mechanical and electrical connections as well as procedures for connecting devices. For example, the number of pins a network connector should have and how each pin should be wired.

Activity

It is sometimes hard to remember the order of the layers. Making up a silly sentence with seven words, each of which starts with the letter of the appropriate layer can help. For example, **A**ll **P**recious **S**ardines **T**urn **N**ice **D**olphins **Ph**obic.

○ Now make up you own – something that you will remember!

Development of protocols and standards

Formal standards

Some standards are formally introduced, often after considerable deliberation by a committee. ASCII is an example of such a standard. Others, known as de facto standards arise through historic precedence or as a result of marketing and sales success of a particular product.

De facto standards

Often de facto standards have evolved, not because they are technically the best but due to commercial or other pressures. In the 1980s there were two types of video recorder, VHS and Betamax. Betamax was widely regarded as being the better quality but VHS became more popular due to better marketing. Betamax flopped while VHS became the standard.

A similar situation is happening in IT. PCs have a huge share of the market yet many people swear by the Apple Macintosh. Microsoft MS-DOS and Windows have such a dominant market share, they have become the standard operating system for a PC. It doesn't mean they are the best. However, developers of new software are unlikely to be interested in producing new software for, say, the Linux operating system while the potential market is so small.

Case Study 1

Setting a standard for mobile devices

More than 200 technology companies have formed the Open Mobile Alliance to develop universal standards for mobile devices so that hand-held computers and mobile phones should all speak the same language.

They wish to replace the WAP standard and look to develop an open standard for the software code used to create wireless platforms.

However, Palm, the biggest hand-held manufacturer, is not part of the Alliance. It has developed a new operating system for its devices that will accommodate better audio and graphics for multimedia users. It allows users to do many new things with handheld computers.

- What is a standard?

- Why do the Alliance want to set up standards for mobile devices?

- Why do Palm not want to join the Alliance?

- Use the Internet to research the current state of standards for mobile devices.

- The standard that the Alliance wishes to establish would be called a 'formal standard'. Explain, with reference to this case study, how a 'de facto' standard could arise.

Summary

- Data is said to be **portable** if it can be transferred from one computer platform to another or from one software application to another.

- **OLE** provides a means of linking or sharing information between different Windows programs.

- Standard binary formats for storage have developed for the interchange of text, numeric data and graphics.

- **Protocols** are the formal rules and procedures that need to be followed to allow data to be transmitted, received and correctly interpreted.

- Some standards are developed **formally**. **De facto standards** grow out of historic precedence.

- The **OSI** model provides a framework for the development of standards to enable different types of computers to be connected.

Portability of data questions

1. Give three examples from everyday life that illustrate the use of standards. *(3)*

2. With the growth in computer systems being purchased for use on networks, there is a greater need for manufacturers to conform to standard protocols.
  a) What are protocols and why are they required? *(4)*
  b) The application layer is one of seven layers in the OSI model. Name three other layers. *(3)*
  c) Briefly describe the role of the application layer in this model. *(3)*

NEAB 1997 Paper 5

3. An IT consultant wrote in a trade journal: 'The growth in technologies such as personal computers, the World Wide Web and WANs has only come about because manufacturers and suppliers of network hardware and software have adopted standard communications protocols. The OSI seven-layer model has been a key factor in this development...'

Discuss this statement. Particular attention should be given to:
  • the meaning of 'communications protocols' and why they are required
  • the OSI model and a description of the role of three of its layer
  • the benefits and limitations of standards.
Illustrate your answer with specific examples. *(20)*

NEAB 1999 Paper 5

4. Users may encounter problems when software manufacturers upgrade a software package. With reference to specific examples describe two such problems. *(4)*

5. Two users are using two different versions of the same word-processing package. When user A sends a file on disk to user B there are no problems in reading the file. However, when files are transferred the other way the transfer is not successful. Explain why this may happen and how to overcome this problem. *(4)*

NEAB Specimen Paper 2

6. A freelance reporter who regularly contributes articles to various newspapers and magazines is considering which word-processing package she should purchase. A friend has said that most modern application packages enable users to produce files which are portable.

With the aid of specific examples discuss this statement. Include in your discussion:

  • an explanation of what portability means in this context
  • why portability is important
  • how the IT industry can encourage this portability. *(16)*

NEAB 1996 Paper 2

7. 'The rise of de facto standards due to commercial sales success can only benefit organisations and individuals.' Discuss this statement. Particular attention should be given to:
  • operating systems
  • portability of data between applications
  • portability of data between different computer systems.
Illustrate your answer with specific examples. *(16)*

NEAB 1999 Paper 2

8. A journalist wrote in a recent edition of a computer trade journal 'The growing use of IT networks places a greater need than ever on manufacturers to conform to standard protocols....'
  a) What are protocols and why are they required? *(4)*
  b) The physical layer is one of the seven layers in the OSI model. Name **three** other layers. *(3)*
  c) Describe the role of the physical layer in this model. *(3)*

AQA June 2000 Paper 5

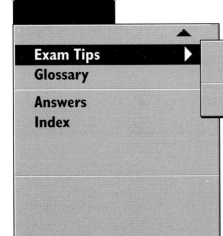

Exam tips: writing an essay

A2 exams normally contain an essay question worth 20 marks. Examples of essay questions are questions 3 on page 52 and 2 on page 207.

The question normally includes around four bullet points. Writing about each bullet point will gain up to four marks per bullet point. The final four marks are for the quality of language used.

In writing an essay it is important to:

- cover all the points in the question
- have a structure to the essay.

An essay must have a beginning, a middle and an end. The beginning is a brief introduction describing the topic, the middle covers all the bullet points in turn. The end is a conclusion.

The best way to ensure that the essay is well structured is to spend five minutes planning the essay. Even though you are likely to come under time pressures in the exams, this is time well spent.

Plan by brainstorming and writing down as many points as you can related to the question. Then link them to the bullet points in the question. A spider diagram may help. (See the example.) The plan should ensure that your essay will be in a logical order.

Example:

1. An international company wants to set up a new computer network. Although many staff currently use stand-alone desktop systems the company has no experience of networking. As an IT consultant you have been asked to prepare a report for the company directors outlining the issues and the potential benefits to communications and productivity that such a network could bring. Your report should include:

- a description of the various network components which would be involved
- a description of the relative merits of different types of network which could be considered
- a description of the security and accounting issues involved

- an explanation of networked applications which could improve communications and productivity within the company.

Quality of language will be assessed in this question. *(20)*

The diagram below has four 'spiders' – one for each bullet point in the question. The idea is to write down items to include on that point in your essay. When you have sufficient items for every bullet point, you can start writing your essay.

Keep to a logical order by covering each bullet point in turn. Write at least one sentence on each of the items in your spider diagram.

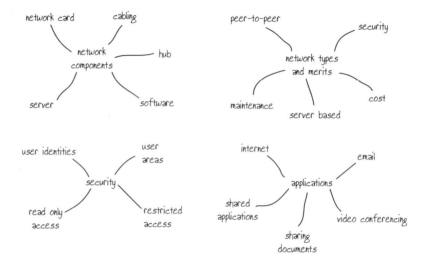

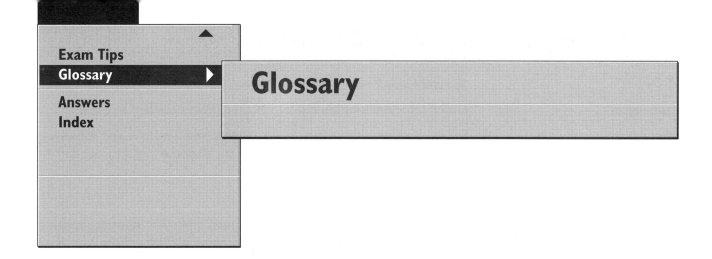

Exam Tips
Glossary ▶
Answers
Index

Glossary

Ad hoc report	A 'one off' report that needs only one particular situation.
Alpha testing	Software testing by the company that wrote the software.
Alphanumeric characters	Letter, numbers or other character, for example punctuation marks.
ASCII	(American Standard Code for Information Interchange). The binary code used in computers to store alphanumeric characters.
ATM	(Automatic Teller Machine). The official name for cash machines outside banks.
Audit trail	An automatic record of computer transactions.
Backup	To make an extra copy of stored data in case the original is lost or corrupted.
Bandwidth	Physical limitations of a communication system (usually bits/sec)
Batch processing	A form of processing where all the data is collected together before being processed.
Beta testing	Testing carried out by real users before software is released.
Bit	(Binary digit). A binary number which can only have the value 0 or 1.
Bitmap	An image which stores the colour of every pixel.
Bridge	A device that is used to link two LANs.
Broadband	A data transmission method that involves several channels of data and so is faster than older methods.
Browser	A program that allows the user to access a database (typically the Internet).
Buffer	Memory where data is stored while waiting to processed, typically in a printer.
Bugs	Errors in computer programs.
Byte	A group of eight bits, normally storing one alphanumeric character.
Cache	A very fast but more expensive computer memory.
Caching (relating to Internet use)	Storing Internet files locally – usually on the computer's hard drive – to enable the files to load quickly if revisited.
CAD	Computer Aided Design.

CD-ROM	(Compact Disc-Read Only Memory). A small plastic disc used to store data.
Compression	A method of reducing the size of a file, typically to use less disk space.
Configure	To set up a computer system for the appropriate hardware and software. A system will need to be configured for the printers, sound cards and so on.
CSV	Comma Separated Variable.
Cyber-	A prefix alluding to computer communication often with reference to the Internet as in cybershopping (shopping by computer) cyberspace (everything accessible by computer communications).
Database	A structured set of data stored on a computer.
Data integrity	The reliability of data, that is ensuring it is accurate.
Data security	Keeping data safe from loss.
DBA	Database Administrator.
DBMS	Database Management System a set of programs allowing the user to access data in a database.
DDE	Dynamic Data Exchange. Shared data in two packages is linked so that when it is updated in one program, it is automatically updated in the other program.
De facto standards	Standards that have evolved historically due to convenience or commercial reasons rather than due to technical reasons or a planned approach.
Debug	Remove bugs from a program.
Desktop	An icon-based user interface that enables the user to load software easily. When you load Microsoft Windows, you see the desktop.
Digital	Something that is represented in numerical form typically in binary numbers.
Direct-mail	Advertising a product by sending details directly to potential buyers through the post.
Directory	An area (usually of a disk) where files are stored. A disk may have several directories and sub-directories to make finding files easier and to aid security.
Distributed system	A system where processing is shared between different computers on a network.
Dongle	A piece of hardware, for example, a lead that has to be plugged in to the computer before software will run. Usually used to protect copyright.
DOS	Disk Operating System.
Dot.com	A company usually trading exclusively via the Internet.
dpi	Dots per inch – describes the performance of a printer.
e-banking	The use of the Internet to communicate with your bank.
e-commerce	The use of computers and electronic communications in business transactions, including web-sites, EDI, on-line databases and EFTPOS systems.

EDI	Electronic Data Interchange. Transferring information such as orders and invoices electronically between two organisations.
EFTPOS	Electronic Funds Transfer at Point of Sale. The system where customers can pay by debit (e.g. Switch) card and the money is taken electronically from their bank account.
e-learning	Using electronic methods to teach someone.
e-tailors	Retailers who do business on the Internet.
e-shopping	Using the Internet to purchase goods and services.
Embedding	Including one file (such as an image or a document) in another file. See OLE (Object Linking and Embedding).
Encryption	To scramble data into a secure code to prevent it being read by unauthorised users.
Extranet	The linking of two intranets usually to assist business transactions, for example linking a customer and a supplier.
FAQ	Frequently Asked Question. A file containing answers to common questions, for example, about using a program.
Fax modem	A modem that enables a computer to send and receive faxes.
Fibre optic	A cable made out of glass fibre and used in communications.
Filters	An option in a program enabling the user to import files from or export files to another program.
Flatbed scanner	A scanner in which the item to be scanned is placed on a flat piece of glass.
Floppy disk	A small removable disk in a hard plastic case, used to store data.
Gigabyte (GB)	A measure of memory capacity equal to roughly 1,000,000,000 bytes (it is exactly 2 to the power 30 or 1,073,741,824).
GUI	Graphical User Interface, for example Windows. It is sometimes pronounced 'gooey'.
Hacking	Unauthorised access to a computer system, possibly for criminal purposes.
Hand scanner	A small device, held in the hand and dragged over the item to be scanned.
Hard disk	A magnetic disk inside a computer that can store much more data than a floppy disk. Usually it cannot be removed but removable hard disks are becoming more common.
Hardware	The physical parts of the computer, such as the processor, keyboard and printer made up of electronic circuits.
HCI	Human-Computer Interface.
HTML	Hyper Text Markup Language.
HTTP	Hypertext Transfer Protocol. The standard protocol for sending and receiving data on the Internet.

Integrated package	A package which combines several different applications such as a word-processor, a graphics package, database, communications software and spreadsheet.
Interactive	A system where there is communication between the user and the computer.
Internet	An international WAN providing information pages and e-mail facilities for millions of users.
Intranet	A private internal network using Internet software, that can be used for internal e-mail and information.
IP	Internet Protocol.
IRC	Internet Relay Chat. A function of the Internet allowing users to send and receive real-time text messages.
ISDN	Integrated Services Digital Network. A telecommunications digital network which is faster than an analogue network using a modem.
ISO	International Standards Organisation.
ISP	Internet Service Provider. A company that offers a connection to the Internet.
Java	A programming language used for utilities on web pages.
JPG or JPEG	Joint Photographic Expert Group. An ISO standard for storing images in compressed form. Pronounced jay-peg.
Kilobyte (KB)	A measure of memory capacity equal to 1024 bytes.
LAN	Local Area Network.
Licence agreement	The document which defines how software can be used, particularly how many people can use it.
Macro	A small program routine usually defined by the user.
Magnetic disk	A small disk coated with magnetic material on which data is stored. It can be a floppy disk or a hard disk.
Magnetic tape	A long plastic tape coated with magnetic material on which data is stored.
Mail-merge	A feature of a word-processing program that combines details from a file of names and addresses into personal letters.
Master file	The file where the master data is stored. Data from this file is combined with data from the transaction file.
Megabyte (MB)	A measure of memory capacity equal to 1,000,000 bytes (it is exactly 2 to the power 20 or 1,048,576).
MICR	Magnetic Ink Character recognition. The input method used to read cheques.

MIS	Management Information System.
Modem	Modulator/demodulator. The device that converts digital computer data into a form that can be sent over the telephone network.
MS-DOS	Microsoft Disk Operating System. The operating system developed for the PC.
Multi-access	A computer system allowing more than one user to access the system at the same time.
Multimedia	A computer system combining text, graphics, sound and video, typically using data stored on CD-ROM.
Multi-tasking	A computer system that can run more than one program simultaneously.
Network	A number of computers connected together.
Normalisation	The process of breaking down complex data structures into simpler forms.
OLE	Object Linking and Embedding. A method of taking data from one file (the source file) and placing it in another file (the destination file). Linked data is stored in the source file and updated if you modify the source file. On the other hand, embedded files are part of the destination file.
On-line processing	Processing while the user is in contact with the computer.
Open systems	Systems that can be used on any computer platform.
Operating system	The software that controls the hardware of a computer.
Package	A program or programs for a specific purpose.
Palmtop	A small handheld computer around the size of a pocket calculator.
Peer-to-peer	A type of network where there is no server, with each station sharing the tasks.
Pentium™	A processor developed by the Intel Corporation™ for the PC.
Peripheral	Any hardware item that is connected to a computer such as printers, mice or keyboards.
PIN	Personal Information Number. Used to check that the user is the person they claim to be, for example at an ATM.
Platform	Used to describe a hardware or software environment.
Port	A socket usually at the back of the computer.
Portability	The ability to use software, hardware or data files on different systems.
Primary key	A unique identifier in a record in a database.
Protocol	A set of rules for communication between different devices.
QBE	Query By Example. Simple language used to search a database.

RAM

Random Access Memory. The computer's internal memory used to store the program and data in use. The contents are lost when the power is turned off.

Redundant data

Data that is repeated unnecessarily (in database).

ROM

Read Only Memory. Part of the computer's memory that is retained even when the power is turned off. Used to store start up program and settings.

Serial access

Accessing data items one after the other until the required one is found. Associated with magnetic tape.

Server

A dedicated computer that controls a network.

Shareware

Software that can legally be distributed freely but users are expected to register with and pay a fee to the copyright holder.

Smart card

A plastic card, like a credit card, with an embedded microchip. The information in the chip can be updated, for example when cash has been with drawn from a ATM.

Software

A computer program or programs.

Software copyright

Laws restricting copying of software.

SQL

Structured Query Language.

Systems analyst

A person whose job involves analysis of whether a task could be carried out more efficiently by computer.

TCP/IP

Transmission Control Protocol/Internet Protocol.

Toggle switch

A switch or button which if pressed once turns a feature on. If pressed again it turns the feature off. The Caps Lock button is an example.

Transaction file

A file containing new transaction details or changes to old data, which is merged with the master file.

USB

Universal Serial Bus – a port on the back of a computer used to connect peripherals such as scanners or a palmtop.

USB hub

A device that plugs into the USB port that enables several peripherals to connect to the computer at once.

URL

Uniform Resources Locator – the Internet address, for example, www.hodder.co.uk

Vector graphics

Image system that stores lines by the length and direction rather than the individuals pixels (as in a bit map).

WAN

Wide Area Network.

WIMP

Windows, Icon, Mouse, Pointer.

Windows™	A GUI for the PC produced by Microsoft.
Wireless network	A network that uses radio waves to transmit data rather than cables
WWW	The World Wide Web.
WYSIWYG	What You See Is What You Get.

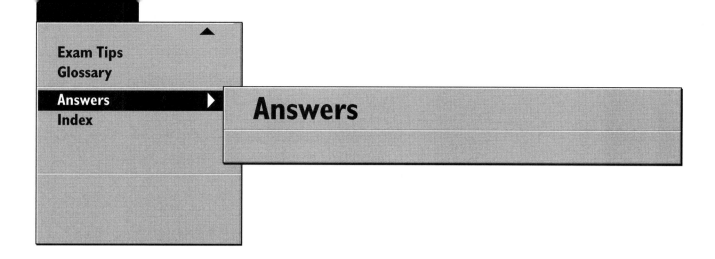

Answers

These answers are only intended to be a brief guide. A level answers often require a full explanation or description. In many cases, other examples exist as well.

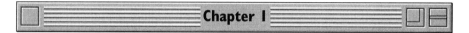
Chapter 1

1. See chapter details.

2. See chapter details.

3. (a) flat
   (b) flat structure has **fewer levels** to go through, **not so many obstacles** to delay communication.

4.

Advantages		**Disadvantages**	
1	Save on wages.	1	Redundancy pay and other issues.
2	Fewer levels in the structure mean a shorter chain of command.	2	Managers will have a wider span of control.

5. E-mail is immediate, you don't have to leave the office, it can be sent to many people at once, recipients can reply straight away.

6. See chapter details.

7. Concerns may include:
   - What will it cost?
   - Will I have to make staff redundant?
   - Will it improve the performance of the company?
   - Will staff cope with the change?
   - Will staff skills be redundant?
   - Will it lower staff morale?

8. See chapter details.

9. See chapter details.

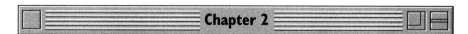
Chapter 2

1. Possible reasons include:
   - inadequate analysis/testing/life cycle stage

- lack of management/end-user involvement in design/testing/development
- concentration on low level data processing
- lack of management knowledge of ICT and its capabilities
- inappropriate or excessive management demands
- lack of team work
- lack of standards
- problems with changeover.

2. (a) Data processing – precise/low level/electronic data capture/used for repetitive routine business activities.
   Examples: Stock control/payroll calculations/invoices/point-of-sale.
   Information System – collection of data to improve performance/aid to decision making/support for management.
   Examples: Sales information system/Financial info system/stock summary.
   (b) Tactical – affecting short-term operational decisions e.g., how many tills to open.
   Strategic – long-term decisions e.g., where to locate new stores.
   (c) The data from the POS system can be used to show who buys what, at what location and at what time.

3. See chapter details.

4. See chapter details.

5. (a) To provide managers with information.
   (b) To enable effective decision-making.
   (c) see Chapter 2.

6. (a) A system that converts data into an appropriate form for managers.
   (b) See Question 1.

7. (a) See Question 5a).
   (b) See Chapter 2.

8.
   - inadequate analysis
   - lack of management involvement in design
   - emphasis on low-level data processing
   - lack of management knowledge of IT systems/capabilities
   - inappropriate management demands
   - excessive management demands
   - lack of professional standards.

9.
   - Strategic: used to inform the business plan to assist decision making e.g., projected income per income stream.
   - Personnel: senior management/board level
   - Operational: used to assist daily tasks e.g., outstanding total of invoices
   - Personnel: mid-management/clerical level.

10. See chapter details.

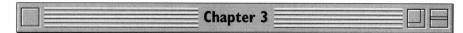

1. (a) • current system no longer fit for purpose/is ineffective
   • changes in business methods
   • new legislation forces changes
   • technical developments
   • current system inflexible/too expensive to run
   (b) • technical issues
   • economic issues
   • legal issues
   • operational issues
   • schedule issues
   • training issues
   • changeover issues.

2. See Chapter 3.

3. See chapter details.

4. See Chapter 2 Question 1.

5. You may have different ideas here!
   (a) phased changeover
   (b) direct changeover
   (c) direct changeover
   (d) direct changeover
   (e) phased changeover
   (f) pilot changeover.

6. The answer should include observation, interview, questionnaires, etc.. The analyst would gather current documents, examples of the current system in action.

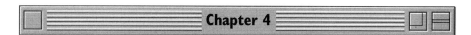

Chapter 4

1. The answer should include network requirements, the ability to share files, compatibility issues, licence issues, support issues, …

2. See Question 1.

3. A system with fully documented/agreed procedures. The answer should state stages of flow/control/exception handling/distribution and give a suitable example, e.g., business letter.

4. A supermarket cashier scans a bar code on a product. The code is sent to the store's computer. The price and name of the product is sent to the till and printed on the receipt. Details of the sale are immediately stored in a transaction file. Every hour the transaction file is sent to the store's warehouse to update stock levels.
   (a) The bar code on the product.
   (b) Operational.
   (c) Also operational but this information can be used for strategic and tactical applications.

5. See chapter details.

6. See chapter details.

7. Helpful: fast system of sending messages, can send attachments, can set up a group of e-mail addresses, etc.. Unhelpful: computer may crash, possibilities of viruses, staff may use e-mail exclusively at the expense of face-to-face.

8. See chapter details.

Chapter 5

1. real time: cost of pair of shoes – needed by sales staff working at operational level when selling shoes to customer;

   daily: total money taken – needed by shop manager to check against sales – operational;

   monthly: total sales of each type of shoe – used by head office buyers at a tactical level to decide which shoe types to continue stocking;

   annually: annual turnover of each store – used by senior management to see if any store has become unviable due to low sales and may therefore need to be closed down (strategic).

2. details of other luxury cat foods on the market including sales and pricing (external);

   details of sales, costs and profits of own new luxury dog food (internal);

   size of potential market (external);

   estimate of development costs of new product (internal).

3. See chapter details.

4. (a) Operational, future information
   (b) Historic operational information
   (c) Current operational information
   (d) Current operational information
   (e) Current operational information

5. Strategic information: information concerning current room usage, potential growth in student numbers, budget forecasts – needed when making strategic decision to build new classroom block; Tactical information: A2 results for previous cohort in ICT, AS results for current cohort needed when deciding whether to enter cohort for ICT4 in January or June; Operational information: attendance rate, test scores of a student who needs to decide whether or not to progress form AS to A2.

6. Data ageing during the improvement stage. Overcome by setting up the model first with test data; perform export once fully tested.

7. Strategic: to decide where to locate warehouse need detailed geographical information on the region including potential sites and transportational details.

    Tactical: information regarding progress of stages of building; operational: information regarding materials required.

8. All levels of management require information on which to base decisions, to organise, to plan and to control. Whilst timing is important, other features such as completeness, accuracy and relevance are equally important in assessing the value of information to an organization.

    Clearly the quality of management information is directly related to its timing, but this in itself is linked to the particular situation giving rise to the need for such information.

    To illustrate the following examples are given:

    Provision of historical information – into this category comes annual accounts where there is no conflict between speed and accuracy, as time is taken to produce the information required.

    Provision of information for control purposes as, for example, in production or quality control. Speed and accuracy are important to avoid costly delays or poor production.

    Provision of information for planning purposes: here the time scale may be years and thus there is less pressure on time and no need for a fine degree of accuracy.

9. See chapter details.

10. See chapter details.

11. See chapter details.

12. See chapter details.

13. See chapter details.

14. See chapter details.

Chapter 6

1. (a) Scanner to read card with bar code; scanner to read card with magnetic stripe.
   (b) Police could track an individual's movements whoever they are.
   (c) To replace cash; as a driving license.

2. Could be mistyped or misread from original document.

    OCR

    Examples: induction course: one of 2 values Y or N; homework marking: number in range 1 to 5;

    (d) Could type Y when N was written – Y is a valid entry but not correct in this case.

(e) Information: % studying subject at GCSE – will influence the amount of time spent covering basic concepts; homework turnaround: make necessary changes to homework setting and marking if a high number of students found the current system unsatisfactory.

3. See chapter details.

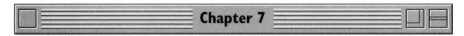
Chapter 7

1. (a) Some suggestions: the surveyors will be able to: use e-mail; use a shared diary system; access reports and documents directly. The drawing packages can be used to produce plans that can be speedily amended. Use of financial packages will speed up accounting process. If a secretary is on holiday or sick another secretary will be able to access the files from own workstation. The filing process will be simplified with a suitable computer based system. The office junior will not need to spend so long acting as a runner, as e-mail will reduce the flow of documents. As a receptionist, the junior will be able to access the diaries of the partners.

   (b) The junior may fear that there is no longer a real job for him; secretaries may fear a loss of autonomy and a decrease in personal contact with their Partner. The Partners may fear that their lack of IT skills will be shown up and that they will lose job satisfaction.

   (c) Need to examine current procedures and work out new ones as appropriate, involving all staff. All staff need to undergo appropriate training. The Partners need to embark on the new project with enthusiasm.

2. Factors: attitude of management and workforce; skill levels and 're-skilling'; structure of organisation and key roles; conditions of service; internal procedures for operations; external image; culture of organisation.

3. See chapter details.

4. See chapter details.

5. See chapter details.

6. See chapter details.

7. See chapter details.

Chapter 8

1. (a) legal requirements: refer to DPA
   (b) inform staff through initial training, handbook, appointment of DP Officer to oversee use and register
   (c) health and safety legislation

2. (a) College must apply for registration under the DPA. Adequate protection should be applied to the system and the data. The registration will specify the data use and how long data can be held. Only authorized users should have access to the data as specified under the registration. The college must supply details of the data held to the data subject upon request.

   (b) There should be an in-house policy to inform staff of the college terms of registration. This may include a list of 'good' and 'bad' practice points for staff. Examples: handling data and disks, access levels changing passwords.

3. See chapter details.

4. See chapter details.

5. See chapter details.

6. See chapter details.

7. See chapter details.

8. See chapter details.

Chapter 9

1. Risk analysis should highlight: how likely breakdown is to occur, what would be effects of such a breakdown, and associated costs.

2. Disasters can bankrupt businesses. Threats include: physical security, document security, personnel security, hardware security, communication security and software security. Contingency plans include backup strategy, employing a specialist disaster recover company, fault tolerant hardware.

3. Information systems are more secure to threats such as fire and flood, as it is possible to duplicate all data off site. To combat unauthorized access some measures (lock doors, identifying authorized personnel etc.) are common to both. However, electronic data is vulnerable when it is transmitted over public networks, large quantities of data can be copied and transported in a small space compared to paper. On the other hand, access to information can be restricted to authorized users by the use of individual identification, passwords and access rights.

4. See chapter details.

5. See chapter details.

6. See chapter details.

7. See chapter details.

8. See chapter details.

9. See chapter details.

10. See chapter details.

11. See chapter details.

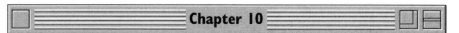

Chapter 10

1. (a) Operating system, software version, problem description, error message, registration number of software, call reference number.
   (b) i) Online access to data, (can do walk-through testing), can run online software upgrade, can run online data fix, easier to distribute upgrades.
      ii) Software house may change data without authorisation.

2. (a) More staff at peak times, use of e-mail for non-immediate case, provision of FAQs on bulletin boards.
   (b) See Question 1a).
   (c) Time to respond to call, length of call, number of repeat calls from the same person.

3. (a) See Question 1a).
   (b) Having an FAQ page/bulletin board for staff, internal e-mail within staff for sharing problems, staff training.
   (c) i) not wasting time on phone, get a hard copy of the response
      ii) less stress, can share ideas.

4. (a) See Question 2c).
   (b) See Question 1b).

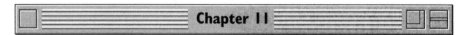

Chapter 11

1. (a) ● level of detail for level of user/type of use of training
      ● staff familiarisation with hardware and software
      ● staff IT literacy
      ● strategy for new staff.
   (b) ● help desk/phone line
      ● on-site technical support
      ● user guides/books/documentation
      ● bulletin boards
      ● online technical help
      ● on-screen help.
   (c) ● CBT
      ● video/interactive video
      ● online tutorial
      ● self-study/step through guides
      ● formal external course.

2. (a) ● Low tech: user completes form on paper, given to main office by a set time each day to form a batch of messages for display.
      ● High tech: user completes online template, e-mailed to the main office by a set time each day.
   (b) Online tutorials, user guide, formal training courses, interactive video.
   (c) Urgent message – some vetting process, signed by senior member of staff.

3. (a) Operator level e.g., inputting account payments.
   Supervisor level e.g., producing reports.
   Management level e.g., fundamental review of structures.
   (b) Previous (relevant) experience, functionality of this package (which parts they need to use) difference between skill-based and task-based training.
   (c) Upgrades/new functionality, users develop new needs (continual need for refresh), new legislation.

4. (a) See Question 3b).
   (b) See Question 3c).

5. (a) i) School managers, teachers, administrative staff, technical staff.
   ii) Managers would need access to grouped reports on progress, teachers to enter data for their classes, administrative staff to add new pupils, technical staff to install the software.
   (b) See Question 1c).

6. See chapter details.

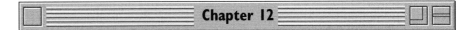
Chapter 12

1. See chapter details.

2. See chapter details.

3. See chapter details.

4. See chapter details.

5. See chapter details.

6. See chapter details.

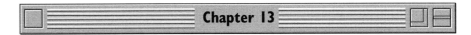
Chapter 13

1. Bill has not given impartial advice. He has broken the BCS code of conduct.

2. (a) See chapter 12
   (b) See chapter details.
   (c) See chapter details.

3. Possible issues: personal use of computer (e-mail, Internet use etc.); security measures, including choice and changing of passwords, not leaving a computer logged on; use only of authorized software; ensuring all personal data stored complies with DPA.

4. See chapter details.

5. See chapter details.

6. See chapter details.

Chapter 14

1. See chapter details.

2. A computer user has bought a large number of packages for a NEAB PC computer. Due to increasing workload it becomes necessary to replace this model with a more powerful computer. The user has a choice of

   either: buying an NEAB SUPERPC machine which is compatible with the NEAB PC,

   or: buying a MEGAMACHINE which is a completely different piece of hardware but provides the software emulation of the NEAB PC.

   (a) User will still have software for the NEAB PC that will need to be run on the new computer
   (b) See chapter details.
   (c) Changeover to SUPERPC will be very straightforward; old software will still run and new software can be introduced as appropriate. However, it is likely that the new hardware will not be as advanced as the MEGAMACHINE and will not run as great a range of new software with new features. As long as the bulk of software run is the old software, the SUPERPC will be a better buy as the use of emulation software will cause the programs to run slower. However, the more powerful computer will come into its own as new software is introduced.

3. IT support will be needed – inappropriate to support non-standard software, might need special training; could cause compatibility problems with other systems; site license for similar software might already be held.

4. See question 3.

5. A company has been running a large number of application packages on a personal computer. Although the computer works and has no hardware faults, the manager of the company now wishes to upgrade to a more powerful computer to run the same type of application packages.

   Need to run more advanced software than hardware will support – e.g. speed and memory capacity for graphics;

   hardware hard to maintain as parts not available;

   company image requires up to date equipment use.

   (b) See chapter details.

   (c) See question 2.

6. See chapter details.

7. See chapter details.

8. See chapter details.

9. See chapter details.

Chapter 15

1. Database files – need to be able to recover rapidly. Use of incremental dumping and logging of all data transactions that occur between dumps. Alternatively the files could be duplicated on an alternative site. System needs to be shut down while a backup is taken.

   Program files: periodic dump to tape using the generations system – needs to take place before any program maintenance or upgrading takes place

2. A separate strategy is needed for database and program files (see question 1). Incremental backup preferable to full backup for database files – full backup would be very time consuming; tape is an inappropriate medium for database; for a more appropriate rotation system see chapter; use of mirrored disks.

3. See chapter details.

Chapter 16

1.

Criterion	Reason
Functionality	The software will have to provide statistical functions so that the research company can produce the relevant analysis.
Robustness	The company will be dealing with vast quantities of data and the software will have to cope without crashing.
Performance	The company will require results to be produced in a reasonable time so the software package must be more efficient than current methods.
Support	The company will require access to support initially as training, but also in future if things go wrong.
Portability	The company may use other software to present the results of their analysis, and so this package must have an export function.
Transferability	Any existing data the company holds that is useful for analysis should be available to the new software package without the need for re-entering data.
Appropriateness/ suitability to end-user	Cannot guarantee ICT literacy level of end-user. Company wants old and new employees alike to use the package quickly.
Future proofing/ upgradeability	The software will have to be of use for a significant length of time so the company will not have to have further investment in the same area in the future.
Compatibility	The company will have systems in place (hardware and/or software) and the new package will have to function effectively with these.
Cost benefit	The company may be prepared to pay extra in order to gain extra functionality.

2. (a) See Question 1.
    (b) See Question 6.

3. (a) New organisational needs, change to a common network platform, additional features in software, current software may no longer be supported by manufacturer, current software may not function with new hardware, to maintain competitiveness.
    (b) See Question 1.

4. (a) ○ to enable an unbiased and objective comparison between systems
        ○ to allow a comparison between user needs and software capabilities
    (b) ○ Functionality: need to establish tasks the software will carry out and tasks that are essential to user in order to decide whether the software meets clients needs.
        ○ User support: ability of user to support software with existing staff skills, scope of software support available from software house, user base and scope of support from user groups, organisational training strategies, etc..
        ○ Hardware resource requirements: cost of upgrading current hardware to cope with new software, e.g., memory demands of each package, possibility of different hardware platforms, minimum spec to run system, demands etc..
    (c) See Question 1.

5. (a) ○ Performance – speed of loading, doing calculations, printing payroll, etc..
        ○ Robustness – does it fall over at all, e.g., on different platforms.
        ○ User support – phone line, cost, Internet support, … .
    (b) cost, compatibility with present data, training needs, ease of use, … .

6. What needs to be found out and why:

    ○ end-user requirements
    ○ the nature of the systems that are currently in place
    ○ functionality available
    ○ available alternatives
    ○ budget restraints
    ○ will the company make use of an ISP or host the website themselves?

Evaluation criteria examples:

Criterion	Reason
Functionality	Will the software provide the functions required by the company?
Performance	Does the company have access to the resources required to cope with the demands of the user/does the server have enough capacity to deal with the increased workload?
Compatibility with existing software base	Can the software integrate with the already established database?

Report:

- purpose – to show how the proposed solution would measure up to the needs of the company
- methodology used to produce the report
- evaluation
- recommendation.

Chapter 17

1. GP --- treats --- << Patient --- possesses --- Medical Record

   Child >> --- has --- Mother

   Hire Car >> --- is hired by --- << Customer

   Borrower >> --- borrows --- << Library Book

   Footballer >> --- plays in --- Team >> --- is a member of --- League

   Teacher >> teaches --- << Pupil >> --- is tutored by --- Tutor

   Newspaper >> --- is delivered to --- << Customer >> --- are located in --- Round --- Paperboy

2. (a) Borrower [id (key), Name and other details]; Book [Book id (key), ISBN, Title, Author]; Loan [id, Book id date due (joint key)].
   (b) Borrower --- << loan >> --- book
   (c) Use of Queries enables overdue books to be selected – using criteria of a due date < today's date. Links to Book and Borrower tables provide access to details of loan.

3. See chapter details.

4. See chapter details.

5. (a) Customer names are repeated when same customer hires 2 cars; town of company is repeated every time a company is referenced.
   (b) See chapter details.
   (c) Lease >> --- Customer >> --- Company

6. (a) See chapter details.

7. (a) See chapter details.
   (b) See chapter details.

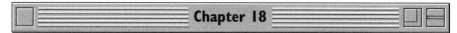

1. (a) See Chapter 18.
    (b) See Chapter 18.

2. To provide access to the Internet for subscribers using standard telephone lines, ISDN lines, broadband cables, …

3. A powerful, fast computer, a large amount of disk space for storing e-mails, hardware to enable fast access – broadband cabling, hubs, routers, etc..

4. See chapter details.

5. See chapter details.

6. See second part of Question 8

7. The nature and significance of a distributed information system:
    - WAN rather than LAN
    - likely to include microwave/satellite/land-based links
    - communications protocols exist to determine how information is transferred
    - distributed control as well as distributed data – control lies with computers at each location
    - need for high bandwidth
    - distribution of control and data is transparent to the user.

    Types of information systems:

    - Internet access
    - company intranet
    - public networks
    - e-mail
    - closed user groups by subscription only
    - company wide applications.

    Data you would expect to be distributed:
    - customer records
    - vehicle records
    - vehicle hire records.

    Advantages:
    - faster data processing – fewer delays communicating with a central server
    - data is stored on the node where it is needed
    - no reliance on a single server.

    Disadvantages:
    - more complex system
    - difficult to back up entire system
    - increased security risks
    - risk of viruses.

8. Advantages:
   More robust system, no reliance on a single server, faster data processing as data is stored on the node where it is needed, power is at the local node, data is stored where it is needed so less delays communicating with central server.
   Limitations:
   More complex system means there is a larger management overhead, good backup strategy required because each area is responsible for its own data, vulnerable to security breaches due to multiple points of access, risk of virus – all nodes need to have up-to-date virus protection, reliance on telecoms equipment.

Chapter 19

1. (a) log in screen, increased communication using the machine, more disk drives on screen, user may now find that they have no right to access files they could previously, extra cable connected to machine, inability to customise interface
   (b) i) e.g., video-conferencing – managers will be able to see each other without the need for travel costs
      ii) risk of unauthorised access – confidential information may be accessible
         risk of viruses – all nodes need to have up to date antivirus software
      iii) ○ use up to date antivirus software
         ○ provide user login and password

2. ○ Network cards in workstations to allow connection to cables, routers to link network segments together, switches, bridges, repeaters, types of network cable, servers, gateway, hub.
   ○ Contrast of LAN and WAN, server-based or peer-to-peer, need for routers, repeaters, bridges etc..
   ○ Need for password system, different types of access can be allocated, accounting – record which users are logged on, accounting – record use of resources, need for organisational code of conduct.
   ○ E-mail, Internet, intranet, work groups, distributed databases, video-conferencing.

3. Create a log in ID or password to identify user, different access rights, accounting log to track misuse, controlled access to peripherals, ...

4. e.g., sees network screen when switches on, need to enter number and password, access to shared software, Internet, shared files, etc..

5. ○ unauthorised access in surgery – passwords
   ○ receptionists seeing patient records – different access levels
   ○ virus damage – antivirus software
   ○ loss of data – backed up regularly
   ○ hacking from outside if Internet connected – firewall
   ○ users failing to log off – auto log off if not used for ten minutes.

6. (a) i) Username, software used, station used, date and time.

ii) Monitor who is doing what – planning new equipment, planning time usage, check no abuse, legal implications.

(b)

Peer-to-peer	Server-based
Has no server	Has server
Software and files stored locally	Software and files stored centrally
Cannot get files at any station	Can get files at any station
Software installed lots of times	Software just installed once
Weak security	Good security
Management relatively easy	Management difficult

7. (a)
- a record of facilities used by each person including processor time
- no of pages printed or disk space used
- details files stored/updated/deleted
- details of e-mail usage
- duration of log in
- ID of logged in users
- network address/station ID
- failed log on attempts.

Why it is useful:
- provide systems administration with information about network load
- enable administrators to deal with network performance problems
- facilitate sensible distribution of resources to users
- to limit use of scarce resources, possibly through a charging system
- inform decisions about any upgrade or systems enhancement
- dealing with network misuse.

(b)
- allocation of hierarchical password to all
- different access rights for different users, e.g., read-only, read-write
- restricted physical access to hardware
- restrict sensitive applications to certain terminals
- organisational codes of practice
- staff training to raise awareness of security procedures/issues
- existence of appropriate security procedures
- audit of security procedures
- auto-log off
- restrict access to hard copies/printouts.

8.
- students – no access to software
- teaching staff – access to software, read-write access to their own classes, read-only access to other classes

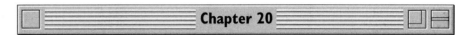

- office staff – read-write access to all classes for latecomers, access to reports on today's absentees, percentage attendance, regular non-attenders, etc.
- senior managers – read-only access to all classes, access to same reports but in particular strategic information – statistics, comparison with previous years.

Chapter 20

1. See chapter detail.

2. Macros can be assigned to buttons to provide a front end for the user, which hides the detailed workings of the package from him. Data can be entered via a dialog box and a macro used to up the sheet in an appropriate manner. All sorting of reports can be automated in a similar way.

3. See chapter details.

4. (a) Volume of text to be displayed on the screen; use of colour; position of pop up menus and help and error messages
   (b) Sophisticated graphics require large amounts of RAM and hard disk space and fast processor

5. See chapter details.

6. (a) See chapter details.
   (b) See chapter details.

7. Clear data entries; useful help messages; logical grouping of data on screen; use of meaningful icons; uncluttered screens, clear instructions for use.

8. See chapter details.

9. (a) i) Same look and feel at different computers. Easy to restore if lost.
      ii) Does not meet specific needs; will need to make same changes (e.g. select font) every time software loaded.

10. See chapter details.

Chapter 21

1. (a)
   - user written – internal development team
   - buy a specific purpose applications package
   - bespoke package written to users specification.
   (b) development time – generic may take less time to develop compared with other methods
   development costs – how do external costs compare with an in-house team

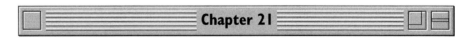

compatibility with existing hardware/software – need for new system to interface with existing applications robustness/reliability – e.g., generic package tested on wider audience than in-house solution.

2. (a) ○ user written/internal development team
    ○ external software house
    ○ customised generic package
    ○ specific, i.e., purchased from a company that specialises in software for examination boards.

  (b) Cost of alternative solutions, development and testing time, compatibility with existing software, ease of use, transferability of existing data files, quality of documentation provided, software licensing, user support, appropriateness of solution, corporate strategies, interface with other generic packages.

3. See Chapter 16 Question 3.

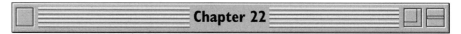
Chapter 22

1. development costs limited, need to meet time deadlines, to be ahead of competition, hardware released after software testing, user has used product in a way that no one has previously, inadequate test plan.

2. (a) ○ bugs in the program – **corrective**
    ○ improvements in the old program – **perfective**
    ○ changing to fit differing needs – **adaptive.**

  (b) i) alpha testing – testing in-house with data provided by software house needed to test implementation against design spec.

     ii) beta testing – off-site/real user testing, using live data, needed to detect errors not detected at alpha stage, involves a wider audience and different environments.

3. (a) e.g., simply the software may not load.
  (b) Because the software has not been tested on this particular type of machine or specification of machine.
  (c) No other alternative software, price is suitable....

4. See Question 2.

5. ○ Adaptive maintenance due to changes to original requirements, e.g., changes in tax legislation/euro.
  ○ Perfective maintenance adding extra features/functions to the system to increase performance of the system.
  ○ Corrective maintenance to fix bugs/logic errors/coding errors.

6. Software will be tested on different configurations, live data used, user independant, many hours of testing can be achieved easily, may uncover bugs overlooked by in-house testing, users may use the operating system in a way that was not envisaged by the manufacturer.

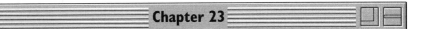

Chapter 23

1. See chapter details.

2. See chapter details.

3. See chapter details.

4. Incompatibility – old files cannot be used; the way in which the user carries out certain operations might have been changed: some features may no longer be available; training in the use of the new software may be needed.

5. User B is using a newer version of the software that can read files produced from earlier versions. However, the old software used by user A is unable to read the newer file. To get around the problem the new version should offer the option to save data in the format of the old version.

6. See chapter details.

7. See chapter details.

8. See chapter details.

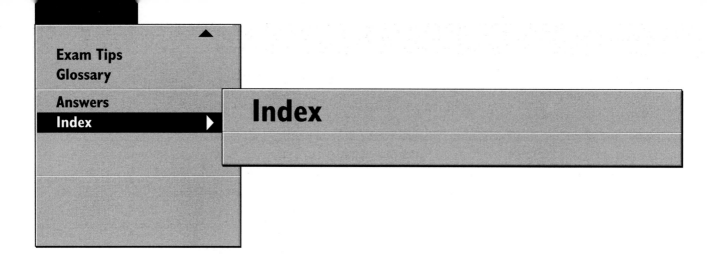